EIFFEL

For Rose Harvie
and
Maggie Anne Cullen Harvie

EIFFEL

THE GENIUS WHO REINVENTED HIMSELF

DAVID I. HARVIE

SUTTON PUBLISHING

This book was first published in 2004 by
Sutton Publishing Limited · Phoenix Mill
Thrupp · Stroud · Gloucestershire · GL5 2BU

This paperback edition first published in 2006

British Library Cataloguing in Publication Data
A catalogue record for this book is available from the British Library.

ISBN 0 7509 3309 7

Typeset in 10/12.5pt Iowan.
Typesetting and origination by
Sutton Publishing Limited.
Printed and bound in Great Britain by
J.H. Haynes & Co. Ltd, Sparkford.

Contents

Acknowledgements   vii

Introduction   ix

1   Beginnings   1
2   'Iron, iron, nothing but iron'   11
3   The Bridge-builder   32
4   'The shapes arise!'   51
5   Liberty   65
6   'A tower of very great height'   76
7   The Tower Rises   102
8   'Unique, strange and truly grandiose'   126
9   The Panama Plunder   151
10   New Directions   185
11   The International Icon   211
12   Whither Tallest?   235

Appendix 1   Works by Eiffel's Company   246
Appendix 2   Eiffel's Honoured Scientists   255
Appendix 3   Films Featuring the Eiffel Tower   258

Notes and References   260
Bibliography   275
Index   281

Acknowledgements

When the suggestion was first made to me that I consider writing this book, my interest was immediately attracted by both the subject and his period in history. I believe there is always something especially curious and attractive about those people and events that have not long ago slipped over the horizon of the direct experience of anyone still living. The tantalising sense of intangibility that often precedes the fully rooted and well-understood place in history has an attraction of its own. In Britain at least – where Eiffel is surely less well known than he deserves – I hope the book's subtitle will offer an intriguing hint of the progressive and public-spirited way in which he reacted to the extraordinary events that befell him and which caused him to reorganise his working life.

In addition to Eiffel's many published works (some of them dauntingly heavy with technical and mathematical detail) and contemporary sources from France, Britain and the United States of America, I have drawn on previous books on the life of this internationally significant polymath. Many of these have now been long out of print. In particular, I draw attention to four volumes: François Poncetton's *Eiffel, Le Magicien du Fer*, published in Paris in 1939; Joseph Harriss's *The Eiffel Tower, Symbol of an Age*, published in London by Paul Elek in 1976 (and originally published by Houghton Mifflin the previous year in New York as *The Tallest Tower*); Bertrand Lemoine's *Gustave Eiffel*, published in Paris in 1984; and Henri Loyrette's *Gustave Eiffel*, published by Rizzoli in New York in 1985 (translated by Rachel and Susan Gomme), and originally published in 1985 as *Eiffel – Un Ingénieur et son Oeuvre* by the Office du Livre SA, Fribourg, Switzerland.

I am grateful to the staffs of a number of libraries, including the British Library and the Newspaper Library at Colindale;

Glasgow University Library, in particular the Special Collections Department; the National Library of Scotland in Edinburgh; and the Mitchell Library in Glasgow. I appreciate the hospitality and assistance of both the Librarian and the Archivist of the Institution of Civil Engineers in London; and I acknowledge the assistance of the Agence Roger-Viollet in Paris and the US Library of Congress in Washington in relation to illustrations. Iain Lewicki has tried to ensure that my translations from French have been reasonably accurate and consistent (not always straightforward given the use of technical terms and changes in idiom and style since the 1880s); and I thank Michel Schepens for kindly agreeing the use of the image of a particularly fine film poster. I am grateful to M. Jean Alex Foret of La Société Nouvelle d'exploitation de la Tour Eiffel, who very kindly drew my attention to new information that has come to light concerning the elevator systems for the Tower. This has allowed corrections both to this new edition and to the official Eiffel Tower website. My wife Rose has as usual acted as a kindly critic, and Jaqueline Mitchell at Sutton has brought valuable editorial dispassion.

Introduction

Towered cities please us then,
And the busy hum of men.
Milton, *L'Allegro* 1.117

The urge to build towers is as old as man, and has produced an extraordinary range of structures, spectacularly diverse in both design and purpose. This compulsion to build to a height considerably greater than the structure's width often manifested superiority over neighbour, rival or enemy. Towers have been erected in honour of deities or to gain closeness to them, to celebrate places of worship, and to proclaim spiritual or intellectual resolve. They have also been built to assert position, power, wealth and prestige, to affirm cultural dominance or to intimidate. Towers with such symbolic purposes usually had little strictly practical use, while those with a demonstrable practical purpose, such as the defensive watch-tower, windmill or lighthouse, have generally been relatively insignificant. Often, seen from today's perspective, the original purpose is, if not lost, then blurred by our willingness to admire the after-effect. This is true of the Tuscan hill town of San Gimignano in Italy, where in the fourteenth century feuding families built over seventy successively higher towers to demonstrate their superiority; today, the result of tribal display is admired by visitors for its unique 'townscape effect'.

The oldest man-made towers, on royal castles near the Egypt–Nubia border, may be 5,000 years old, and Sardinia is reckoned to have had over 7,000 *nuraghi*, or round stone towers dating from 1,500 BC (of which 300 remain).[1] The *ziggurat* mountain dwellings of ancient Sumaria, which developed as stepped, man-made, pyramid-shaped structures surmounted by religious temples reaching for the gods, began a tradition that lasted for thousands of years. The name that best survives is probably the Tower of Babel, which was built on the ruins of earlier towers in the sixth century BC at Babylon, in the fertile valley between the Rivers Tigris and Euphrates in Mesopotamia (modern Iraq). A few ancient written references and rather more archaeological evidence together prove the existence of a seven-storey tower of baked, brilliant-blue enamelled brick which did not conform to the 'greater height than width' definition – each side appears to have been about 300ft in length, approximately equalling its supposed height.

The story of the Tower of Babel has come to us (and been mightily recycled) from the biblical tradition, in which a jealous Old Testament God reacts against the arrogance of its collaborating builders:

> And the Lord came down to see the city and the tower, which the children of men had builded. And the Lord said, 'Behold, the people is one, and they have all one language; and this they begin to do; and now nothing will be restrained from them, which they have imagined to do. Come, let us go down, and there confuse their language, that they may not understand one another's speech.'
>
> (Genesis 11: 5–7)

Gustave Eiffel is a national hero in France but is perhaps uniquely remembered in Britain and elsewhere for his famous iron tower, which has survived long beyond its expected twenty years and has become possibly the world's most recognised structure. This extraordinary 986ft tower was deliberately built for Paris's Exposition Universelle of 1889, to be the tallest building in the world at a time when national self-worth was being energetically driven by a series of great international exhibitions. However, before Eiffel had riveted his first two pieces of iron together at the Champ de Mars, he and his proposed tower were publicly pilloried in what became known as the Artists' Protest, when the intellectual elite combined to pour scorn on his proposal. The great battle of Art versus Industry – a battle intended to be annulled by the very concept of the international exhibition – became focused on the tower. However, the impetus behind the 1889 exhibition was enough to forestall the protest, and Eiffel, who had taken personal financial responsibility for the entire 8-million-franc project, proceeded to build what has become perhaps the most iconic structure in the world.

Eiffel was already a supreme exponent of the new 'art' of engineering design and construction in iron. *'Le magicien du fer'* had an international reputation, for bridge-building in particular. He had constructed iron bridges, great and small, all over Europe, Russia and the Far East; other iron structures – railway stations, churches and all manner of industrial buildings – had been designed and built for locations in Peru, Bolivia, the Philippines and Algeria. Another of his more unusual achievements was his design and construction of the hidden, internal iron skeleton of Frédéric Bartholdi's famous 155ft Statue of Liberty Enlightening the World, which stands on a 150ft-high plinth on Bedloe's Island at the entrance to New York harbour. Eiffel's own favourite project had been a huge, innovative floating and rotating dome for the observatory at Nice; this was achieved in collaboration with Charles Garnier, the designer of the classically ornate Paris Opera, who would become his most bitter opponent in the battle of Art versus Industry, or as it became known, 'stone versus iron'.

Yet, as he was beginning his prodigious efforts on his great tower, Eiffel became ensnared in what was to become the greatest political and financial scandal in French history. In 1880, public subscription was opened in Paris for shares in the Compagnie Universelle du Canal Interocéanique. The elderly retired diplomat Ferdinand de Lesseps was planning to repeat his famous success in leading the construction of the Suez Canal by excavating a 45-mile ship canal across the narrow isthmus of Panama. Regrettably little attention was given to the catastrophic experiences of the Scottish adventurers who had tried to secure a trading settlement in that unforgiving, disease-ridden landscape 200 years before; the Darien disaster should have been a prophetic warning. The canal was expected to become a great triumph of French engineering and project administration, but it ended in total failure, with 20,000 men dead (mostly of yellow fever and malaria), and almost one and a half billion francs (250 million dollars) lost.

Gustave Eiffel had been opposed to the original plan to construct a sea-level canal without locks, and it was only much later, when constructional, financial and political setbacks threatened the project, that Ferdinand de Lesseps persuaded Eiffel to design and construct a series of ten locks for a revised project. Within a year, matters had deteriorated significantly, and attempts to raise ever-greater sums of money to keep the project alive collapsed. The company was dissolved, and although Eiffel had a signed and ratified agreement with the liquidator that clarified and agreed the limits of his financial liability, he was sucked into the rapidly escalating scandal. In the midst of an erupting political backlash, during which the future prime minister Georges Clemenceau fought a duel with pistols, Gustave Eiffel was charged with breach of trust and swindling. Found guilty, he was fined and sentenced to two years in prison. Although this verdict was to become notorious, and the sentence was later quashed by the French Supreme Court, Gustave Eiffel was deeply hurt by the experience, feeling that his public reputation had been tarnished, by association if not directly. He resigned his position with his own company and never built another structure during the rest of his life; but this extremely wealthy, restlessly inquisitive man did not retreat into secure retirement; he reinvented himself. He had always insisted that his great tower was not simply a temporary, frivolous side-show for the 1889 Exhibition, but a structure of great practical value. He now decided to put it to use as a scientific instrument in his new life as a theoretical and practical scientist.

He immediately began a series of experiments on the wind resistance of falling bodies, employing equipment he himself designed. These experiments measured the velocities of specially-produced instruments in free-fall from the top of the tower. Trials were also conducted in the earliest radio transmissions, between the tower and the Pantheon; and by establishing a series of meteorological stations throughout France, he built the scientific basis on which the future of French meteorology would operate. His work on meteorology and air resistance was extended into the new science of aerodynamics, and Eiffel built a pioneering wind tunnel at the Champ de Mars.

The Eiffel Tower remained the tallest building in the world until 1930, when the superb art deco Chrysler Building was erected in New York. The skyscraper race was under way; within a year the Empire State Building had taken the title. The scramble to join the sky bandwagon became intense, and the only question that now mattered was, 'how high can we go?' Many of the proposals never made it further than the frothy publicity launch party, as designers and developers raced to join the frantic new game. In the autumn of 2003 the tallest building in the world became 'Taipei 101', at 1,667ft. Many of the world's tallest buildings are either in, or planned for, the Far East, and there are proposals for buildings reaching to four times the height of the Eiffel Tower in India and Tokyo, while further 'conceptual' plans exist for a 2-mile-high sky city of 500 floors. Although ideas for such seemingly impossibly high buildings seem distinctly of our time, the concept for the first mile-high building came as long ago as 1956, when the visionary American architect Frank Lloyd Wright proposed such a building for Chicago. Even the atrocity that destroyed the Twin Towers of the World Trade Center in New York in 2001 has not dulled the age-old desire to build higher than anyone else. Techniques will improve and new materials will be devised, and the obsession, it seems, continues.

This book not only gives an account of an individual of international importance (who is perhaps much less well-known in Britain than ought to be the case), but aims to set him within the turbulent and exciting times that Europe, and France in particular, were experiencing during his life. As a graduating student he stepped into a world that, through the establishment of the series of great international exhibitions, was trying to foster international brotherhood and to unite the seemingly irreconcilable cultures of

Art and Industry. At a time when France regarded her sense of taste and style as her greatest and most important contribution to international intercourse, Eiffel embraced that idea wholeheartedly. Yet in his most iconic, innovative work he was bitterly accused of exacerbating wounds by the self-appointed cliques who wanted to hold on to their perceived right to dictate the cultural landscape. Eiffel's later involvement in France's most prestigious international demonstration of her engineering prowess – which turned into her biggest political and financial scandal – and his subsequent reinvention of himself are nothing less than startling features in the story of one of Europe's most brilliant and enduring champions.

ONE

Beginnings

Gustave Eiffel's family name, now so intimately associated with everything French, was Germanic rather than French in origin. In the early eighteenth century his great-great-grandfather, Jean-René Boenickhausen, came from the village of Marmagen in Westphalia, 37 miles south of Cologne; he settled in Paris and for convenience adopted the surname Eiffel, after the name of his native region of Eifel. (Legally, the family remained Boenickhausen-Eiffel until 1880, when Gustave Eiffel took action in court in Dijon to annul the German prefix.) Jean-René made a good marriage in 1711 with Marie Lideriz, the daughter of his landlord, and became a forester; he died only eleven years later, at Saint-Valérie in Picardy, but his widow later remarried and eventually the children married into middle-class Parisian life, and the family prospered as master weavers and owners of a successful tapestry studio.[1] Throughout his life, Gustave Eiffel collected many examples of fine eighteenth-century tapestries and took considerable pride in his family's mastery of the traditions of a vocation that became recognised as characteristic of the continuing French expertise in fine arts and crafts:

> The tapestry weaver's profession was an elite trade; it has left us, in that delicate branch of the art of furnishing, delightful patterns which we admire and still copy today as one of the most precious products of French taste. The weavers of that period, one of the most brilliant in the 18th century, were true artists.[2]

The family craft of tapestry-weaving came to an end with Gustave's father, Alexandre, who in 1811 at the age of sixteen

1

rejected craftsmanship in favour of a military career in Napoleon Bonaparte's imperial army. This was a time when France consisted of 130 separate administrative regions, overseeing half of Europe. Alexandre saw service in Italy, and during the period when he taught at a military school at Saumur he wrote several books on military affairs. In November 1824, when he was stationed at Dijon, he married Catherine-Mélanie Moneuse, the daughter of a timber merchant. Catherine Eiffel was totally different in character from Alexandre. Throughout their marriage she remained business-orientated, and was largely responsible for the family's financial success and prosperity. Alexandre was a learned man who read Greek and Latin and had a spirited, ironic, humanistic outlook on life; in one account he was compared in character to Charles Dickens.[3] He had already left the army and become a civil administrator in the *préfecture*, or local government department, by the time their first child and only son, Alexandre Gustave, was born on 15 December 1832; his two sisters, Marie and Laure, were born in 1834 and 1836 respectively.

Dijon, the ancient capital of Burgundy, situated at the confluence of the Rivers Suzon and Ouche, lies some 200 miles south-east of Paris. Long recognised as one of France's great wine-producing centres, Dijon is now often associated with the production of mustard, vinegar and chocolate. However, its history is closely associated with the duchy founded in 1015 by Robert, Duke of Burgundy, when court patronage attracted the best of French architects, musicians and artists. In the eighteenth century, the city was the centre of French intellectual life, but by the time Alexandre was born in the nineteenth century, the coming of the railways had opened up the area and it had become an important centre of the transport, mineral and related heavy industries.

Gustave's mother decided to increase her commercial commitments after the birth of her son. She had continued a charcoal business begun by her parents, but now took up the opportunity to become the principal distributor of coal from the mines at Epinac in Saône-et-Loire, and later those at Saint-Eloy near Commentry. Blast furnaces had recently been established in the surrounding area, and coal was much in demand in preference to the charcoal of earlier years. Le Canal de Bourgogne had been completed in the year of Gustave's birth, and related industrial expansion required considerable movements of massive quantities of coal. Linking the Atlantic with the Mediterranean via the Rivers Yonne and Saône, the 150-mile Burgundy Canal was a major factor in that industrial prosperity. Madame Eiffel appears to have had considerable business acumen, and although her commitment to these commercial activities meant that Gustave lived for much of his childhood with his blind grandmother in Dijon, his mother was very close to her son and had considerable influence over him until her death. Although she was a spirited and strong-willed woman whose authority in business affairs was widely recognised, she did not dominate her family; to both parents, their children were of paramount importance. Gustave later paid homage to his parents' fortitude and commitment:

Right at the canal port she set up large coal depots, which were regularly restocked by a succession of overland deliveries. A great bustle pervaded these depots, and my father soon had to give up his place in the *Préfecture* to join my mother, alongside whom his time was more usefully spent. My young imagination was deeply impressed by their strenuous labour to expedite the unloading of ships, and the loading of carts, whatever the weather, which obliged them to leave the little house they lived in, on the very bank of the canal, at daybreak and which did not stop until after nightfall.[4]

By 1843 the family had become wealthy, but some poor investments led Catherine to decide to close the coal business, a profitable asset that sold for a substantial sum. Keeping some savings in the charcoal and steel industries, they made new investments in the brewery of Edouard Régneau and took up residence as tenants in a small eighteenth-century château, where they lived for the next twenty years. Despite the Eiffels' prosperity, they were regarded as somewhat inferior incomers by the patrician families who constituted the influential layer of Dijon society. Even their solid Parisian background did not protect them from the insular snobbery that was fundamental to the local social order. (Much later, Gustave was to attempt a marriage with the daughter of a Bordeaux family, but the union was condemned by the girl's parents, who were insulting about the standing in 'society' of the Eiffel family. Even the intervention of a Dijon attorney failed to substantiate the Eiffels' good middle-class reputation.) These humiliations bypassed Gustave the child, however, and he led a happy if quiet, provincial childhood, which he later recalled with affection as providing him with 'much sharper memories than of other times of my life'.[5]

The part of his childhood that Gustave did not enjoy was school, which left him with 'the most wretched memories'. He was apparently an undistinguished pupil for most of these years, and complained of boredom and of having his time wasted in the smelly, cold schoolrooms of the Lycée Royal, where he was compelled to learn useless lessons by heart.[6] He was rescued in his last two years at school by two teachers, M. Desjardin and M. Clémencet, who taught him history and literature respectively. They persuaded the young Eiffel to work hard enough to make up for a wasted year, and he was eventually successful in taking *baccalauréats* in science and humanities, enabling him to attend the Collège Sainte-Barbe in Paris as a preparation for going on to further study at the prestigious Ecole Polytechnique.

There were compensations for an imaginative child in his nearby surroundings: he discovered workshops, a contractor's depot, an eccentric scholar whom he was unable properly to characterise as either alchemist or sorcerer, and two grand houses inhabited by people who would not speak to him or any of his family.[7] One of his great pleasures in these years was in forming a close relationship with his uncle, the rather fierce Jean-Baptiste Mollerat, who lived near his grandmother, and whom he later regarded as a second father. Mollerat, a determined anti-monarchist who continually assured the boy that 'All kings are rascals!' had suffered a deep disappointment as a young man. He had fallen for a young woman whose parents disapproved of him; nevertheless, they swore allegiance to each other, and Jean-Baptiste went to America to seek his fortune. When he returned, he discovered that the girl had married someone else. He drowned his sorrows in the study of chemistry, and it was only years later that he married a sister of Gustave's mother. Mollerat devised a process for the distillation of vinegar and wood spirits, and opened a large factory at Pouilly-sur-Saône, near Dijon. As well as the informal education he obtained from his uncle, Eiffel also benefited from a friendship with one of his uncle's friends, Michel Perret, a well-known chemist who owned mineral mines near Lyons. Perret engaged him in philosophical and theological discussion and encouraged Gustave to accompany him to his underground caverns, which produced copper minerals used in the manufacture of sulphuric acid. Perret had a virtual monopoly of this process in France, and happily encouraged the youth to learn as much as he wished, not only about industrial chemistry, but of 'extraordinary things such as mesmerism, which he practised on his servant, or philosophical themes such as theological arguments or the theories of Saint-Simon'.[8] The liberal ideas and attitudes he learned from Mollerat and Perret were of lasting influence and importance, and were probably significant to Gustave's rejection of any kind of specifically religious ethos in his life; it was probably their influence that first gave the young Eiffel an insight into the practical value of mathematics.

In 1844, at the age of twelve, he visited Paris for the first time. He had been promised the trip by his father for some time, but in the end it was his mother alone who accompanied him. He was dazzled by the city, visiting the theatre and the opera, and travelling by train for the first time, to Versailles. Six years later, in October 1850, Alexandre finally accompanied his son to Paris, this time to enrol him for two years in the Collège Sainte-Barbe in the Latin Quarter. This time there was no overwhelming feeling of strangeness or alienation. On the contrary, he was impressed both by the vibrancy of the city and its resources and amenities, and a realisation that life in provincial Dijon was quite dull, at a time when revolution was in the Parisian air.

Two years earlier, King Louis-Philippe had been overthrown with the support of the masses (and escaped to England as 'Mr Smith'), a republic declared, and a self-appointed committee affirmed as the provisional government. In November there was an election for the state presidency which was won by Charles Louis Napoleon Bonaparte (a nephew of Napoleon Bonaparte). In December 1851, with political discord continuing and a right-wing move under way to restore the monarchy, Napoleon mounted a bloody *coup d'état*, dissolved the constitution, and became dictator. The Second Empire of Napoleon III was declared in 1852 and continued for the next eighteen years.

Within days of starting at Sainte-Barbe, Eiffel was nevertheless bored and homesick. Later, things seem to have settled, and he wrote to his mother that he had discovered the pleasures of dancing – and English girls, whom he thought were fun and much less reserved than French girls.[9] He also enjoyed the cultural offerings of the city and maintained the interest in mesmerism that had been stirred by Michel Perret by attending seances from time to time.[10] His schoolwork seems to have been quite indifferent. He wrote to his mother after his examinations that he was satisfied that he had done well to come 43rd out of 106: 'You might not find this very good, but I think it isn't bad. There are at least 25 or 30 who are in their third year at Sainte-Barbe; you understand that they will inevitably do best.'[11]

He tried to convince her that he would be happy to maintain that position throughout the year. That was not, however, the view of his teachers; in their opinion he had failed. He was less concerned about this than was his family, possibly because he was beginning to realise that his capabilities lay in practical rather than academic fields. The school was managed on very strict lines, which may well have been best for everyone, given that, during Gustave's time there, the *coup d'état* which brought Napoleon to power raged around the city and was witnessed by him and his fellow pupils:

From two till five o'clock we heard the sound of roaring cannon-fire; that was truly sinister. At a given signal everybody stopped and listened and in the general silence we could hear the distant muted sound of cannon-fire; it was frightening. M. Blanchet came to tell me that there were many killed yesterday. In our area, it didn't amount to much, as the district is disarmed; nevertheless all the streets are occupied by soldiers. All night we heard their infernal racket; they have hacked down all the wooden boards around the Pantheon and set huge fires in the middle of the street. Yesterday they were wild with drink, singing disgusting songs all night, to my deep sadness.[12]

In his second year he felt sure that he had performed well enough in his examinations to obtain the necessary certificate allowing him to enter the Ecole Polytechnique, but there was apparently a dispute among the examiners over his performance, and he was made to face them in an additional interview.[13] It appears that petty squabbles among the examiners prevailed, and he succeeded only in obtaining passes sufficient for the Ecole Centrale des Arts et Manufactures (the state school of civil engineering), regarded as more vocational than the influential Polytechnique that had been his original goal. Instead of joining the sons of the bourgeoisie in studying maths and science at the highest level, he decided – without any apparent family regret – to go to the equally admirable and rather more liberal Ecole Centrale.

This school had been established as a private institution in 1829 by Alphonse Lavallée, a businessman from Nantes, so that 'the doctors of factories and mills' could be better trained. Eiffel attended the school in its original location in rue de Thorigny in the Marais district of the city, and rented a room just off the Place des Vosges. The Hôtel Salé had been built in the mid-seventeenth century for a salt tax collector, and when the school moved to other premises to the south of Paris it became the Ecole des Métiers d'Art; the building in the Marais now houses the Musée Picasso.

In his youth, Eiffel developed a strong trait of character that was to have a profound influence throughout his life, and which would, in its turn, be of great comfort to him in his own old age: he realised the importance of his family relationships. He had a good rapport with his father, was especially close to his mother, and developed a warm-hearted, protective attitude to his two sisters. Marie was his favourite, and he was careful to satisfy himself that when she was courted by Armand Hussonmorel, a successful flour miller, she was making a decision that would ensure her future comfort and happiness. When Marie married in 1852, he wrote to his mother, asking her to tell Marie not to forget him. Likewise, when, two years later, Laure married Joseph Collin, a foundry manager, Gustave displayed deeply affectionate concern.

The French have long idolised Eiffel as '*le magicien du fer*' and it is perhaps a surprise that his field of study had no connection whatsoever with metallurgy or engineering. He is generally described at this period as being a rather prim, timid and conventional youth who nevertheless had a modest charm, which he retained until his death at the age of ninety-one. His years at the Ecole Centrale seem to have been unremarkable, his work generally diligent and his progress steady. The work was onerous, quite different from what he had been used to at Sainte-Barbe, with only two days' holiday in the year, and the discipline ferocious in effect and often petty in character. He had a particular weakness in technical drawing (a subject of some importance for someone who would become a construction engineer) achieving only 17 per cent on one occasion. He complained to his mother that, '*je crois que le professeur me donne de mauvaises notes par habitude.*' ('I think the teacher gives me bad marks out of habit'.)

In his second year, he was required to select a subject in which to specialise from a list including metallurgy, mechanics, civil engineering and chemistry. It seems astonishing, in view of his later achievements, that Eiffel chose to concentrate on chemistry. This appears to have been a wholly pragmatic decision resulting from the fact that Jean-Baptiste Mollerat, with no children of his own, had nominated Gustave as his successor in taking charge of the successful vinegar and industrial spirit plant at Pouilly-sur-Saône. His uncle's political stance (he claimed the reputation of having been present at the guillotining of Robespierre) was at odds with the Bonapartist position of Gustave's father, who had spent much of his life in a series of military appointments. This difference opened up into a bitter family quarrel when a young man of republican views began to court Gustave's sister and Alexandre brought the affair to an end, provoking his uncle Jean-Baptiste to respond with hostility. The two branches of the family permanently divided and Gustave's opportunity to take over the running of the vinegar factory disappeared. When his uncle died the following year, the factory was acquired by a niece, and almost immediately began to fail:

> The plant from the Pouilly factory was scattered and sold like old scrap. All the buildings were demolished and the site given over to cultivation. So the plough was driven over this factory where the industrial genius of one man had created a source of wealth for the surrounding area as well as for himself.[14]

And, he might well have added, for Eiffel also. His hopes of an easy entry into a career in chemistry, for which he would be properly qualified, evaporated. He had been one of the best students in the subject, but luckily the Ecole Centrale did not allow total specialisation, preferring to produce students with a broad technical education. Eiffel completed work on a range of additional subjects, including the processing of soda, zinc and linen. In August 1855, during a visit to Paris by his sister Marie and her husband Armand, they were able to telegraph Madame Eiffel with the happy news that Gustave had received his diploma.

In a move that was to prove highly significant to his entire future, he asked his mother to buy him a permanent season ticket for that year's Exposition Universelle. This second major international exhibition was ostensibly to demonstrate the superiority of France in material and cultural affairs and to promote international understanding and cooperation. It was allegedly the initiative of Napoleon III, designed to advance his own regime and to answer the success of Britain's Great Exhibition of four years earlier. Who can say to what extent the

22-year-old with the rolled diploma under his arm may have been impressed by the structure of Barrault's iron Palais de l'Industrie? He was one among many young men graduating from college who were ready to take on the world in any discipline, taking as their inspiration the exciting range of industrial and commercial activity generated by the exhibition.

Giving preliminary consideration to a new career in some aspect of metallurgy, Eiffel decided to take advice from his brother-in-law Joseph Collin, who managed the iron foundry at Châtillon-sur-Seine. The outcome was that, totally unprepared by any form of training, Eiffel became apprenticed to his brother-in-law on a voluntary, unpaid basis. He wrote to his mother, saying that he was happy with the move, but that he wanted to be sure it would only be for a limited period.[15] He made considerable efforts to observe and learn as much of the technical, administrative and financial aspects of the iron-founding business as he could, but he also began to seek out the means of finding a permanent job. It is likely that his formidable, business-like mother, to whom he was still very close, was involved in this task, and that she sought out contacts in the mining and metallurgical industries with whom she had business dealings. In any case, Eiffel gathered whatever references and letters of introduction he could, and sought his future in a Paris that was reaping the many industrial and commercial benefits conferred on her by Napoleon III's Exposition Universelle.

TWO

'Iron, iron, nothing but iron'[1]

When Eiffel left college with his diploma at the age of twenty-two in 1855, he had already been in Paris for five years. However, during a short holiday in Switzerland with family and other friends, it emerged that he was in debt to his landlord to the extent of 800 francs. He had hoped to conceal the situation in the general family merriment and congratulation surrounding the award of his diploma, but his mother was incensed – less by the amount owed than by his duplicity in concealing it – and he was bluntly accused of letting money run through his fingers. Gustave confessed his wrongdoing with contrition in the mood of celebration for his sister Laure's imminent wedding, the fault was forgiven and he returned to Paris. He had the season ticket for the Exposition Universelle that his mother had bought for him, and probably sated himself at the exhibition, appreciating the quality of the engineering exhibits in the huge iron Palais de l'Industrie. Nevertheless, he kept his arrangement to start work at the foundry under the supervision of his brother-in-law, although it is likely that he already knew that his future would lie in Paris.

The city which he now knew so well was in a state of high excitement, with the Exposition attracting visitors from across the country and around the world; public enthusiasm for such spectacles was now deep-seated. Although London's Society of Arts had offered prizes for specimens of manufactured goods – particularly such 'artistic' items as tapestry, carpets and porcelain – as early as 1756, France was quicker off the mark in establishing a tradition of exhibitions. The marquis d'Avèze had opened up the Maison d'Orsay and its grounds in Paris to an exhibition of 'a great many objects of taste and vertu' in 1798. Later, modest expositions celebrating French art and industry were held on the Champ de Mars (the huge military parade-ground across the Seine from the Trocadero Gardens), in the quadrangle of the Louvre, the terrace of the Hôpital des Invalides, and the Place de la Concorde. By the time an exhibition was held on the Champs-Elysées in 1849, the number of exhibitors had reached four and a half thousand.

When Napoleon III, Emperor of France, decided to hold a universal exhibition in Paris in 1855, the public motive was to celebrate the forty years of peace since Waterloo and to stimulate material and cultural progress. However, among other items on the hidden agenda was the vital necessity to surpass the success of London's Great Exhibition.[2] The French had been mortified by the huge success of the London event – regarded as the first of the modern 'world fairs' – and needed to regain what they regarded as their superior position in the sphere of national self-regard. One French commissioner was icily succinct: 'The brazen imitator England has stolen from us the idea of a universal exposition.'[3] However, the concept was now widely accepted, not least politically, as a vital means of declaring national prowess. Almost every such event produced momentous 'firsts' in the introduction of new products of lasting impact: London in 1851 saw the introduction of the Colt revolver, the elevator first appeared in Dublin in 1853, the sewing machine and the first production of aluminium in Paris in 1855, the calculating machine in London in 1862, the telephone in Philadelphia in 1876, the Ferris Wheel in Chicago in 1893 and 'moving pictures' in Paris in 1900.

London's 1851 Great Exhibition of the Works of Industry of all Nations 'for the purposes of exhibition, of competition and of encouragement' was presided over by Prince Albert in the manner (according to his detractors) of the royal master toying with his plaything. Six million people passed through the huge iron gates, cast at Coalbrookdale, to visit 17,000 exhibits containing 100,000 products in Joseph Paxton's spectacular iron-and-glass Crystal Palace at Hyde Park.[4] The importance of this first international exhibition of manufactured products was hard to overstate. It paved the way for the worldwide promotion and development of many features of modern society, such as art and design, international trade, foreign relations and the blossoming new industry of tourism. Charlotte Brontë noted after her visit that 'Its grandeur does not consist in *one* thing, but in the unique assemblage of *all* things', although it is said that the exhibit that caught the public imagination more than anything else was James Nasmyth's massive steam hammer. The exhibition also signalled to the public the synthesis of art and industry, as design came to be regarded as an increasingly important feature of the manufacturing process. The purely functional was fine, but the French in particular were demonstrating that the concept of good design could increase the value, desirability and the practical performance of products. What had previously been patronisingly referred to as 'the mechanical arts' were now to be called 'the useful arts'. The Great Exhibition was also to become the model for the many international exhibitions that were promoted in the following century.

London's Great Exhibition of 1851 was by far the biggest event of its kind, and Paxton's central creation was almost 2,000 feet in length, covering 19 acres, excluding 217,000 square feet of galleries (the building was so huge and slender that the Astronomer Royal, Professor George Airey, declared that it would collapse). Nevertheless, the French were justifiably proud of their pre-eminence in fine art and in sophisticated industrial design and production. They regarded style as the quintessentially priceless aspect of French civilisation. It was such confidence that enabled their 1,740 exhibitors to threaten English dominance of the medal tables at the Crystal Palace, with porcelain, agricultural machinery, fine silks and furnishings, and examples of imaginative technology including a prototype submarine.

There was a prevailing sense of pacifist internationalism abroad, and the international exhibitions were expected to act as a potent social cement for the brotherhood of nations. The *Art Journal*'s *Illustrated Catalogue of the Exhibition* addressed this intention on its first page:

Whatever be the extent of the benefit which this great demonstration may confer upon the Industrial Arts of the world, it cannot fail to soften, if not eradicate altogether, the prejudices and animosities which have so long retarded the happiness of nations; and to promote those feelings of 'peace and goodwill' which are among the surest antecedents of their prosperity; a peace, which Shakespeare has told us,

> Is of the nature of a conquest;
> For then both parties nobly are subdued,
> And neither party loses.[5]

Napoleon III had already begun to change Paris. He came to power after the successful *coup d'état* of 1851 (his earlier attempts to gain control had seen him exiled to America and imprisoned in France). A man of liberal social conviction with a well-developed concern for people's living conditions, he soon embarked on a renewal of the city. In the thirty years from 1852 came new sewers, water pipes, bridges, railways and other public works; and, with dramatic vision, the financier, town planner and *préfet* of Paris, Baron Georges Eugène Haussmann, swept away miles of chaotic slums and began planning and constructing grand new boulevards and public monuments, creating the superb classical townscapes that endure today. In his promotion of the Exposition Universelle, Napoleon espoused all the fine sentiments and values of the 'brazen imitator'. In his inaugural speech he was to proclaim that 'With great happiness I hereby open this temple of peace that brings together all peoples in a spirit of concord.'[6] However, some things in the world had changed. The fierce struggle with Russia was raging in the Crimea, and Britain, France, Italy and Turkey were fighting a very dirty war. Consequently, imperial Russia was not to be represented, although individuals were (and, curiously, Russian prisoners of war were allowed to attend).[7]

The entire exhibition would be contained inside one spectacular building, the Palais de l'Industrie, to be constructed on the Grand Carré de Marigny, a promenade beside the then relatively undeveloped Champs-Elysées. The chosen architect and engineer, Jean-Marie Viel and Alexandre Barrault, collaborated on a scheme with distinct echoes of the Crystal Palace. The light, iron-framed building with reinforced glass canopies (the Emperor's 'temple of peace') was 820ft in length by 354ft wide and 115ft high. Viel is said to have taken as his inspiration the Bibliothèque Sainte-Geneviève by Henri Labrouste, and planned a similar structure displaying the benefits of combining iron behind a masonry façade. However, cost considerations meant that the masonry was severely reduced and had to be braced with additional iron columns. Barrault observed that '. . . all complicated arrangements are unattractive and denote inaccuracy of construction or poor distribution of material.'[8] Some critics thought, however, that Barrault had lost his nerve.

The emergence of iron as an architectural material in the Palace of Industry was by no means universally popular. The radical writer Octave Mirabeau described the blight of its domination of the Champs-Elysées as like 'an ox trampling through a rose garden'; and Charles Garnier, the celebrated architect of the equally celebrated opera house, was similarly scathing when the Palais was demolished to make way for the exhibition of 1900 – he said then that no architect of note in Paris wanted its retention. Under construction, the Palais looked like being a disaster. Despite being erected at considerable speed, it was still unfinished on the opening day; it was too small to house comfortably the 21,000 exhibitors, and was very badly ventilated; two substantial additional buildings had to be hurriedly erected at the last minute. The exhibition was half as big again as London's Great Exhibition, and cost twice as much, although attendance was significantly lower than that at the Crystal Palace.

Queen Victoria came to Paris herself and was received with great enthusiasm. After centuries of bitter antagonism (if not outright war) between the two countries, this constituted an extraordinary and passionately celebrated peace treaty. Both France and Britain celebrated their new brotherhood by displaying for the first time the produce and cultures of their respective colonial empires. The Exposition Universelle again proved that Britain was the leader in heavy industry and basic processing and manufacture, while the French excelled in design and quality of finish. Given the intention to devote considerable space to painting and sculpture, it was the French exhibits in the fine-arts building that attracted the most visitors and the greatest critical notice.[9]

The Paris Exposition Universelle of 1855 was not, however, one which gave undue significance to works of art of interest to the wealthy, or machinery and technologies for the attention only of bloated businessmen. There were also thousands of cheaper goods designed to appeal to the meritorious and democratic French concept of *bon marché* promoted by the man who would devise the department store, Aristide Boucicaut. For the first time, at the insistence of Napoleon III, all goods had a price label; conforming to the idea of a popular market place, every item could either be bought or ordered on the spot. Napoleon insisted in his final *Rapport sur l'Exposition* that all such future exhibitions should be committed to the egalitarian concept of *'plus d'aissance au profit du plus grand nombre'* ('the greatest good for the greatest number').[10] To this democratic end, considerable efforts were made to encourage mass popular attendance, and the original entrance charge was reduced from five to two francs; special trains were organised in order that not only Parisians, but people from the provinces and the wider countryside could attend. There were critics, however, who condemned the idolisation of consumerism, and regretted the fact that the population was being encouraged to pay money to gawp at diamonds. In a spectacular event in the final days of the exhibition, Hector Berlioz, the great French composer who ironically had a bigger reputation in Britain, Germany and Russia than in his native country, conducted a magnificent performance of his cantata *L'Imperiale*, his *Symphonie triomphale* and his *Te Deum*.

After Gustave Eiffel's broad education at the Ecole Centrale, and the brief but welcome flirtation with the iron industry, thanks to his brother-in-law, he was anxious to discover precisely where his mainstream in life would lie. As it happened – and it may have been nothing more or less than luck – he landed right in the heart of the most dynamic industry not only in France but throughout Europe – the railways. Since the earliest days of the Industrial Revolution, the railways had been the driving force behind industry, transport and employment, and not the least of the changes they brought about was the possibility of mass transport for people who had hitherto often never ventured further than the village or township of their childhood. Main lines had been constructed from Paris to the industrial north in the early 1840s, and in the five years after 1852, 8,000 miles of track were laid and six major French companies were established. However, it had been the Scottish and English engineers William Mackenzie and Thomas Brassey who had constructed the important line from Paris to Le Havre in 1846. Crucially, these burgeoning railway lines were to need an architectural and engineering infrastructure, in particular, bridges.

On 10 February 1856, Gustave Eiffel called at the workshops of Charles Nepveu at 36 rue de la Bienfaisance in the Quartier Saint-Augustin, in the 8th arrondissement near the Gare St-Lazare in the north of Paris (Nepveu also owned a separate railway-carriage-building workshop a little further north, at Clichy). This seems to have been essentially a chance visit by Eiffel to one of several potential employers, with no particular expectation on his part; it was to prove momentous. Although nowadays Saint-Augustin is an unremarkable part of the inner city, it had a reputation at that time as a run-down area inhabited by transient, impoverished incomers, and was referred to as 'Little Poland'. However, as a member of the French Society of Civil Engineers (of which, much later, Eiffel would become president), Nepveu was a well-known and highly respected figure in the business of designing and constructing steam railway engines, rolling stock and track. He offered Eiffel the job of private secretary at a salary of 150 francs per month, with the opportunity to study a number of specific issues, such as the building of foundations in rivers.[11] The two men seem to have struck an immediate rapport, and Eiffel responded with enthusiasm, renting a room in a large house nearby.

Initially left to his own devices, he was given complete freedom to make himself familiar with all the company's activities, which he quickly realised were considerable. Soon after starting with Nepveu, he described in a letter to his mother a routine that involved his still being at work until late at night, usually accompanying the tireless Nepveu.[12] Eiffel himself worked hard and diligently, and on Sundays he took private lessons in economics at the Ecole des Mines (School of Mines). He clearly thought that with Nepveu he had found the ideal position in which to learn everything that would fit him out for his working life. But very soon, things went wrong. Nepveu seems to have been rather highly strung, and certainly less capable as a businessman than as an engineer. The previous year he had exhibited a new steam locomotive of his own design, and the unsuccessful project had considerably drained his barely sufficient finances. One day in May, he unaccountably didn't appear at his office; invoices were unpaid and the business was insolvent. Eiffel's letters reveal his concern that Nepveu might have killed himself, as he had left the previous day without any money, carrying only his papers and pistols.[13]

Nepveu had made no arrangements to warn or protect his workers against such an adverse situation. However, fifteen days after his dramatic disappearance, he was brought back from Geneva by Professor Emile Trélat, of the Conservatoire des Arts et Métiers, a close friend to whom he had previously introduced Eiffel. Although Eiffel received no explanation of the disappearance, which seems to have been regarded as due to a temporary nervous breakdown, he and Nepveu greeted each other happily. The two men needed each other, in different ways, and Eiffel remained with Nepveu, unpaid, while the business was formally wound up, writing to his mother to assure her that his employer remained a man of substance with good prospects for the future. Nepveu for his part found his protégé a good position in August 1856 with La Compagnie des Chemins de Fer de l'Ouest. This company, owned by the Pereire brothers, financial wizards taking daring advantage of the new climate brought about by Louis-Napoleon, owned the Gare St-Lazare and many of the principal French railway lines. They were followers of the theories of the French socialist-philosopher Claude Henri de Ronvroy, the comte de Saint-Simon (1760–1825). He is regarded as the founder of French socialism, and promoted the organisation of a society led by science and industry – what he called the 'new Christianity'. The brothers Pereire were also involved in establishing railways in Spain, Austria and Russia, and in promoting a multitude of other industrial activities throughout France, all based on their allegiance to the new democratic concepts of Saint-Simon.[14]

Eiffel was paid 125 francs a month and immediately given responsible duties to carry out. He had the opportunity to work with the company's highly respected chief engineer, Eugène Flachat, who had just completed a huge extension to the Gare St-Lazare[15]; he had also completed the first sheet-iron bridge in France, at Clichy, modelled on the principles recently established by Robert Stephenson on the Britannia Bridge over the Menai Straits, linking Anglesey to north-west Wales. Eiffel later wrote of his debt to Flachat, who had pioneered the use of sheet iron fixed by rivets, rather than pins and bolts as had been favoured until 1850:

In France, the introduction of sheet-metal bridges dates from the bridges at Clichy and d'Asnières on the Saint-Germain Railway in 1852. It is to M. Flachat, at that time engineer-in-chief of the railway, that are attributed the first iron constructions, which were later applied on a very large scale in the building of the railways of southern France.[16]

After the erection by Baltard of Les Halles in the mid-1850s – the first time in France that a building prominently proclaimed its mode of construction (and it was the *new* material) – iron began to be considered for a wide range of structures in France, from railway stations to markets, halls, factories and pavilions. Although iron had been used for a few arched bridges, there was not yet an established tradition of using iron in bridge-building. France's use of iron in structural engineering was delayed by cost considerations, and the fact that most of the progress in iron-founding, and in techniques such as riveting and plate-rolling, was being made and patented in England, which in any case had a much longer history of iron-working. Gustave Eiffel himself often acknowledged the fact that England was far ahead of France in the use of iron:

> Sheet-metal bridges, that is to say, bridges composed of laminated iron in which the pieces are assembled by means of rivets, did not make their appearance till well after cast-iron bridges and suspension bridges, and it is again in England, the land of metal, that we must look for their origin.[17]

Eiffel's own first-ever design, for a small, 72ft cast- and sheet-iron bridge for the Saint-Germain Railway, was soon finished and accepted, and there were hopes that the company would win the contract for a big new bridge at Bordeaux. Nepveu, meanwhile, was trying to arrange the sale of his own company to the Compagnie Belge de Matériels de Chemins de Fer, directed by the Pauwels family of industrialists. He was also trying to position himself for what he knew would be an important construction contract for the bridge across the Garonne river at Bordeaux. As it happened, the outcome could hardly have been better for either Nepveu or Eiffel. The Belgian company paid handsomely for the Paris and Clichy workshops, which were renamed la Compagnie de matériels de Chemins de Fer. Nepveu was retained in charge and arranged that, within the new French branch of the business, Eiffel should have a senior position in his own right, rather than function as a possibly short-lived personal assistant with insecure tenure of office; he was appointed head of research at the main Paris workshops at a salary of 250 francs per month. This promotion delighted Eiffel; for the first time he had a permanent, responsible position in a large, successful company, which had no financial restraints or impediments. He wrote to his mother of being wary of becoming involved in another situation in which he might find himself suddenly pushed out on the street again.[18] Although he was close to Nepveu, and had great respect for his enterprise and imagination, he was relieved to be free from the inevitable acquiescence which he owed to his mentor.[19]

The move away from timber and masonry to iron and steel in large structures was a momentous change in building construction. This was first established in bridges, then in iron-framed buildings such as the Crystal Palace and Palais de l'Industrie; the trend continued later in structures such as Les Halles and the Eiffel Tower in Paris, in railway stations and in the use of steel framing and steel-reinforced concrete in most of the world's skyscrapers. The change is notable also for the fact that, whereas wood and stone are essentially 'building' materials, iron and steel were 'constructional'; in that semantic difference perhaps lay the explanation for the inspirational achievements of the new breed of civil engineers who pioneered the great metal structures. Iron and steel did not simply replace the traditional materials, they demanded wholly new designs and methods.

Iron, the fourth commonest element on earth, was first produced in China from about the sixth century BC, and was introduced to Europe around 1500. Cast iron was produced by reducing the mineral ore in a smelting furnace heated by charcoal (later coke or coal) and limestone (as a flux to promote the liquid flow). With sufficient time and heat, the molten iron was sweated from the particles in the ironstone and dropped to the bottom of the furnace, from where it could be tapped at the appropriate time into cooling channels to form solid bars of pig-iron. The pig-iron bars could later be re-melted for pouring into shaped moulds prepared in earth or sand, from which cast iron products were formed. Since production appeared to work better in winter rather than summer, cold air was blasted over the molten iron in the mistaken belief that it improved the quality. Much later, in 1828, James Beaumont Neilson in Glasgow patented the 'hot blast' method,[20] which certainly did improve matters while also using two-thirds less fuel; however, this progressive method was quite at odds with erroneously accepted practice, and took some years to come to fruition. Cast iron contained approximately 3 per cent carbon, small quantities of silicon and manganese, and even smaller amounts of other impurities such as phosphorus and sulphur, which imparted its greatest and characteristic weakness: brittleness. Like stone, cast iron was of poor tensile strength, but its compressive strength made it an important load-bearing structural material, commonly in the form of vertical pillars. (More modern forms of cast iron have been devised which, by careful production chemistry, are more malleable.)

Wrought iron was softer and more pliant, and unlike cast iron its strength lay in tension rather than compression; in constructional terms, this made it ideal for use in horizontal beams. After the large-scale production of steel began in the mid-1850s, the uses of wrought iron again returned to the more decorative. As it could be shaped only by being hammered, bent and rolled, wrought iron has a long history of use for decorative purposes in such items as railings, grilles, balconies, church screens, and so on; it was also used for the production of tools and items such as nails.

On St Valentine's Day 1784, Henry Cort patented a process for 'shingling, welding, and manufacturing iron and steel into bars, plates, and rods of purer quality and in larger quantity than heretofore, by a more effectual application of fire and machinery'.[21] He produced wrought iron in what were called 'puddling-furnaces'; about 5 hundredweights of pig-iron bars were melted in the furnace, and over a two-hour period an experienced man operating a puddling rake would introduce oxygen with the purpose of burning off most of the carbon (the main constituent causing brittleness). This 'industrialised' production of wrought iron was difficult, and highly dependent on both the introduction of production improvements and the diligence of the iron-worker. From the furnace, short wrought bars had to be further subjected to hammering and rolling before they were regarded as of sufficient quality. The more hammering and rolling cycles, the better the finished quality; these factors made wrought iron considerably more expensive than cast. The best-quality wrought iron resists corrosion, although it has a fibrous structure which leads in time to flaking. Cort's process was to enable wrought iron to remain the major structural material until the end of the nineteenth century, when improvements in production methods allowed steel to take its place. At the time of the Great Exhibition of 1851, the annual output of pig-iron in Britain was almost 3 million tons, most of which was converted into wrought iron; by the 1880s there were 4,500 iron furnaces at work in Britain, producing nearly 8 million tons of pig-iron.

In 1855, the demands of the Crimean War prompted Henry Bessemer to action. Bessemer was an inventor and metallurgist of Huguenot stock, whose father had been a member of the French Academy of Sciences. He lived near Hitchin in Hertfordshire, and had invented perforated dies which rendered the stamps used on official deeds incapable of fraudulent use, thus saving the government up to £100,000 each year (at 1833 values). He held patents covering a bewildering range of interests including the production of glass, printing-type, composing machinery, railway carriages, paints and oils, and sugars. After inventing a gun with a rifled barrel, Bessemer decided to try to further reduce the carbon content of iron, and to achieve a stronger, more malleable and cost-effective metal. Over a fifteen-year period from 1854 to 1869, he registered a great number of patents covering his successive improvements in producing high-quality, reliable steel on a commercial scale.

From his workshops at St Pancras, Bessemer produced a long series of improvements to his original idea of running the melted pig-iron from the blast furnace into a 'Bessemer converter' or large, cylindrical chamber lined with fireclay, during which the 10 hundredweights of molten iron was subjected to a blast of hot air at 15 pounds to the square inch pressure. In 1856, Bessemer demonstrated his results to the engineer George Rennie, who was so impressed that, in his capacity as president of the Mechanical Section of the British Association for the Advancement of Science, he arranged for Bessemer to address a meeting of the British Association, to be held in Cheltenham on 13 August. His paper on the economic production of steel was entitled 'On the manufacture of malleable iron and steel without Fuel'; it was seen as momentous.

Iron was first used as a structural material in England. The Darbys of Coalbrookdale made metallurgical progress by changing from charcoal to coke and coal as iron-founding fuels, thus enabling a more powerful furnace blast. But it was Abraham Darby III who shook the world of engineering in 1777 with his daring, imaginative and handsome cast-iron arched bridge over the Severn near the village of Broseley; this was the first time iron had been used in a structural role. Darby used iron dovetailing of radial members into ribs, as if the material was wood; the individual iron components were designed and made to pass through one another using mortise and dovetail joints secured by wedges; no bolts or rivets were used anywhere in the structure. This was to parallel the infant Industrial Age with a new Iron Age.

The French had made several attempts to introduce iron in bridge-building, but had failed largely because of the difficulty of casting large masses of iron; expense had been another factor, and stone and timber both remained significantly cheaper. The first success was with a bridge at Lyon in 1755, when one of the principal 82ft arches was actually assembled in a workshop, but high costs dictated that the bridge was eventually completed with timber. When Darby had become involved in the project to build the bridge near Broseley, it had been designed by Mr Pritchard, its Shrewsbury architect, to be built of stone with a cast-iron 'keystone' a few feet in width. However, this design was soon shelved, and the entire 100½ft ribbed arch was cast at Coalbrookdale; the bridge was constructed and erected between 1777 and 1779. Unlike masonry, its open structure allowed the common winter flood-water to pass through, and for that reason this first iron bridge was the only one of many crossings on the Severn to survive.

The next plan for a substantial iron bridge came from a surprising source, and was staggering in concept. Tom Paine, the famous English radical author of *The Rights of Man*, had been a stay-maker in his native Norfolk, a schoolteacher, a marine, an exciseman at Lewes in Sussex, a tobacconist and a would-be inventor of smokeless candles. He went to America in 1774, became a friend of luminaries such as Benjamin Franklin and Dr Benjamin Rush, served in the army and rose to become Secretary to the Committee for Foreign Affairs. Later, he became involved in

French politics as a member of the National Convention, and was imprisoned. While he was in America, one of his many interests was the use of iron in bridge-building. In 1787, a bridge was proposed for the Schuylkill river, between downtown Philadelphia and what is now Valley Forge National Historical Park. The river became choked with ice every winter, so the bridge had to be constructed without the use of piers. Paine patented a design[22] for an iron bridge with an astoundingly ambitious single arch span of 400ft. He obtained Franklin's support, lobbied the French Academy of Sciences in Paris and sent copies of his plans to Sir Joseph Banks for presentation to the Royal Society in London. Confident of appropriate support, he went to Rotherham in Yorkshire, where he had the bridge sections cast, after which the parts were transported to London and partially erected for public display in Paddington. While Paine was distracted by other affairs, his principal American backer became bankrupt, and Paine was temporarily arrested; thereafter, he naively went to see his Jacobin friends in Paris at the time of the Revolution. This was a mistake, since they put him in prison and he escaped the guillotine only by the fall of Robespierre. Needless to say, in such circumstances, the business of the bridge lapsed.

Meanwhile, the public exhibition in Paddington had attracted attention. The foundry in Rotherham agreed to retrieve the parts of the bridge to offset their debt, and in 1796 parts of Tom Paine's bridge were incorporated in a high-level bridge with a 236ft span (exceeding that of any bridge then known) over the River Wear at Sunderland, nominally designed by Rowland Burdon, MP for Castle Eden.[23] Robert Stephenson, who replaced the Wear bridge in 1859, said of the original:

We must not deny to Paine the credit of conceiving the construction of iron bridges of far larger span than had been made before his time, or of the important examples both as models and large constructions which he caused to be made and publicly exhibited. In whatever shares the merit of this great work may be apportioned, it must be admitted to be one of the earliest and greatest triumphs of the art of bridge construction.[24]

Although Paine returned to America and became involved in promoting the principles of constructing iron bridges, he never succeeded in carrying out any of his plans in practice. However, Darby and Paine undoubtedly started a new discipline in Britain. Also in 1796 came the first iron bridge by Thomas Telford, over the River Severn at Buildwas, halfway between Shrewsbury and Bridgnorth. This was a single span of 130ft, and much lighter than the first Darby iron bridge; it survived until 1906. Telford went on to build many more iron structures; his beautiful 1814 Craigellachie Bridge (the Gaelic place-name meaning 'the Rock of Separation') over the turbulent River Spey in Scotland is the oldest surviving of what have been claimed to be the most technically accomplished bridges of their period. The iron ribs for this bridge of two 152ft, nearly parabolic, trussed-iron arches (the upper arch of greater radius forming the roadway) were cast in Denbighshire in Wales.

In 1797, a rich landowner in Lower Silesia built the first iron bridge on the Continent, with a small 43ft span, over the Strieguer Wasser, near Laasan. In France, the first iron bridges were built in Paris in the early nineteenth century: the Pont des Arts of 1803 and the Pont d'Austerlitz of 1806, both crossing the Seine.[25] All these bridges, from Darby's onwards, although built of iron, were arched bridges formed in the manner of their predecessors. Next came a series of suspension bridges, following the innovative Chinese, who had been using chain-suspended bridges for a very long time. The first modern wrought-iron chain suspension bridge was erected in 1796 in North America, and the oldest surviving such example is the 240ft-span bridge of 1809 over the Merrimac River in Massachusetts. In Britain, Thomas Telford had built the Menai Suspension Bridge and the Conwy Castle Bridge by 1826, and Captain Samuel Brown, RN (later Sir Samuel) built a number of suspension bridges, notably the Union Bridge over the River Tweed at Berwick, using forged and bolted wrought-iron bars.

Following cast-iron arched and suspension bridges came a number of cable suspension bridges, first in North America in 1816, then in Switzerland and France, where the engineer Marc

Séguin was responsible for many such structures throughout the country.[26] In 1847, after a number of faulty bridges were constructed by early railway engineers, the British government instituted an official commission that took evidence from engineers, designers and iron-founders, providing an authoritative understanding of the use of iron in bridge building in the years immediately prior to the introduction of steel. The next major construction period saw the introduction of wrought-iron arched and girder bridges, of which the earliest and most important example was Robert Stephenson's still extant Britannia Bridge of 1850 over the Menai Straits. There were two spans each of 460ft over water, and two each of 230ft over land; the structure was composed of tubular girders built from wrought-iron plates and angle irons. An original design feature allowed for the addition of suspension chains if necessary, but they were never applied. Gustave Eiffel, in praising 'this fine piece of work' said that from the beginning England had achieved what had not been equalled since: 'At the first attempt the engineer, Robert Stephenson, has managed a master-stroke.'[27] This audacious structure inspired a two-volume work by Stephenson on its conception and construction; this work was followed by the efforts of several outstanding engineers to formulate what became the new science of materials. These initiatives were led by Sir William Fairbairn, prominent in marine and mechanical fields, and his partner the mathematician Eaton Hodgkinson; together they calculated the properties of different forms of iron and methods of design and construction.

During this period of bridge-building, tunnelling under the English Channel was also a daunting challenge for engineers. Nicolas Desmaret in 1751 and Albert Mathieu half a century later both planned tunnels for horse-drawn road traffic. The potential use of iron increased the likelihood of success; in 1851, Hector Horeau planned a seabed tunnel of cast-iron sections, with a natural incline which he hoped would avoid the use of steam engines; somewhat fancifully, the ends of his tunnel were to be held in position at the surface by paddle-steamers. The most persistent engineer was Thome de Gamond, whose various plans for a sectional iron tunnel were placed before Napoleon III and Queen Victoria, but became ensnared in the mutual political suspicions of both governments. Some of his ideas were adopted by Sir John Hawkshaw, the builder in the 1880s of the 4½-mile-long Severn Tunnel. Hawkshaw was consulting engineer to the first English Channel Tunnel Company, established in 1872, but resigned after he came to the conclusion that such a tunnel would be to Britain's military disadvantage.[28]

As Gustave Eiffel considered the design of his first major work, he had before him several earlier Parisian examples to influence him. The Pont des Arts of 1803 linked the Louvre with the Institut de France across the Seine. Referred to as a *'passerelle'* by Parisians – it was for pedestrian use only – it was fitted with chairs to sit on and small glasshouses filled with exotic plants in which to shelter. In 1839 had come the important building, combining masonry with iron, that would show the way to new uses for iron in France. The Bibliothèque Sainte-Geneviève in Paris was designed by Henri Labrouste in 1845 and constructed between 1845 and 1851. While the outer walls of this handsome classical building are of conventional stone, the massive double-vaulted roofs and supporting pillars are all of wrought and cast iron. Labrouste believed that architecture should reflect society, and followed the precepts of Victor Hugo, who insisted that architecture, like literature, ought to be capable of organic phases of construction to reflect the rationalism of industrial society. Labrouste – whose work was especially admired in the USA – also designed the Reading Room in the Bibliothèque Nationale.

The famous Paris market area, Les Halles, had its origins in the twelfth century, when Philippe-Auguste had 'la foire St-Lazare' moved to what is now the area between the rue du Faubourg Saint-Denis and Boulevard Magenta – the site of the Gare du Nord. In 1851, the area was redeveloped by Victor Baltard, an architect devoted to the ideals of the glorious classical ruins of Greece and Rome. However, his masonry structure infuriated the progressive Napoleon III who, with the support of Baron Haussmann, insisted that the market ought to resemble 'big umbrellas', and ordered that the buildings be demolished and that the architect think again.[29] Baltard came back with designs for twelve spectacular iron-and-glass pavilions perched on slender cast-iron columns. The effect was magnificent, and Les Halles became one of the most-loved features of the city. Zola referred to the building as the only original monument built in Paris in the nineteenth century, and Mies van der Rohe described the market as 'the symbol of the golden age of French building techniques'.[30] Sadly, Baltard's masterpiece was demolished in 1972 (one building has been retained for display at Nogent-sur-Marne, outside the city). Baltard went on to produce other fine cast-iron buildings, in the old slaughterhouse area of La Villette in the north of Paris, where his former veterinary hall has been restored as 'la maison de Villette'.

As Gustave Eiffel and Charles Nepveu contemplated their newly assured future and the possibility of benefiting from the imminent contract for the Bordeaux Bridge, Eiffel was experiencing something of a crisis in his relationship with his mother. They remained amicable, but as a consequence of the unhappiness brought about by his earlier debt, his mother had refused to make further advances to him at a time when he felt he needed to be more settled after six years of moving from apartment to apartment. There was also disagreement over items of family furniture promised to him, which he felt would have helped establish him in his own home. His life was entering a period of uncertainty, and to make matters worse, he was staying in a shared apartment with an Italian sculptor, to whom Mme Eiffel apparently took an instant dislike. Eiffel seemingly won his mother over with tender pleadings of affection for her and his father, and the explanation that they should no longer look on him as a child, but as a young ambitious man stepping out into the adult world.[31] His timing was perfect.

When the Compagnie de l'Ouest became the subject of commercial intrigue and malicious whispering, resulting in 1857 in the controversial dismissal of Eugène Flachat, Nepveu successfully negotiated the contract for the bridge at Bordeaux for his new Belgian masters. The bridge would provide an important strategic rail link between the separate systems of the Compagnie d'Orléans and the Compagnie du Midi. Hitherto, passengers between Paris and Bordeaux had to leave each train at the Gare de La Bastide terminus and cross the river by an old stone bridge, either on foot or by carriage, before joining the train of the other company at the Gare du Midi for the 250-mile journey to Sète on the Mediterranean Golfe du Lion; the transfer of freight was even more time-consuming and costly. Soon after the contract was signed, at the beginning of January 1858, Charles Nepveu honoured his protégé, when the 25-year-old Eiffel was given overall charge of the metal assembly. This would be no insignificant contract; the demand was for a 1,640ft iron bridge on six 79ft piers standing in turbulent, fast-flowing water. The most critical factor, and the one most likely to damage the young Eiffel, was the time-scale; the bridge had to be completed in two years. Within a year, Nepveu had resigned and left Eiffel in sole charge of the project. Luckily, he had attracted the interest and support of Stanislas de La Roche-Tolay, the chief engineer of the Compagnie du Midi, with whom he had worked closely on the designs for the bridge. Despite such backing, the next two years would be a defining time for the young engineer and his iron-building ability, with all eyes scrutinising his every management decision and constructional move.

Years later, Eiffel wrote of his appreciation of England's premier position in terms of iron-bridge-building experience, but he demanded recognition for France's creative abilities:

> . . . we have had the honour, in France, of by far overtaking them in the theory and of creating methods which were opening up to progress a self-confident approach free from empiricism. We have, up to recent years, remained faithful to this precedent, in which German science has done nothing more than follow, and it is our great construction companies which have, up to recent years, built the greatest works of art in iron in all the countries of Europe.[32]

Any remaining lethargy in adopting the new forms of iron construction in France was to be swept away as the young *'magicien du fer'* in charge of the building of the 1,640ft railway bridge across the Garonne at Bordeaux started work. He knew the challenges that awaited him, but also understood that there would be some who would not be slow in pointing the finger of blame and disgrace should he fail.

THREE

The Bridge-builder

R ight from the start of his professional career, Gustave Eiffel adopted a methodology that would remain with him, and be further refined, throughout his working life. He abhorred the trial-and-error approach of other engineers and demanded, of himself and others, a disciplined execution based on well-conceived planning and forethought. His first major problems as construction began on the Bordeaux bridge in the summer of 1858 were to construct a wooden service bridge and to establish workshops at La Bastide, where the metal sections would be constructed. Although the piers for the Bordeaux bridge were to be of masonry, Eiffel was interested in the methods used in a similar, large iron bridge opened the previous year in South Wales. This was the Crumlin Viaduct over the steep Ebbw and Kendon valleys. At 1,658ft, the viaduct was almost identical in total length to the Bordeaux bridge, but was much higher, at 200ft. It was composed of ten wrought-iron trusses supported on eight cast-iron piers, each of which was formed by fourteen round cast-iron columns held together by diagonal wrought-iron braces – *les croix de saint André*, which would also feature on the Bordeaux bridge. According to Eiffel, the Crumlin Viaduct was the first such structure to employ cast-iron piers.[1]

Eiffel introduced the technique of hydraulic pile-driving into the river bed, which had been used for the first time two years earlier. He had encountered this device with Nepveu, but it was not yet in common practice in France. He used cylindrical caissons (hollow, open-topped water-tight chambers) 6ft in diameter, which were driven into the river bed; at the bottom of each caisson was an airlocked working chamber. Compressed air was fed into these chambers, the pressure being adjusted to correspond with external water pressure. Workers, and the spoil they excavated, were brought out through an air lock at the top of the chamber, and as work proceeded, the chamber would be driven further downwards, to depths of up to 82ft, adjustments being continually made so that the top of each caisson was always above water level.[2] The method had been invented in 1830 by the extraordinary Thomas Cochrane, later tenth Earl of Dundonald (and, as Admiral Sir Thomas, the 'Sea Wolf') to enable coal mining under the River Forth at Culross. It was used by Brunel during the construction of his Royal Albert Bridge over the Tamar at Saltash, on the Devon–Cornwall border, but had first been employed in bridge foundations in 1851 by William Cubitt and John Wright at Rochester on the River Medway. Eiffel visited the Kehl bridge on the Rhine at Strasbourg, where similar techniques were being used, but was rather scathing of the vast amounts of money that were being expended. The use of caissons was to become a common technique in Eiffel's later bridge work, where he rejected the solid iron-plate designs of Eugène Flachat for an open lattice design in which vertical members were held together by 'St Andrew's cross' diagonal bracing.

Eiffel proved himself an astute manager and an inspired organiser. The works continued without any adverse incidents of note, and he assured himself that his position with the Pauwels company was secure and likely to progress. Only one accident seems to have occurred, when a riveter fell into the Garonne, apparently after a liquid lunch. Eiffel, a strong swimmer, immediately removed his coat and shoes, dived into the swift-flowing water and rescued the man. He gathered his workers together afterwards and instructed them to ensure that they were securely roped in future. Possibly as a result of that incident, Eiffel built up a strict safety regime among the men who would work for him in later years, in particular with regard to alcohol. He was perceptive in understanding the issues that would become important in the construction industry, and many of his safety innovations became standard practice. When starting construction on his tower in 1887, he was faced with vocal opposition from objectors who regarded the project as far too dangerous, but he was able to show that he had instituted methods and practices designed to make the erectors safer than they had been on low-level bridges.

Not long into the construction, Eiffel discovered that his sister Marie's husband had made some bad business decisions and was on the verge of bankruptcy. Reacting with his characteristic sense of family solidarity, he arranged for his brother-in-law Armand to take up employment on the bridge project, and he and Marie were soon installed with him in Bordeaux, where the arrangement proved to be highly successful for all concerned. When the bridge was completed – within the extremely tight schedule – Eiffel's workmen came together to present him, as a token of their admiration and respect, with a specially designed medal depicting the bridge on one side and the hydraulic pile-driving apparatus on the other. The people of Bordeaux, who apparently referred affectionately to the bridge as 'the footbridge', now had a structure of immense economic and strategic importance. In early 2006, the Eiffel family was attempting to secure the future of the Bordeaux bridge, which was under threat of demolition by Réseau Ferré de France (France's railway network), which wanted to build a new four-track bridge. In the face of claims that 'the Passerelle Eiffel' was too expensive to renovate and maintain, RFF was willing to sell the bridge for one euro, but no-one had yet taken up the offer.

Eiffel had been very lucky, as such a young engineer, to supervise the bridge over the Garonne, but he was nonetheless anxious to secure for himself a good future in the construction industry. Although he was an employee of the Pauwels company, the Bordeaux bridge project was typical of much of his work, being contracted by competing railway companies who were collaborating on specific joint projects; in practice, his services seem to have been available by arrangement, with clients seeking out their preferred designers and engineers for individual contracts. De La Roche-Tolay, the engineer with whom he had collaborated in designing the Bordeaux bridge, and who had a very high regard for his abilities, introduced him to other influential men in the railway construction business who were becoming aware of his good reputation. Meanwhile, the Pauwels company was clearly impressed with Eiffel, and in September 1860 promoted him to the position of engineer-general to the group's railway division, responsible only to the main board in Brussels. He was rewarded with an annual salary of 9,000 francs and 5 per cent of the profits of any projects he directed; his contract could only be broken by a year's notice in advance.[3]

During his time in Bordeaux, Eiffel pursued a number of eligible young women with a view to marriage; in at least one such case he was apparently rejected by the family on grounds of 'standing'. He seems to have had a clear eye on a settled domestic situation, however, and turned his attention back to his home town of Dijon. As it happened, he fell in love with a girl he had known since childhood. He described her to his mother as '. . . having a modest dowry, a passable figure, but on the other hand great kindness, a steady humour and simple tastes'.[4] She was Marie Gaudelet, the seventeen-year-old granddaughter of Edouard Régneau, the brewer in whose business his parents had invested, and whose tenants they had become. They were married on 8 July 1862 and intended to set up home in Paris. In August the following year, their first child, Claire, was born; two other daughters, Laure and Valentine, and two sons, Edouard and Albert, were to follow. Within the family, his wife was known as Marguerite, to distinguish her from Eiffel's sister Marie, and as time progressed, Gustave formed a very close relationship with her grandfather M. Régneau. The marriage seems to have been entirely happy and contented, despite Eiffel's almost incessant absence on business – a concern about which he confided to his mother.

Soon after his marriage, when Eiffel was given further promotion as director of the company's workshops at Clichy at an annual salary of 12,000 francs, he and his wife were able to set up home in a large house in the north of Paris. However, it was not long before things at Clichy began to turn sour. At first, Eiffel thought that the sluggishness in business was part of a general industrial downturn after the boom of the 1850s, but by the summer of 1863 there was a substantial loss at Clichy, and by the end of that year he was forced to begin laying workers off. To protect his own position, he managed to secure the opportunity of private work on the concourse of two railway stations, while at the same time attempting to deduce the true state of the Pauwels company. He discovered that the business was underfinanced and realised that he ought to leave this 'half-dead' company as soon as possible, before he was involved in the liquidation process. He was asked to become a consultant at a reduced salary, but declined in favour of setting up on his own, cushioned somewhat by work that he had already negotiated. During this unsettling period in his professional life, he was to experience a series of domestic difficulties and disappointments. His sister Laure, who had been ill for some time, was in need of constant care and moved into the home of Gustave and Marguerite, and he was deeply distressed by her death in August 1864 at the age of 28; this was to be the first of several grave family losses that would affect him deeply in the next few years.

Eiffel was fortunate to obtain a contract for the supervision of the building and delivery of thirty-three locomotives for the Egyptian government. Notwithstanding an extended visit to Egypt in April 1865, this was a contract he could largely manage 'at a distance', and he was paid all expenses and 25 per cent of the profits – a comfortable situation which he reckoned would give him a 10,000-franc share. In parallel, he would be able to handle other work and negotiate the details of further contracts. During his stay in Egypt he visited the Suez Canal, then being constructed by the French aristocrat Ferdinand de Lesseps (the canal was to open in 1869). This visit was professionally instructive for Eiffel, but in view of his later association with de Lesseps, he might retrospectively have regretted not understanding more of the entrepreneur's character and business methods. In 1866, Eiffel's assumptions about the viability of the Pauwels railway engineering company were proved correct, as the Paris workshops were closed.

In an attempt to boost the stagnating economy, the French government promoted a second universal exhibition, to be held in

1867. Eiffel seized the opportunity and became extremely interested in the construction of the main exhibition hall. Luckily, the director of works was Jean-Baptiste Krantz, with whom Eiffel had formed a good relationship on earlier railway contracts. Since he had not yet established his own workshops, Eiffel could not expect to be given substantial construction contracts, and his practical work for the exhibition was limited to relatively minor work on the Galerie des Beaux-Arts et d'Archéologie. However, he was appointed technical assistant to Krantz, and also designed the main arch-girders for the Galerie des Machines, a superb iron-framed ellipse which at the time was the largest structure of its kind. In the course of this design work, he produced, with the assistance of Henri Tresca, director of the Conservatoire des Arts et Métiers, the calculations that formed the basis for all wrought-iron construction. This was a labour of love closely linked to his lifelong insistence on rigorous discipline and his contempt for the guesswork that was still common in engineering construction. His new formulae for the elasticity principles applicable to iron structures would enable him to develop his hallmark design features – strength, rigidity and lightness – and to pioneer iron architecture characterised by light, open structure rather than heavy, solid mass. He also developed a strong mathematical base from which to understand his own work; this would be an enduring obsession. In a lecture that he was to deliver twenty years later, he explained his thinking on large-scale metal construction; while he was a faithful exponent of wrought iron, he concluded that, despite its drawbacks, steel was probably the metal of the future:

I have mentioned, so far, only wrought iron, but metal constructions can also be established out of cast iron or steel. Those out of cast iron are oldest, then came iron constructions and, more recently, those of steel. If one compares these three metals, one can say that, in large work, the use of cast iron has tended to disappear, except for columns or supports, because it resists tractive forces very badly. In addition, it is in general so brittle that under the influence of vibration its breaking-point is heightened.

The properties of steel are more difficult to define; it is a metal of very variable resistance and properties; its breaking strength can double, according to its mode of preparation; its impact resistance is generally weaker than its elevated breaking-point. The resistance of the steel used today in the construction industries is not much higher than that of iron, but its superiority lies in its elastic limit; i.e. the point where the deformations persist under the effect of a load is much higher than for iron. We can thus be reassured on the future fate of our steel constructions, on condition, of course, that they are preserved from the rust which is their mortal enemy.[5]

If Gustave Eiffel was to succeed in obtaining construction contracts, he needed to acquire substantial iron-working premises, and so, towards the end of 1866, with the help of a loan, he took a twelve-year lease of workshops at 48 rue Fouquet in the Levallois-Perret district of northern Paris, not far from the closed works of the Pauwels company at Clichy. The whole St-Lazare/Clichy area had been planned in 1822 by Jacques Perret, and later developed by Nicolas Levallois in 1845 from a suburban wasteland into a disordered district dominated by small workshops and a diversity of industrial enterprises. The chaos was heightened by the fact that people still lived in close proximity to the industrial noise and dirt – in 1880 there were 30,000 inhabitants, and twenty years later, 50,000. Eiffel's publicity material, giving little hint of the huge structures and international success that were to come, described a modest range of iron constructions of which he claimed experience – works such as market halls, reservoirs, gasholders and boilers. But his timing, still within the period of the massive expansion of the French railways (the network increased during the period 1840–80 from 310 to 16,780 miles), meant that his prosperity would derive, initially at least, from the railways. However, the first ten years were not easy, and Eiffel's progress was, as for everyone else, disrupted by the fall of Napoleon III's Second Empire and the bloody civil war that filled the streets of Paris during the period of the Commune of 1871.

Apart from the galleries for the 1867 exhibition, Eiffel undertook a number of relatively small projects around this time. There was a small bridge in Paris, another at La Rochelle, and forty-two small railway bridges on the railway line from Poitiers to Limoges; he also constructed gasworks at Versailles, Passy and Boulogne. More unusually, for the City of Paris he constructed the exterior iron framework of the synagogue in the rue de Tournelles, in the Jewish Marais district near the Bastille, and the attic structure of the church of Notre-Dame-des-Champs in the boulevard Montparnasse. In 1863, the Paris-Orléans railway company extended its network, specifically to link up its lines on either side of the Massif Central. To that end, it obtained the rights to construct a line from Commentry to Gannat, near Vichy. This was a relatively short 37-mile section of railway on a route from Lyon to Bordeaux, but the critical feature for Eiffel was that the terrain demanded tunnels, bridges and viaducts. The chief engineer in charge of the project was Wilhelm Nordling, who remembered Eiffel from his work on the Bordeaux bridge.

In 1867, along with several competitors, Eiffel was considered for various construction works on the line; he was successful in winning the bid to build two viaducts and in having his designs accepted for other works which would be undertaken by other companies. The two viaducts, at Rouzat on the River Sioule north of Clermont-Ferrand, and at Neuvial, were to be constructed to Nordling's designs, but Eiffel made a number of significant changes, with Nordling's agreement. The Rouzat viaduct (590ft in length and 197ft high) was shorter but similar in design to the viaduct at Crumlin in Wales, which Eiffel had admired. The two piers were composed of cast-iron columns with wrought-iron bracing, and Eiffel devised a new method of riveting the braces to the columns in order to produce a lighter but stronger joint than the conventional bolted structure. He also employed a novel method of rolling the prefabricated deck sections out towards the next pier, ensuring that during the movement the weight was evenly distributed across the rollers. Eiffel later wrote of one of the most important lessons learned in this project:

These viaducts on the line from Commentry to Gannat led to serious progress because of the care and attention with which their engineer, M. Nordling, studied the different forces that occur in structures of that type. The dangers of insufficient study of these forces were shown a few years ago at the great Tay Bridge in Scotland, where a violent wind, acting on the deck, overturned the cast-iron piers supporting it, just as a train was crossing.[6]

While completing the two viaducts, in October 1868, Eiffel signed deeds of partnership with Théophile Seyrig, a brilliant and well-to-do young German graduate of the Ecole Centrale, to establish G. Eiffel et Compagnie, with a capital of 200,000 francs. The young engineer, a junior rather than an equal partner, nevertheless contributed the larger sum of 126,000 francs to the partnership, which it was agreed would last for five years.[7] Seyrig ran the theoretical design side of the business with considerable flair and diligence while Eiffel controlled practical matters. The agreement was later renewed, but the partnership was dissolved in 1879, when Eiffel came to the conclusion that Seyrig was too financially demanding. A few years later, Seyrig instituted – and lost – a long-drawn-out legal dispute over the disposal of the partnership's assets. At that time, Eiffel changed the name of the company to the Compagnie des Etablissements Eiffel. (In 1895 it would change again to La Société de Construction de Levallois-Perret, and again in 1937, some years after Eiffel's death, when his name was restored to his company, re-formed as 'Anciens Etablissements Eiffel'.)

Although Gustave Eiffel is remembered for a few specific constructions, of which the tower is the most noted, the work of his company for many years revolved around more bread-and-butter commissions, some of them in the far-flung French colonies. He was to evolve a particular expertise in a variety of bridges for railway and military use, and throughout the early years he built up enormous experience of innovative ways of both designing for iron construction and carrying out assemblies themselves. This wide experience underpinned the emergence of the rigorous concepts of mathematical calculation and highly controlled planning and execution that were to become his guiding principles.

Despite Eiffel's knowledge of, and expertise in, bridge-building in all its forms, he was intrigued by the problems and fascinated by the prospect of constructing iron-framed buildings. Although there had been a few such structures in France in the early nineteenth century, he knew that it was not until the time of Stephenson in England and the many railway stations of the 1840s that the necessary techniques were developed. He was of the opinion that Exchange Station in Liverpool (he called it Tithe-Barn Street after the adjacent road), built in 1850 with a span of 140ft, was the most important.[8] From that example, he believed, followed all the great station constructions, accelerated, at least in France, by the development of the Polonceau Truss – named after the French engineer who invented it (Eiffel would use that formation himself in his first great 'train shed' at Budapest in 1875–7).

After the completion of the two viaducts in 1869, Eiffel was dejected by losing several contracts, for lighthouses in Egypt, a market at Dijon, and a station and large bridge in Italy. Such setbacks were becoming widespread, with political disruption in France (and especially Paris), and climactic revolutionary events erupting on to the streets. The heady days of Napoleon's empire had turned sour, with foreign policy errors and a growing opposition to liberalism provoking intense public reaction. In the elections of 1869, opposition seats in the national legislature doubled, and political mishandling of a crisis the following year over the succession to the throne of Spain resulted in France declaring war on Germany. This political turmoil notwithstanding, during 1870 Eiffel's company constructed several railway bridges for the Compagnie du Midi, a swing-bridge at Dieppe and the large playground and courtyard, covered in iron and glass, of the Lycée Carnot in Paris. Two years later came the main bridges of Chinon and Thouars on the River Thouet, and several bridges on the railway from Tours on the Loire via Poitiers to the seaside resort of les Sables-d'Olonne on the Bay of Biscay, where Eiffel et Cie also constructed a casino.

The political situation deteriorated; the royalist National Assembly, elected to make a peace treaty with Germany, was suspected by republicans in Paris of trying to restore the monarchy, and after some weeks of mounting opposition among the various factions, communes were established in a number of cities. Most of these were suppressed by the Versailles government, but the Paris Commune survived until *la semaine sanglante*, 'the bloody week' at the end of May 1871, when troops entered an undefended area of the city. Street battles ensued, the archbishop of Paris and other public figures were executed, public buildings such as the Tuileries Palace and the Hôtel de Ville were destroyed, and 20,000 insurrectionists killed. A final desperate stand was made in the Père Lachaise Cemetery, where the last remnants of resistance were massacred. In the aftermath, government repression was harsh, and tens of thousands were arrested or deported to penal colonies.

At Easter 1871, Eiffel's brother-in-law Armand Hussonmorel died in New York. The following year, however, Eiffel was delighted for his beloved sister when in February she married Dr Albert Hénocque, a highly respected Parisian specialist in haematology. Eiffel's business was at a critical stage during this period, and he appears to have had no sympathy whatsoever either with the republicans or the disruption to the city that their uprising caused. He sent his family out of the city, and was made a sergeant in the national guard. As with other manufacturers, he arranged temporary workshops within the city fortifications, and began to make munitions. He complained in a letter to his father about having to work surrounded by the sound of machine-gun fire, shouting and fighting in the streets; at one point, he was prevented from reaching his workshops at all by the closure of the city.[9]

Despite the fragile economic situation in France, Eiffel et Cie was successful in winning contracts abroad. Having a long-standing interest in obtaining work in Peru, Eiffel arranged for one of the company's directors, M. Lelièvre, whom he had known and trusted for many years, to depart for South America in June 1871 with the intention of acting as his agent and generating lucrative contracts.[10]

Meanwhile, other foreign deals were completed: between 1872 and 1875 the company built bridges in Romania, a footbridge in Cairo, locks on the Moskva river in Russia and the iron framework for a church in Manila in the Philippines. Lelièvre appears to have had considerable success, and as numerous projects came to fruition in South America, he announced that he expected to remain there for four or five years. The company constructed a custom-house (now the Casa de la Cultura) and pier at Arica in Chile, a gasworks at La Paz in Bolivia, railway bridges at La Oroya and a church at Tacna, in Peru. The iron church of San Marcos at Arica in Chile, like those at Tacna and Manila, was entirely built at the Eiffel workshops in Levallois-Perret, dismantled, and despatched for erection on site. It was initially erected further up the Chilean coast and was only moved to Arica after a tidal wave had destroyed all the town's churches. The experience of constructing complete buildings in Paris for re-erection several thousand miles away necessitated total accuracy of planning and design, and great diligence in casting and pre-assembly. There could be no 'nipping back to the foundry' for a new or replacement part. That experience provided exactly the demanding discipline that Eiffel was already interested in, and which would be the principal reason for his success with the tower. Sadly, hopes of further success in South America were dealt a savage blow with the death of Lelièvre in November 1873. Eiffel wrote that he would never again have such a devoted friend. He was to face another personal blow the following year, when Marguerite's grandfather, M. Régneau, died.

In 1875, the company was successful in winning two substantial contracts, each of which could on its own be described as the biggest and most important to date. The railway station at Pest (now Budapest) in Hungary was the terminus of the main line from Vienna, but it was small and had become inadequate. The authorities wanted a new, larger station on the same 15,550-square yard site; this would be more practical and also prestigious, as befitted a great national capital. The Austrian railways were French-controlled, with Wilhelm Nordling in a senior position, so Eiffel and Seyrig returned from Vienna in March 1875 with a contract signed and sealed; Eiffel's proposals for a train shed that allowed its iron structure to be boldly visible and which also enabled the prominent use of masonry and glass had been accepted. The contract was worth just under 3 million francs, and Eiffel quickly subcontracted aspects of the masonry, carpentry and ancillary work. The station was to be twin-sided, with arrivals and departures on opposite sides, and the overall plan for the rectangular covered nave with pitched glass and iron roof was similar to that supervised by Nordling six years before for the Gare d'Austerlitz in Paris. In order to allow railway services to continue without disruption, the entire structure surrounded the original station, which in the final stages was quickly demolished. The solid administrative buildings adjoining the train shed – to designs by the company's own architect – are heavily baroque in style, with pavilions topped by mansard roofs, towers and octagonal domes; but the startling feature is the frontage of the main concourse and train shed, which presents a glass-fronted gabled-end wall 246ft high, with an iron-and-glass pavement canopy supported on iron columns. Eiffel completed Nyugati (West) Railway Station in two years, and exhibited its plans and photographs at the Universal Exhibition of 1878. He declared that the materials ought to be deliberately exposed rather than hidden:

> . . . we sought to capture the clarity and simplicity of composition which a building of this type should show. We have carefully brought out the role and the nature of the various materials used as clearly as possible.[11]

In 1875, the Royal Portuguese Railways held a competition for the design and construction of a railway bridge over the deep River Douro at Oporto on the Atlantic coast in the north of the country, saving a 7½-mile detour. The surrounding geology was difficult: a gorge with steep sides in which the water was frequently very rough, with rapid currents, recurrent flooding and a very sandy bed. This would have to be a high bridge with a long, single span; the sandy bottom and 65ft depth of the river prohibited any form of central pier. The resulting total length of the bridge was 1,158ft, with a single span of 195ft, and the bridge deck 204ft above the river. It was to be the fourth longest single-span bridge in the world, after the St Louis Bridge over the Mississippi (519ft), the Kuilenbourg Bridge (492ft) over the Rhine in Holland, and Robert Stephenson's Britannia Bridge (459ft).

There were competitive plans submitted by four experienced companies, one English and three French; none of them adopted the suspension principle that was so favoured in the USA and which was then being exemplified by Washington Roebling's construction of the massive Brooklyn Bridge in New York to the design of his late father John Roebling. The Eiffel et Cie plan, conceived by Seyrig, was for a large trussed parabolic arch anchored in abutment masonry on each bank. The railway deck was supported by two latticed iron piers on the banks, one rising from the abutment on each side, and others rising from the arch itself; the bridge spanned the river at an oblique angle to offset wind resistance. Eiffel wrote to his mother saying that it would be one of the biggest bridges in Europe, claiming that if he got the contract his company also would be among the most important. At 965,000 francs, his price for the work was just over a third of that of the most expensive of his competitors – 1,410,000 was the next cheapest quote, and 2,760,000 francs was the quote from the English company.[12] Three months after winning the agreement to construct the Budapest station, Eiffel signed a contract with the Portuguese Railway Company, which demonstrated unusual confidence and trust in accepting such a low price from a still relatively small construction company that was already committed to a contract for another major work abroad. However, Eiffel's proposals were accepted and he rewarded that trust by building the bridge almost exactly as drawn (the contract price was increased a little to accommodate agreed modifications to the design). Seyrig played a major role in his own right in the design of the bridge. Nevertheless, it was this project that would sow the seeds of dispute between Eiffel and Seyrig, and the experience on this bridge raised a question over Eiffel's ability to deal fairly with collaborators that would resurface more than once in the future. As work began, he hoped to be able to return a favour by employing his brother-in-law Joseph Collin, who had been unsuccessful since leaving the foundry, but the arrangement did not work out, and Collin was dismissed for gross inefficiency.

Unusually, Eiffel decided that he wanted to persuade Marguerite to abandon Paris and join him in Portugal. She and their five-year-old daughter Valentine were established in a house in the country, some distance from the site of the bridge. This arrangement was new to both of them. Perhaps Eiffel was becoming tired of being alone for long periods; he had always felt a degree of regret and guilt that he was so often away from his family. Maybe there was a premonition; at any event, the weather was cold, wet and humid, and Marguerite was wracked by coughing fits. Later in the year she showed signs of being seriously ill.

The Douro arch was the biggest in the world at the time, and its topographical situation brought an immediate problem: scaffolding could not be erected in the deep, fast-flowing water, thus preventing the use of a false wooden arch upon which to launch the ironwork. Eiffel therefore decided to build the two halves of the iron arch out towards each other from the abutment on each bank, temporarily supporting the ironwork by the use of steel cables fixed to the piers. This was a method first used in the USA during the construction of the similar-sized arch of the St Louis Bridge. Accurate mathematical calculation was required to ensure that the two halves of the arch met high over the middle of the river without distorting the structure. Equally accurate manufacture in Paris of the designed parts was vital, as was a sense of teamwork. Eiffel recruited Emile Nouguier to supervise the works, and Jean Compagnon to be in charge of assembly; both these men, who had socialist Masonic sympathies, would remain with him through many other works and would be important in realising the tower.[13] As the arch progressed, the horizontal deviation was found to be only about one centimetre, although a greater vertical margin was planned in order to permit the supporting cables to lower the two sections slightly, enabling gravity to assist an accurate fit. Work on the bridge began in January 1876 and was completed on 31 October the following year. Eiffel's successful completion of the bridge, on time and within such a very tight budget, no doubt enhanced his reputation considerably. On 4 November, the bridge was ceremonially opened by King Luís I of Portugal and Queen Maria Pia, after whom it was named. (The Maria Pia Bridge over the Douro was replaced in 1984 by a new cantilever bridge, known as the Ponte de São João.)

Eiffel was forceful in insisting that the design of the bridge be a bold example of the art of the structural engineer and not intrude into the natural landscape; in bypassing the accepted rules of architecture it defined a new means for a new material to assert its right to its own simplicity of form, and to be considered beautiful. This was an argument frequently used by engineers who built the great iron structures, and Eiffel himself would initially be forced into a defensive use of it in relation to his tower. Claims had been made in France as early as 1849 for the importance of iron architecture, and in England fulsome agreement came from Sir George Gilbert Scott (architect of Glasgow University, the India Office and St Pancras station in London, among many other buildings). Despite his status as the undisputed master of Gothic, Scott wrote that it was 'self evident . . . that the triumph of modern metallic construction opens out a perfectly new field for architectural development'.[14] The Maria Pia Bridge certainly attained an immediate success, and achieved a prominence that made it a popular and instantly recognisable symbol for Oporto. Théophile Seyrig was also an authoritative promoter of the bridge and of its design. The year after it was opened, he presented a paper on its calculation and design to the French Society of Civil Engineers in which he claimed that 'the form of the arch has been judged the most elegant of all time.' He was also outspoken on the significance of the bridge in the landscape, pointing out that it was unusual to come across any great work that elevated the beauty or character of its position.[15] There is uncertainty as to just how much the design can be fairly attributed to Eiffel. He himself credited as collaborators firstly the distinguished structural engineer Henry de Dion[16] (who had vigorously supported Eiffel's imaginative application to the railway company) and Seyrig. However, after the latter presented his paper and appeared to claim a principal role in the design, Eiffel published his own *Notice sur le pont du Douro à Porto*, and allegedly began to 'systematically suppress' Seyrig's name.[17] This inflamed the quarrel that would split the partnership within a year. A sympathetic view might be that Eiffel was over-anxious to seize any opportunity to promote the young company that bore his own name; however, the dispute bore similarities to difficulties in years to come that suggest Eiffel had some uncertainty in acknowledging collaborative relationships.

In the economically depressed aftermath of the civil war, and with the intention of declaring that republican France was still glorious, another, rather hurriedly arranged, Exposition Universelle was mounted again in Paris in 1878. Eiffel used the opportunity to boost his reputation by extolling his own virtues and promoting some of the work that was now beginning to receive public as well as purely professional interest. He exhibited a 1:50 scale model of the Maria Pia Bridge, together with drawings and descriptions of Nyugati station in Budapest and several other projects, such as the Vianna do Castello combined road–rail bridge in Portugal; the 1,764-ton deck had been built onshore and launched in one piece on to its nine masonry piles. Eiffel had his eye on some of the dedicated structural work for the exhibition itself, but his principal competition entry was a failure, as indeed were those of his competitors. The aborted idea was for a covered bridge linking the Champ de Mars with the Trocadero and passing over the existing Pont d'Iéna; it was indicated that this was not to be a purely functional footbridge, but in its own right a significant architectural feature of the exhibition. The *cachet* of being able to advertise his most recent work in the centre of Paris was too good to miss, and Eiffel unsurprisingly decided to propose a smaller version of the Maria Pia Bridge, with a single span of 492ft. The bridge would have led to a grand entrance hall surmounted by a glass cupola. However, his estimate for the cost was three times that for the Maria Pia Bridge itself. For this reason (and the potential ruination of the view of the new Trocadero Palace), none of the competition entries was accepted, and that particular project was abandoned.

Despite his disappointment, and perhaps thanks to Jean-Baptiste Krantz being the exhibition's general commissioner, Eiffel et Cie was heavily involved in three substantial structures. The Great Iéna Entrance Hall and Machine Gallery was opposite the Trocadero, extending for 984ft, with three surmounting domes. The most notable feature of this building was that it employed, for the first time, roof trusses without tie-beams, which had been designed by de Dion (who unfortunately died before he saw his creation). This huge step forward in the perfection of iron structures meant that unsightly and disruptive secondary support mechanisms were wholly unnecessary. The size and decorative features of this building were widely criticised, and even though Eiffel's ironwork was noteworthy, disappointment with the architectural aspects meant that little credit came Eiffel's way.

The City of Paris Pavilion, 260ft by 80ft, collaboratively designed by the city architect, Henry de Dion and Eiffel et Cie, was a principal venue for the display of models of works and buildings being undertaken by the city after the ravages of the Commune. The huge hall had a glass ceiling supported on triangular roof trusses resting in turn on wrought-iron pillars, and was so designed as to allow certain pillars to be repositioned, enabling the disposition of spaces in the hall to be changed to suit different exhibits. Eiffel was particularly pleased that the pavilion was a fine example of the use of terracotta and enamelling as decorative features of the ironwork.[18] The pavilion outlived the exhibition and was moved to the opposite side of the Seine until it was demolished before the Expo of 1900. The work on the small iron-and-brick pavilion for the Paris Gas Company is interesting, mainly because Eiffel found himself working with Stephen Sauvestre, the intended designer of the abandoned entrance hall who would later be the architect for the tower. The exhibition was a triumph for Eiffel; he was awarded the Cross of the Légion d'Honneur, and quickly learned the value and techniques of keeping his name in the public eye. Despite the difficulties with Seyrig, Eiffel et Cie had completed several large and significant public projects as well as a considerable number of smaller, bread-and-butter commissions. These included gasworks at La Villette and Clichy in northern Paris, a pier in Peru, numerous railway bridges in France, Spain and Portugal, and a novel mobile revolving iron crane. By 1879, Eiffel felt that he was at last in his element, with a firmly established public reputation.

Not everything was rosy, however. He had endured a troublesome relationship with Seyrig; much more grievously, his happy marriage came to a tragic end with the death of Marguerite in 1877, just before the completion of the Maria Pia Bridge. The chronic pneumonia to which she was prone had become very much worse following her visit to Porto two years earlier, and the last month of her life was devoted to a frantic attempt, guided by Dr Albert Hénocque, to obtain the best medical advice that Paris could offer. Despite this care, she died at home in Paris at the age of thirty-two, leaving Gustave with the youngest child only seven years old. He never remarried, but in later life (at his insistence) was looked after by his eldest daughter, Claire – a duty that was imposed and accepted regardless of her marriage to Adolphe Salles. (Such a potentially disastrous filial arrangement in fact proved to be mutually agreeable, and Salles became Eiffel's devoted friend and collaborator.) For now, in the immediate aftermath of his wife's death, Eiffel set out for the almost-completed Maria Pia Bridge, accompanied by the fourteen-year-old Claire. Despite the terrible personal misery, Gustave Eiffel's eyes were on the future: he was about to build another bridge, which he believed would be the most important structure ever built in France.

FOUR

'The shapes arise!'

In 1856, Walt Whitman, the great idealist-become-realist American poet, described such themes as nature, industrialisation and endurance in his long poem 'Song of the Broad-Axe', in which he depicted how

> The shapes arise!
> Shapes of factories, arsenals, foundries, markets,
> Shapes of the two-threaded tracks of railroads,
> Shapes of the sleepers of bridges, vast frameworks,
> girders, arches . . .[1]

After the success of the bridge over the Douro and the exhibition of 1878, and with the split from Seyrig appearing permanent, Eiffel was now moving towards dazzling success in bringing art to massive iron structures; yet he had his feet sufficiently on the ground to ensure that there were manageable works in the pipeline before seeking another dramatic project.

During 1879 and 1880 he worked again for his oldest client, the Compagnie des Chemins de fer du Midi, for whom he constructed several bridges in the shadow of the Pyrenees, using his compressed-air system. There were also road bridges further north, bridges on the Beira–Alta railway in Portugal; there were two bridges in Romania, a road bridge in Algeria, and a railway bridge over the Tagus on the line from Cáceres to Estremadura in central Spain. Seyrig, meanwhile, was preparing to make a bid to undertake a large bridge on his own account, a second bridge over the Douro not far from the Maria Pia.

In the Place Le Corbusier in the rue des Sèvres, in the 7th

arrondissement, the famous fixed-price department store Magasin au Bon Marché, founded by Aristide Boucicaut in 1852, was in the course of a long twenty-year period of demolition and refurbishment of its five upper floors and two basements. Apart from his desire to avoid the use of wood, for reasons of fire prevention, the architect Louis-Charles Boileau was an advocate of the use of iron, and Eiffel was contracted to complete the framework for the last series of departments on the rue Babylone. Eiffel's involvement here has been described as his finest architectural work:

> The Boileau/Eiffel section of the Bon Marché was penetrated and articulated by spectacular light wells, bridges and baroque staircases. Equally integrated into the structure were light metal catwalks running over the high-pitched ferro-vitreous roof covering the major voids.[2]

Although the ornamental detail was distinctly of a past age, the use of iron was bold, and the refurbished Magasin au Bon Marché was widely regarded as a prototype for many of the greatest department stores, both in Paris and elsewhere.

Despite the difficulty with Seyrig, Eiffel's reputation and business were thriving, and his annual turnover was about 5 million francs.[3] His work on the Maria Pia Bridge had been widely noticed in engineering and railway circles, and early in 1879 he was approached by the company that operated the railways in the Massif Central, south of Clermont-Ferrand. They were contemplating a line on a difficult 56-mile route between Marvejols and Neussargues. In order to save a lengthy detour, it would require bridging the deep gorge of the turbulent River Truyère at Garabit, 10 miles from the town of Saint-Flour. The problem was that the viaduct would have to be 400ft high, almost exactly twice the height of Maria Pia; it would be the highest arched bridge in the world and 1,854ft in length. Eiffel proposed a single parabolic arch standing on five trussed-iron piers, similar to the design used on the Maria Pia Bridge. He relished the publication of a drawing graphically displaying the height:

To give an idea of the height of 122 metres, I have compared the Vendôme column placed on top of Notre Dame; the railway track is at a greater height than the superimposed monuments.[4]

He immediately knew that scaffolding would be impossible, and that as with the Maria-Pia, both halves of the huge arch would have to be cantilevered out from opposite banks, with steel cables stayed on the towers and anchored in masonry. The project would demand great precision of design calculation, manufacture and assembly. Although the railway company had its own architect, Léon Boyer, supervising the construction of the line, the bridge project was clearly regarded as belonging to Eiffel. Because of the size of the enterprise, the project required the permission of the French Ministry of Bridges and Roads, which apparently considered that Eiffel was the only engineer conceivably able to construct such a bridge. Clearly impressed by his work on the Douro bridge, they agreed in the summer of 1879 to award the contract to Eiffel, without proceeding to public competitive tender:

> . . . because only M. Eiffel has constructed a similar work, and only he has the experience of the new assembly methods of which he is in large part the inventor, and for which he also has the equipment which was used to erect the bridge over the Douro.[5]

Two weeks after this announcement, Eiffel took the decisive move to break his partnership with Seyrig, which in theory still had nine years to run. This move seems brutally deliberate in its timing, as Seyrig must have considered that he was due some share of the Garabit contract, given his considerable contribution to the earlier, Maria Pia design. Seyrig's legal attempts to get what he thought was his fair share of the assets of the partnership dragged on for twelve years, and he was finally awarded nearly four times his original investment in the company.[6]

Although Eiffel's professional life was beginning to appear extremely promising, the personal agony of his wife's early death continued to haunt him, despite the fact that his sister Marie and her second husband, Dr Albert Hénocque, were of great help and comfort to him, becoming closely involved in supporting Eiffel's children. He endured further heavy loss with the death of his mother in February 1878 at the age of seventy-nine. On the first anniversary of her death, he wrote lovingly to his father, regretting his solitude and sadness and suggesting that it would have been better if they had been together at such a time. Six months later his father also died.[7] However, with five young children to bring up Eiffel looked forward to countering despair by applying himself both to their happiness and security, and to his own particular elixir – hard work.

Because of the isolated location of the Garabit construction site, a substantial work camp had first to be provided, with dormitories, offices, canteens, materials stores, stables and even a school for the children of the workmen, many of whom would be on-site for several years, accompanied by their families. Work began in January 1880. Scaffolding and a temporary low-level wooden bridge provided access between both river banks. Iron assembly started in August 1882, and the arch itself a year later; the bridge (originally scheduled to be completed in two years) was finished in late 1884. The materials used give some idea of the scale of the construction: 3,169 tons of wrought iron, 23 tons of cast iron, 41 tons of steel, 678,768 rivets, 719,390 cubic feet of masonry and 38 tons of red paint.

Two of the triumvirate of close collaborators for this project, Emile Nouguier and Jean Compagnon, had been with Eiffel on the Douro bridge contract, and the third would also be a vital member of the team that would build the tower ten years later. The 24-year-old Maurice Koechlin was born at Guebwiller in Alsace and had studied at the Swiss Polytechnikum in Zurich under Karl Culmann, the celebrated German-Swiss railway engineer and engineering theoretician. Koechlin filled the void left by Seyrig, and together with Nouguier, Compagnon and Jean-Baptiste Gobert (who had already been with Eiffel as his assistant for three years) would form the core of the team that would remain with Eiffel during the rest of his engineering life.

Karl Culmann is credited with influencing the young Eiffel with his analysis and explanation of 'graphic statics' in relation to structural ideas. (This was the concept of the pictorial representation of forces acting on a structure, especially useful in calculating the response of structures to external actions.) Culmann himself had learned the concept of 'biomimicry', which had also attracted Joseph Paxton, from Hermann von Meyer, professor of anatomy in Zurich, and ideas linking bone structures with the mathematics of load-bearing were clearly employed by Eiffel in his tower.

As Eiffel started work on the Garabit Viaduct, calculating in his usual meticulous way the tiniest detail not only of the structure itself but of his methods of production and assembly, the Tay Bridge collapsed in Scotland. In 1871, the North British Railway had commissioned Thomas Bouch to proceed with his design for a bridge across the wide and often stormy Firth of Tay between Newport in Fife and Craig Pier in Dundee. Bouch had a reputation among the English engineering elite for being both underqualified and somewhat reckless, rejecting heavy iron plate in favour of lattice girders carried by slender columns – what one contractor referred to as 'muscle without flesh'. His bridges always seemed to be constructed very quickly, while adhering to tight budgets. At the time, the Tay Bridge was to be the longest in the world, built of wrought-iron lattice girder trusses supported on cast-iron columns that rose from masonry piers in the sea. The two miles would be covered in sixty-five spans at a height of 100ft above the Firth, with thirteen box-shaped 'high girders' forming the central section.

After the ceremonial opening for Bouch's Tay Bridge on 31 May 1879, 600 guests sat down to a banquet in Dundee's Albert Hall. The following month, Queen Victoria ordered that the royal train should cross the bridge on its way south from Balmoral, and Bouch was able to note in his diary for 26 June, 'Attending at Windsor for Knighthood.' Only six months later came the catastrophic collapse of the bridge: during a ferocious storm on the evening of Sunday 28 December 1879, the afternoon train from Edinburgh to Dundee plunged into the fury of the Firth of Tay, along with over 1,000ft of the 'high girders' at the centre of the bridge and all seventy-five passengers and crew.

At the ensuing court of inquiry, much of the iron was found to have been of inferior quality, sometimes badly cast, with long cracks in the iron columns due to shrinkage; other evidence suggested deliberate substitution of best by inferior materials. Many defects in the columns had been filled with 'beaumontegg', a mixture of wax and iron filings with the convenient characteristic of looking just like solid iron when burnished with a stone. A fatal error attributed to Bouch was that he had ignored the question of wind pressures. When Bouch was offered the comfort that he couldn't be blamed for lack of knowledge of wind pressure, Wreck Commissioner Rothery said:

> Be it so, yet he knew, or might have known, that at that time engineers in France made an allowance of 55lb per sq ft for wind pressure, and in the United States an allowance of 50 lb.[8]

Yet, although Bouch had been advised to ignore the matter, he had in fact sought guidance from the Railway Inspectorate. He had also consulted the Astronomer Royal, Sir George Airey (who had been erroneously insistent that Paxton's Crystal Palace would collapse in 1850), over his early plans for the Forth Bridge. Airey had glibly claimed that 'The greatest wind pressure to which a plane surface like that of the bridge will be subjected in its whole extent is 10lb per square foot.'[9] Immediately after the disaster, Airey lost confidence in his earlier ideas, and began to recommend assuming a wind pressure of 120lb per square foot. Asked about this at the inquiry, when it was suggested to him that there was no scientific basis for such an assumption, he replied, 'I cannot say how it is, but ideas do not always come into one's mind.'[10] His entire approach to the problem seems to have been based on uninformed guesswork.

In early July 1880, after sitting for twenty-five days in Dundee and London, the court of inquiry published its verdict in a report of over 1,000 pages. It concluded:

The bridge was badly designed, badly constructed and badly maintained. For these defects both in the design, the construction and the maintenance Sir Thomas Bouch is in our opinion mainly to blame. For the faults in design he is entirely responsible. For those of construction he is principally to blame in not having exercised that supervision over the work which would have enabled him to detect and apply a remedy to them. And for the fault of maintenance he is also principally if not entirely to blame in having neglected to maintain such an inspection over the structure as its character imperatively demanded.[11]

Engineers around the world were horrified by the implications of the collapse in Scotland, and Eiffel was no exception. He increased safety factors for the Garabit Viaduct and limited the stress in the trusses under combined wind pressure and train load to 838lb per square inch. In addition to resting the ends of the arches on hinges to allow for expansion, he calculated the effects of temperature changes, and the consequence of lateral wind pressures on the deck with and without the presence of a moving train. Having designed the deck's side girders to rise 5ft 3in. above the rails, he also took account of the partial sheltering of the train against the wind. As with the Maria Pia Bridge, the ribs of the arch were inclined from the vertical, that is, designed and constructed to be wider apart at the bottom than at the top, in order to aid stability and wind resistance. (This difficult technique is most dramatically seen in the huge cantilevers of the Forth Railway Bridge in Scotland; the practice was found in the early twentieth century to be both structurally unnecessary and expensive.) Aerodynamic analysis was becoming something of an obsession with Eiffel, and he ensured that without detriment to the elegance of the design, the Garabit Viaduct would not be allowed to yield to the wind. This project above all others proved his mastery of the aerodynamics of bridge-building, and his ability to design and build light, elegant and extremely strong latticed structures.

The Garabit Viaduct became an experimental laboratory for the processes that would later enable the Eiffel Tower to be realised with such success. Already, Eiffel was insisting on techniques that were entirely different from those soon to be adopted for the construction of the Forth Railway Bridge in Scotland. There, techniques that were common in carpentry were normal; drawings and parts all arrived on the bridge with considerable adjustment and alteration required during final assembly. This meant that sophisticated tools and equipment had to be available to permit critical drilling and bending high on the bridge itself. For his part, Eiffel insisted that every single component arrived accurately forged, shaped and drilled, ready to be assembled exactly in its unique position in the structure; if any part was incorrect or deficient, it was not modified, but summarily rejected.

Although the method of assembly was similar to that used on the Maria Pia Bridge, in the aftermath of the Tay Bridge collapse all safety tolerances were more rigorous. The steel cables that supported the extending ends of the two halves of the arch had maximum load ratings of 85 tons, although no cable bore a load greater than 15 tons. When the arch was completed it was tested under a load comprising a 75-ton locomotive and twenty-two coaches each weighing 15 tons; the 0.3in deflection at the apex of the arch was exactly as Eiffel had estimated.[12] The careful calculation of tension and compression within the components of the bridge certainly resulted in a massive, yet light and supremely strong, structure.

Garabit was the last bridge he built, but in later years, Eiffel was haunted by suggestions that it was in fact the work of Seyrig (although no documentary evidence supports such claims). In recent years, the construction of a dam at the site has raised the river level, and therefore detracted from the dramatic effect of the bridging of the once-deep valley, but the Garabit Viaduct, painted red and floodlit at night, is still claimed as the most graceful of Eiffel's bridges. At the same time, although set in a wild natural landscape, the bridge projected the power of the new industrial age in which function was predominant. The dichotomy between art and industry that had been articulated in the arena of the previous half-century's international exhibitions had simply moved on to a grander scale and into the open air. The division would soon become a raging dispute.

Following the masterpiece of the Garabit Viaduct, Eiffel's new company embarked on a string of contracts abroad. There was the challenging Cubzac road bridge on the Dordogne, which was to be constructed in place of, and using some parts of, an original suspension bridge of 1837 that had collapsed in a storm in 1869. The new bridge was 1,881ft long, constructed in eight spans resting on cast-iron piers built on original masonry piers. Eiffel remained very proud of this commission because he had to devise innovative methods of complying with the contract conditions, involving partly using a new and untried cantilever technique, and partly involving 'rolling out' over changing gradients.

France had extensive colonial interests in Indo-China, some areas of which were French protectorates under local rulers; however, when France occupied Saigon in 1859, an area of the 26,640 square miles known as Cochinchine (Cochin China) was administered directly by France as a colony. In 1880, Eiffel completed the Tan An railway bridge on the line from Saigon to Mytho, one of several railway and road bridges he would construct there. The Tan An Bridge crossed a rapidly flowing river, which necessitated a long central unsupported span of 263ft; this in turn required yet another Eiffel 'first', in pushing two halves of the deck out from each end, to meet in the middle. His work in French Indo-China also resulted in the design of small, prefabricated portable bridges, ideal for military use. They were designed from standardised light steel parts, were relatively inexpensive, could be bolted together in a variety of forms by people with little engineering skill, and were strong enough to support heavy military vehicles; a 70ft bridge could be built in position in one hour. The construction of such bridges had only become possible because of Eiffel's unique mastery of the technique of using accurately calculated and manufactured parts. He patented this method and made considerable sums selling the kits of parts, complete with assembly instructions, largely to the French colonies. Between 1881 and 1884 he supplied over a hundred such bridges to Cochin China alone, at a cost of over a million francs.[13]

Others were sold in Portugal, Italy, Senegal, Java, Greece, Brazil and Peru. His 'economical portable bridges' remained in widespread use until the Bailey Bridge system was devised by the English engineer (Sir) Donald Coleman Bailey in the 1940s.

The workshops at Levallois-Perret buzzed with constant activity as new orders poured in; Eiffel was professionally established and, perhaps inheriting the financial acumen of his mother, well on his way to considerable wealth. The family moved from Levallois-Perret to the Rue Prony near the Parc Monceau, nearer the centre of Paris; a much grander move still would be made in just a few years, when he and his family would own substantial properties in various parts of France. Although he was now well-to-do, and moving in more elevated circles, he did not succumb to the temptations of high society, preferring the comfort and pleasure of his extended family whenever he could temporarily leave his professional responsibilities. If socially dull, he was recognised by his peers as an engineer of great self-confidence, who was unusually interested in professional frankness, always willing to publish his drawings and details of his calculations and procedures. Although he was an engineer first and foremost, the new uses for iron in construction demanded that he develop more than a casual interest in design. But his reputation was still confined to professional circles; if he craved a more public fame, he had only some little time to wait.

In late 1880, Eiffel entered two international competitions for road bridges. He won the first, in collaboration with the engineer Janos Feketehazy, to build a replacement for the Szeged road bridge over the River Tisa in Hungary, which had been swept away in a flood. The design was for four shallow parabolic arches of reducing span on masonry piers. The second competition, for a road bridge at Porto, near the Maria Pia Bridge, turned into a disappointment. All the biggest and best French engineering contractors were in competition, along with two Belgian companies, two English and one Dutch. Not only did Gustave Eiffel fail to obtain the contract, but the man who did was Théophile Seyrig. The Luis I Bridge was to be an elegant wrought-iron tied arch similar to the Maria Pia, with a span of 565ft and at 3,000 tons almost twice its weight; it had a double deck for road and pedestrian traffic, the upper deck running over the top of the arch and the lower suspended at the level of the springings. The bridge has been converted in recent years to carry a metro service.

During 1883–4 came the Tardes railway viaduct on the line from Montluçon to Eyguerande for the Orléans Railway Company. This was another example of unusual difficulty due to the terrain; because of the depth of the valley (328ft at the centre of the span), the track-deck at both ends of the viaduct had to be on a curve. Eiffel decided to use the 'rolling out' method that he had first used on the Sioule Viaduct. However, there was an exceptional mishap because of severe weather conditions. During a stormy night in January 1884, with no one on the site, a 174ft section of deck cantilevered from a masonry pier was blown down. Eiffel was not blamed for this incident, which was compensated for by the state, and the bridge was later completed with no further incident.

The new Eiffel company was extremely busy during the 1880s, with all manner of contracts, of which only the most notable are mentioned; conveniently, the portable bridges were so popular that they became a continuing demand throughout the years, providing a stable and reliable volume of work. In the peak years there were to be company offices opened in Lisbon, Shanghai and Saigon, and agents employed on commission contracts in St Petersburg, Madrid, Naples and Buenos Aires. Eiffel's affinity for introducing innovative techniques enabled him to register patents in France and abroad for a dozen improvements in constructional and design methods. Although bridges of all forms were the mainstay, there was still a wide range of work: a dam on the River Seine at Port-Mort, a market at Bordeaux, another gasworks (at Rennes), and a grand iron hall with balconies on three floors for the Paris headquarters of Crédit Lyonnais – one of the oldest private limited company banks in France, and an important icon of the French economy. Among Eiffel's many advances was his use of steel, building the first steel bridge in France over the Sarthe at Morannes in 1885. Eiffel was not wholly convinced of the pre-eminence of steel over iron, feeling that many of its supposed beneficial properties were too dependent on the vagaries of production; at the same time, he was able to see the trends:

> The manufacture of steel is very delicate, and it is only in recent years that it has been possible to produce a metal of which we can be confident and which perfectly offers the special qualities required. There is a marked tendency in the construction industries increasingly, day by day, to replace iron with steel, and there are already a great number of very important steel structures. One can say without contradiction, I believe, that steel is the metal of the future.[14]

In 1884, Gustave Eiffel embarked on an unusual project that would remain in his mind a particular favourite of his career; it had the added interest of being at the invitation of a giant of French classical architecture who would become one of his implacable detractors during the construction of his tower. Raphael Bischoffsheim, born in Amsterdam and member of a fabulously wealthy banking family, had trained as a civil engineer at the Ecole Centrale in Paris. He went on to become inspector of the railway company, the Compagnie des Chemins de fer du Midi (when he had met the young Eiffel at the time of the building of the Bordeaux Bridge) before eventually becoming part of the family banking empire. He was a highly regarded philanthropist who had an interest in scientific endeavours, and in particular those related to astronomy, a field to which he donated generous sums. He funded observatories in Paris, at Parc Montsouris in the south of the city, where the Bureau des Longitudes was based, and at Pic du Midi, 9,436ft high in the Pyrenees. However, his major contribution to astronomy was his purchase of land at Mont-Gras in the hills above Nice and his endowment, to the extent of 1,500,000 francs, of a new observatory, inaugurated in 1887 and known today as the Observatoire de la Côte d'Azur.

With the intention that the observatory should be not only a scientific marvel but an artistic one, Bischoffsheim called on the architect Charles Garnier to design the entire complex. Garnier had recently designed a large villa for Bischoffsheim at Bordighera in Italy, but his extraordinary fame as an architect of the beaux-arts style was entirely due to his completion in 1875 of his neo-baroque Paris Opera House, which instantly became the most talked-about building of the century. Garnier admired some of Eiffel's work, including an unrealised design for the reconstruction of the dome of the Paris Observatory. He sought him out to design the iron truss-work and exterior of the huge 79ft-diameter dome for the equatorial telescope, 30in in diameter and 59ft long, which would be the centrepiece of the Nice Observatory. Eiffel's huge cupola – larger than that of the Pantheon, it would be the largest unsupported dome in the world – rested on a classical Palladian base designed by Garnier. Other similar structures were usually rotated, very slowly, on rollers, but while Eiffel employed such a reserve system for use during maintenance periods, he designed a typically innovative flotation arrangement. This essentially meant that the weight of the dome was borne by a circular float in a reservoir of water containing non-freezing magnesium chloride; the entire 110-ton weight could be fully rotated by a child in only 4 minutes. The dome and its 620 sections of sheet-iron outer skin were constructed in the Levallois-Perret workshops, then dismantled and transported to Nice for re-erection on Garnier's masonry plinth.

Eiffel's experience was seemingly complete; he had not only built iron bridges, viaducts, buildings and industrial facilities of all descriptions in many countries, but he had learned how to do it, absorbed the knowledge and perfected the techniques. Now, he had collaborated with France's most celebrated neoclassical architect. Charles Garnier would soon become Eiffel's bitter enemy in a debate that was to characterise the 1880s and '90s in France as in other European countries; this would be about a dry, academic, official 'art' and its relationship to the new force that was the driving feature of modern life – industrialisation. Eiffel was becoming the undisputed master of a new and highly technical form of construction that declared itself to be uncompromisingly big and which, as in the Garabit Viaduct, adopted a place in the middle of a natural landscape – a contrast that provoked extreme reaction. The leaders of the traditionalists were painters, and it was one of their fraternity, William Bouguereau, who summed up their stance when he addressed the five Academies of Paris in 1885:

> One is born an artist. The artist is a man of a special nature, who has a particular sense which is to see form and colour spontaneously, together, in a perfect harmony . . . One must first love nature with all one's heart and soul, and be capable of spending hours before it, studying and admiring it. Everything is in nature. A plant, a leaf, a blade of grass are objects for infinite and profound meditation.[15]

The problem for those who insisted on defining the national taste in such a manner was that by 1880 France was on the brink of massive technological change, and the population as a whole (through experiences in factories and elsewhere) was right at the heart of it; they were the first to recognise the change, work with it, and want to redefine all manner of attitudes in the light of it. For the traditionalists, there were appalling new torments such as electricity, newspapers, mass production and mass communication, satire and photomechanical reproduction (of 'art', indeed). The intellectuals who inhabited the salons were being left behind; on seeing this, they became reactionaries. Even the republican political philosopher Jules Simon observed that '. . . the industrial revolution, in occurring just after the social revolution had complicated social change no end.'[16]

Gustave Eiffel would become embroiled in this cultural fury with his tower in Paris in the next few years, and his simultaneous involvement with the charismatic but dogmatic Ferdinand de Lesseps would plunge both him and the French state into deep and infamous crisis, a crisis that would have a profound effect on Eiffel's future. But the project that would give him the first taste of international fame was about to get under way. However, the moves to bring about the Statue of Liberty Enlightening the World had begun fifteen years earlier at a dinner held by liberal republicans in Paris.

FIVE

Liberty

In the summer of 1865, a few months after the assassination of the US President Abraham Lincoln, which had so shocked republican France, Edouard René Lefebvre de Laboulaye, historian, staunch liberal republican and lecturer at the Collège de France, held a dinner for prominent intellectuals and politicians at his home near Versailles. As a student of American government, he conceived the idea of finding an appropriate means of celebrating the birth of the United States of America, the part played in it by France, and the ideals of freedom and independence that were so cherished by both nations and which seemed to have been threatened by Lincoln's murder. One of his guests was the young Alsatian sculptor Frédéric Auguste Bartholdi; he was already known as a sculptor in stone and bronze with a penchant for the interpretation of large patriotic themes. He had visited Egypt for a second time in 1867, where, encouraged by Ferdinand de Lesseps, he had planned a gigantic statuesque lighthouse for the entrance to the Suez Canal. The project never came about, but the concept stayed firmly in his mind. Following the Franco-Prussian War, Bartholdi was again a guest at one of Laboulaye's dinners, when he revealed that he had considered emigrating to America. The whole matter of a link with the USA was under discussion again, and with the centenary of American independence approaching, Laboulaye encouraged Bartholdi to go to America to try to consolidate their ideas.

The young sculptor was enthusiastic and set off for New York in 1871, with letters of introduction from his distinguished fellow guests at Versailles. During the voyage he revived his concept of the huge monument for Suez, and by the time he had his first sight of New York Harbor, he was convinced that he had found the idea that would fulfil the best hopes and intentions of Laboulaye and his friends in Paris. He travelled widely throughout the USA canvassing his proposal, met President Ulysses Grant and numerous politicians, philanthropists, businessmen and newspaper editors. He had particularly useful discussions with Charles Sumner, the politician, lawyer and student of jurisprudence, the naturalist Jean Louis Agassiz, and the poet Henry Wadsworth Longfellow. His final plan was for a colossal 155ft statue of Liberty Enlightening the World, to stand on a 150ft plinth inside the courtyard of Fort Wood on Bedloe's Island at the entrance to New York Harbor.[1]

Bartholdi's proposal was received by Laboulaye and his followers with great enthusiasm, and the Franco-American Union was formed in the autumn of 1875 with Laboulaye as president. Bartholdi immediately began work on a series of preliminary models about 4ft high, and struggled to solve the problems of choice of materials and the mechanics of construction. The great and the good of French society were recruited to the dynamic new international project, and individuals contributed enthusiastically to an open subscription. The state was not to be involved, although the City of Paris made a substantial contribution. A lottery was organised, and in a continuing series of exhibitions, entertainments and modest fundraising schemes organised at all levels of French society, the money required to design and build the statue in Paris and ship it to New York steadily mounted. Individual lottery contributions were symbolically limited to one franc, but the total amounted to 300,000 francs, coming from rich and poor, the artisans of Paris and the industrial cities, and peasant farmers from the rural interior of France. The playwright Émile Guiard and composer Charles Gounod collaborated on a celebratory hymn entitled 'La Liberté Eclairant le Monde' which was presented at the Paris Opera, and an inscribed gold medal was struck and sent to the widow of the murdered American president with the message, 'Tell Mrs. Lincoln that in this little box is the heart of France.'

In the USA a similar subscription was to be established to pay for the massive 155ft masonry plinth, designed by Richard M.

Hunt, on which the statue would stand. Almost immediately, there was confusion in the USA about French government involvement:

> There exists a mistaken idea among the people here that the colossal statue of Liberty, to be erected in our harbor on Bedloe's Island, is to be presented by the French government to the United States. This is not the case; the government has nothing to do with it. The project was started by the French people, and it was intended that the French and American people should, by their joint efforts, raise a lasting monument to celebrate the triumph of liberty in their respective countries.[2]

To help American fundraising, the statue's massive right forearm, hand and torch were sent to a place of honour at the Philadelphia Exhibition in 1876. Many millions saw it there before the pieces were sent for display in Madison Square, New York until 1884, when they were returned to Paris for final adjustments and assembly. The statue was to be by far the biggest in the world, dwarfing earlier icons such as the Sphinx of Giza or the Colossus of Rhodes, with a head 17ft across, an 8ft index finger and a right arm 42ft long and 12ft thick. French subscribers had responded with enthusiasm, and Bartholdi was able to begin work on larger scale models of the various structural elements in the Paris workshops of Gaget, Gauthier et Cie in the rue de Chazelles, where the roof for Charles Garnier's fabulous Paris Opera House had been made. His first model for the figure of Liberty was his elderly mother Charlotte, but the possibly apocryphal but nevertheless attractive story has it that when she tired of the rigours of posing, he substituted his mistress Jeanne-Emilie Baheux de Puysieux, whom he met on his first visit to the USA, and whom he later married. Despite the statue's colossal size, Bartholdi's overriding guiding principle was simplicity of design, and all his refinements made at the model stages were aimed at that objective:

> The details of the lines ought not to arrest the eye . . . the surfaces should be broad and simple, defined by a bold and

clear design, accentuated in the important places . . . it should have a summarised character such as one would give to a rapid sketch.[3]

In the USA, fundraising was much more sluggish than in France, despite the public exhibitions in Philadelphia and New York; it seems that there were persistent misunderstandings as to the international nature of the gift, and that it was to be made to the people of the USA as a whole and not just the city of New York. When the lack of funding became a public issue, cities such as Philadelphia, Boston, San Francisco and Cleveland immediately offered to provide the funds if Liberty could be theirs. A new American Committee for the Statue of Liberty was formed in January 1877; the initial 144 members soon swelled to over 400 prominent citizens, including a co-founder of the *New York Times*, the father of the future President Theodore Roosevelt, John Jay the jurist and statesman, and William Maxwell Evarts, the US Attorney-General, who was chairman. It had appeared likely that the pedestal would have to be abandoned and the generous and imaginative gift of the people of France rejected in whatever conciliatory manner could be devised. However, impetus was added to the project when a legislative sub-committee succeeded in steering a resolution through Congress that recognised that the gift from France was already nearing completion in Paris; accordingly the President was directed

. . . to designate and set apart for the erection thereof a suitable site upon either Governor's or Bedloe's Island, in the harbor of New York; and upon the completion thereof shall cause the same to be inaugurated with such ceremonies as will serve to testify the gratitude of our people for this expressive and felicitous memorial of the sympathy of our sister republic . . .[4]

Progress remained slow, however, with the press largely hostile and demanding to know why people across the country should be asked to pay for 'New York's Lighthouse'. By 1881, little had been achieved, and the sum required was revised upwards by 100 per cent.

Meanwhile, Bartholdi had been deeply uncertain as to what kind of structure would bear the strain of transportation across the Atlantic and re-erection in New York, and be able even to bear its own weight and survive on a windswept site. His plan had been to form the statue in embossed copper sheets 4in thick, fixed to a framework by riveted metal strips. But what kind of framework would be strong enough without condemning the structure to a wholly impractical weight? He contacted the republican architect Eugène-Emmanuel Viollet-le-Duc, who had designed the framework for Aimé Millet's huge statue of Vercingetorix in 1865; Viollet-le-Duc began work, but died with only the internal structure for the head designed.

In 1881, Bartholdi sought the collaboration of Gustave Eiffel, having become aware of his interest in wind-resistance problems. After studying calculations prepared by Maurice Koechlin, Eiffel planned an entirely different interior iron skeleton from Viollet-le Duc's, based on a pylon of four vertical iron beams rising from the granite pedestal. However, he was concerned by the raised arm bearing the torch, which, greatly overhanging the statue's centre of gravity, would be an inherent weakness. He therefore arranged to carry the arm's supporting beam right down through the skeleton to the opposite side, thus providing a counterbalance. However, his interest in the aerodynamics of the statue on such an exposed site persuaded him to go much further in providing stability. Each of the 300-plus shaped copper sheets achieves its stability directly from the framework rather than from either its upper or lower neighbour. Although the copper sheets are riveted together, they are not load-bearing; each piece is uniquely fixed by iron straps to a wooden framework attached to the internal skeleton and is therefore self-sustaining and independently reliant on the framework, rather than on any part of the outer copper shell:

The iron braces uniting the copper shell with the supporting truss-works were forged to the form of the copper sheets after the latter had been entirely completed. The finished pieces were finally carried into the court of the workshop, and there assembled and fastened to the frame.[5]

The copper sheets were also arranged to allow individual expansion, and were insulated from the iron framework to avoid undesirable electrical activity in adverse weather conditions. The weight of copper was approximately 176,400lb, and iron approximately 265,000lb, giving a total weight for the statue of approximately 440,000lb. Eiffel constructed the framework at the workshops in the rue de Chazelles in the 17th arrondissement, where, towering above Baron Haussmann's skyline, the structure attracted great interest, especially after workmen began fixing the shaped copper sheets to the skeleton. Bartholdi wrote to the chairman of the American Committee in December 1882: 'The statue commences to reach above the houses, and by next spring we shall see it overlook the entire city, as the large monuments of Paris now do.'[6] The site overlooking the workshops became a favourite venue for impromptu orators anxious to comment on Franco-American affairs. This attention persuaded the previously reticent French government to take an interest in the project, and conscious of the potential goodwill for the Republic, offered to provide the services of the French navy in transporting the statue to New York.

As work on the pedestal in New York was far behind schedule, the final stages of the statue were slowed down. However, it was finished in the early summer of 1884, and after a celebratory dinner, Bartholdi took an American senator to the opera, where the visitor was astounded to find the recognisable figure of Liberty in their box; it was Bartholdi's mother Charlotte. A further banquet on 11 June, attended by a distinguished company, was held to celebrate Liberty's completion. Edouard de Laboulaye had died the previous year, and had been succeeded as president of the Franco-American Union by Ferdinand de Lesseps, who on 4 July 1884 formally offered the Statue of Liberty to Levi P. Morton, the US Minister to France, saying:

This is the result of the devoted enthusiasm, the intelligence and the noblest sentiments which can inspire man. It is great in its conception, great in its execution, great in its proportions; let us hope that it will add, by its moral value, to the memories and sympathies that it is intended to perpetuate.

Morton concluded his acceptance remarks thus: 'God grant that it may stand until the end of time as an emblem of imperishable sympathy and affection between the Republics of France and the United States.'[7]

The transatlantic voyage was some way off, however. American funding for the pedestal faltered again in the autumn of 1884, when money ran out. Although the substantial foundations had been excavated, what money had been obtained had disappeared in various preliminary contracts. The internal mass of the huge pedestal was to be concrete, but massive blocks of granite from Connecticut were to form the external faces. Despite the lack of real progress, there was lavish Masonic celebration of the official laying of the cornerstone of the pedestal in August 1884 by the Grand Master of the Grand Lodge of New York State. However, hardly any work on the plinth itself had been undertaken when money ran out yet again.

Just when prospects seemed at their worst, a saviour came to hand. The previous year, the *New York World* newspaper had been taken over by Joseph Pulitzer, a Hungarian *émigré*.[8] He quickly turned the newspaper into a popular, campaigning paper with the largest circulation of any in the USA. In the spring of 1885, it began an energetic campaign to raise the necessary $100,000 to complete the gigantic plinth. The paper not only encouraged donations, but vilified the rich and famous who resisted contributing, and attacked the mean provincialism of other areas of the USA that whined about the statue's New York location. It harangued its readership daily and the nation as a whole, and organised a huge range of benefit events; it printed the name of every donor, of whatever amount (many, particularly those of thousands of school-children, were of less than $1), and publicised the sale of authorised commemorative models of Liberty.

Money poured in, especially when word arrived from France that the statue had been dismantled into 350 pieces and packed into 214 specially made crates. The voyage across the Atlantic began on 21 May, as the three-masted frigate *Isère* left Rouen. Five months after launching its campaign, the *World* was able to announce that the funds to enable completion of the pedestal had been achieved. *Harper's New Monthly* bemoaned the sloth in obtaining the American funding for the pedestal, and in common with almost all the American press, congratulated the *World* on its efforts:

> But, except for the assiduity of the *New York World*, which opened a popular subscription and stimulated interest every day by publishing the details of the movement, it is not clear that the grant must not have been made finally by Congress. The *World* is apparently to be credited with the honor of the completion of a work to which unassisted American public spirit seemed to be unequal.[9]

In June, *The Manufacturer and Builder* of New York reported the completion of the statue and its impending arrival in the city:

> From its lofty resting place voyagers from and to our shores may be reminded by the sight of this beautiful and colossal gift, of the friendship of the chivalrous nation to which we owe so heavy a debt of gratitude for her timely aid in our day of sore distress. The statue is now on its way to our shores, and it behoves us to prepare for its reception a monument which shall be worthy to receive so noble a work.[10]

The *Isère* arrived at Sandy Hook, the entrance to New York Harbor, on 17 June, and Major-General Charles P. Stone, the chief engineer of the pedestal, officially took possession of the statue and the accompanying deeds of gift. Several months passed, during which the statue was carefully unpacked and reassembled, using a third of a million copper rivets. The final courses of masonry were added to the plinth, which was officially completed in April 1886, with the stonemasons throwing silver coins from their own pockets into the setting mortar.

On a cold, damp 28 October 1886, the Statue of Liberty was formally dedicated before thousands of people and several boatloads of protesting suffragettes. The celebrations began in the morning at Madison Square, with President Grover Cleveland reviewing a military parade, accompanied by US and French government and civic notables. Parades continued for some hours, terminating at the Battery, when the dignitaries boarded the USS *Despatch*, which led a flotilla of vessels to Bedloe's Island, where several French warships lay at anchor. Two and a half thousand special guests were seated at the base of the pedestal, but accounts suggest that a million people watched the events, as the cream of American and French government and society played their various roles.

Ferdinand de Lesseps, speaking in French, again enacted the ceremonial presentation, accompanied by applause, ships' whistles, gun salutes and military bands. Inside the torch, 300ft above, Frédéric Bartholdi pulled the French tricolour from Liberty's face at the moment of ceremonial climax. President Cleveland gave what was described as a potent and pointed acceptance speech:

The people of the United States accept with gratitude from their brethren of the French Republic the grand and complete work of art we here inaugurate. This token of the affection and consideration of the people of France demonstrates the kinship of republics, and conveys to us the assurance that in our efforts to commend to mankind the excellence of a government resting upon popular will, we still have beyond the American continent a steadfast ally. We are not here today to bow before the representation of a fierce warlike god, filled with wrath and vengeance, but we joyously contemplate instead our own deity keeping watch and ward before the open gates of America and greater than all that have been celebrated in ancient song.[11]

Perhaps confirming the point of view of the suffragettes, the only females allowed near the ceremonials were Bartholdi's wife Jeanne-Emilie, and Tototte, the eight-year-old daughter of de Lesseps. That evening, the torch held high in Liberty's hand was lit for the first time. In 1903, the famous inscription placed on the pedestal of the dignified 'The New Colossus' by the Spanish Jewish poet Emma Lazarus (who had died in 1887)[12] expressed what was the statue's essential value, and confirmed Liberty's true *raison d'être*:

> Not like the brazen giant of Greek fame,
> With conquering limbs astride from land to land;
> Here at our sea-washed, sunset gates shall stand
> A mighty woman with a torch, whose flame
> Is the imprisoned lightning, and her name
> Mother of Exiles. From her beacon-hand
> Glows world-wide welcome; her mild eyes command
> The air-bridged harbor that twin cities frame.
> 'Keep ancient lands, your storied pomp!' cries she
> With silent lips. 'Give me your tired, your poor,
> Your huddled masses yearning to breathe free,
> The wretched refuse of your teeming shore.
> Send these, the homeless, tempest-tost to me,
> I lift my lamp beside the golden door.'

As Eiffel's tower was to become, the Statue of Liberty has undoubtedly been seen as one of the world's great iconic monuments. In later years, replicas of the statue began to appear, initially in highly 'authorised' circumstances. The replica industry began very soon after Bartholdi's original was inaugurated, when on 4 July 1889 the American community in Paris gifted a relatively large 35ft bronze copy to the French people; it now stands beside the Pont de Grenelle, near the Eiffel Tower. Much more recently, there have been 'civic' replicas erected in Budapest, Yokosuka and Bordeaux, and the Boy Scouts of America have promoted the erection of over two hundred 8½ft civic replicas in sheet copper all over the USA and in the Panama Canal Zone, Guam, Manila and Puerto Rico.

Public access to Bartholdi and Eiffel's Statue of Liberty was withdrawn following the attack on the World Trade Centre in November 2001. Substantial security improvements have since been made, and guided access by timed ticket restored to most areas except the Crown (the torch has been closed since 1916). Optimistically, recent political perceptions of Liberty's eyes being depressingly closed will be overturned. However, in an echo of the original fundraising difficulties, allegations have been made that reopening was delayed by government action in response to serious questions over the financial relationship between the Statue of Liberty-Ellis Island Foundation and the US National Parks Service, which administers both monuments.[13] Whatever the circumstances surrounding the reopening, the sentiments expressed by the French Ambassador to the USA in 1916 on the occasion of Liberty's torch being powered by electricity should surely be reconfirmed: 'Not to a man, not to a nation, the statue was raised. It was raised to an idea – an idea greater than France or the United States: the idea of Liberty.'[14]

SIX

'A tower of very great height'

Gustave Eiffel undoubtedly benefited from the linking of his name with that of Bartholdi and the new international icon of the Statue of Liberty; it meant that his reputation came to be increasingly known beyond the confines of the engineering profession. The statue is often regarded as a relatively insignificant feature of his work (partly at least because of the invisibility of his contribution). However, Eiffel himself was pleased with his collaboration with Bartholdi, above all for the knowledge and experience it gave to his understanding of the problems of wind resistance, especially in relation to iron piers.

On completion of the statue project, Eiffel began to turn his attention to the possibilities offered by another French international exhibition. As far back as 1880, the French government under Prime Minister Jules Ferry had proposed an international Paris Exposition Universelle for 1889, recognising an already traditional eleven-year gap since the previous fair; there was also a secondary purpose – to celebrate the centenary of the Revolution. This had been a matter of some delicacy; not all the countries expected to participate (or for that matter all Frenchmen) were thought likely either to recognise or respect the revolutionary anniversary. It was also clear that there were already several international exhibitions planned in various other countries for the year 1888, thus possibly diluting the stock of enthusiasm for an exhibition that might be seen as being a year late. While it had been clearly intended that the three goals were to be reconciliation, rehabilitation and imperial supremacy, government had been keen to find a way to appeal not only to those of republican sympathies (who regarded such events as classic examples of debauched capitalism), but also to those of monarchist leanings, among whom the Revolution was still defiantly seen as disastrous. Ideally, political differences would be suspended for the duration. However, few such events have come into being in less auspicious circumstances, and Britain was one of several countries that regarded the 'international' aspect of the proposed exhibition with suspicion; the only British exhibitors to take part were privately organised and without government support or sanction.

The administration of the exhibition came under the control of a commission presided over by Antonin Proust, Minister of Fine Arts and friend of Edouard Manet. Proust had progressive views on consumerism and the increasing mechanisation of production, and feared that industrial processes alienated skilled employees from their work, and resulted in 'incoherent' design and architecture. However, it was March 1885 before an official prospectus was launched, and well into 1886 before much in the way of practical organisation was under way. Whatever success would be achieved would be thanks more to the energy of the newly appointed Minister of Commerce and Industry. Edouard Lockroy, son of an actor and dramatist, was a militant republican journalist who had been imprisoned at Versailles and Chartres after the Commune, but released without trial. He then became a writer, dramatist and literary wit who moved in the circles of Victor Hugo; he also became a prominent and successful politician who was able to align his natural radical support with more mainstream official republicanism. Funding the exhibition would be a critical issue. While the 1878 fair had lost money, it had more than doubled its attendance over the 1867 exhibition. Lockroy took hold of the planning, and drove through an agreement for a budget to be shared between the government (17 million francs), the City of Paris (8 million francs), and Crédit Foncier, the private company which was proposed to underwrite the project (2½ million francs).[1]

In the uncertain period of the exhibition's administrative birth, during which speculation on an iconic central feature began, the genesis of what became the Eiffel Tower is somewhat shrouded in uncertainty – one of those shrouds under which Eiffel has been accused of hiding his indebtedness to the work of others. Edouard Lockroy, as the responsible minister, demanded a 300-metre iron tower as the central feature of the exhibition. At the beginning of May 1886, he published in the government's *Journal Officiel* an invitation to architects and engineers to 'study the possibility of erecting on the Champ de Mars an iron tower with a base 125 metres square and 300 metres high'.[2] However, it seems certain that he did not devise such a concept himself, nor did he acquire the idea by accident.

The open invitation allowed the absurdly short time of only sixteen days for submission of blueprints before applications closed; surprisingly, in the circumstances, over a hundred serious applications were received. One was from Gustave Eiffel, his two engineering colleagues Nouguier and Koechlin, and the architect Stephen Sauvestre. It may be, however, that there was much more of a preamble to both the application and the announcement of the competition than was revealed at the time. Maurice Koechlin recorded his recollections of these events in 1939. He stated that he and Nouguier had privately discussed the possibility of a tower for the exhibition, and that, working at home as early as May and June 1884, he had prepared preliminary calculations and a sketch for a 300 metre-high iron tower, 'consisting of four lattice girders standing apart at the base and coming together at the top, joined to one another by metal trusses at regular intervals'.[3] As Eiffel had done with his early drawing of the Garabit Viaduct, Koechlin compiled a scale reference composed of sketches of Notre Dame, the Statue of Liberty, the Arc de Triomphe and three versions of the Vendôme columns all piled on top of each other. He showed the draft plan to Eiffel, who expressed no interest in it but gave permission for the two to study it further. Sauvestre became involved, drawing up a large-scale refined architectural drawing showing highly spraddled (therefore efficiently wind-resisting) lattice-work legs and including an arch between the base and the first-level platform, on which was sited a 45,192sq.ft glass-panelled gallery. It showed a 9,685sq.ft gallery on the second level, and a 2,690sq.ft glass dome and exterior balcony at the top; the drawing was later reproduced in a brochure published by the Eiffel Company. The detailed design work was not confined to the niceties of 'how it looked', but implied consideration of the mathematics of weight, gravity and wind forces acting on the individual components. The four great legs are not spread and curved principally for aesthetic reasons, but because Eiffel and Koechlin allowed their computation of the stresses acting against the smallest individual iron part to define the design.

These considerations infuriated the traditionalists, who were outraged that the absolute role of aesthetics was here subservient to what they regarded as the wholly mechanical and commercially driven. They were unwilling to recognise that only new materials, and therefore new methods, could construct something so high; they became obsessed with what for them was an 'industrial' enterprise devoid of 'art' as its central purpose. Lockroy and his fellow administrators did, however, see the uniqueness of such a project as a massive iron tower. Not only that, but they invested it with attributes that seem very much of our own time; the tower would be democratic in style – the product of new cooperation between public and private resources, and the product also of new materials and methods. The key words were to be symbolic: inventiveness, wealth-creating, motivational; the engineering was being perceived to be social as much as mechanical.

Sauvestre's drawing was shown to Frédéric Bartholdi, and Antonin Proust insisted that it ought to be exhibited at an exhibition of decorative arts, which led inevitably to the start of a long period of public discussion and controversy. Having been asked to discuss the drawing with Sauvestre, Eiffel resiled from his earlier indifference; there could be no question of anyone other than Gustave Eiffel himself undertaking such a project, particularly not one emanating from his own employees. But he realised that he would have to recognise the work of the other three, which he did by buying the exclusive patent rights from his three colleagues on 12 December 1884.[4] In return, their names were guaranteed to be associated with the project if it proceeded, and they were to be paid 1 per cent of the cost estimate approved by the exhibition's director-general. (They eventually each received just over 50,000 francs under a settlement made in 1888.) Eiffel later gave his own account of his indebtedness to the other three:

. . . the preliminary draft for the construction of a large 300-metre pylon that two of my company's more distinguish collaborators, MM. Émile Nouguier and Maurice Koechlin, presented to me for the exhibition of 1889 recognised, after our shared study, the problem of a 1,000ft tower. They associated the architect M. Sauvestre with the architectural part of the project. I did not hesitate to assume company responsibility for the enterprise and to devote to its realisation efforts which I certainly didn't believe, at the time, would be onerous. Though I myself directed the final studies and the execution of work with the assistance of the company's engineers, I happily give my usual collaborators MM. Nouguier and Koechlin their due acknowledgement that, neither for the final studies nor for the assembly work, did they fail to deliver a project that has been invaluable to me. M. Maurice Koechlin principally followed all the studies with a scientific zeal to which I gladly pay homage.[5]

Although there is no patent or other formal protection for ideas *per se*, the fact that the three had developed their ideas into a sophisticated architectural drawing may have been something of an embarrassment to Eiffel, given his earlier lack of interest. He was himself working on ideas involving the design of a proposed bridge which would have iron piers with a base of 140ft and height of 400ft.[6] Whatever his true reaction to his employees' proposals, it is indisputable that only he had the knowledge, experience and political clout to consider the construction of such an enormous tower. It is also testimony to his powers of persuasion that eighteen months after he began the promotion of what was now 'his' tower, Edouard Lockroy was able to publish its basic specification as the guideline requirements in the competition for the exhibition's symbolic structure. Right from the start it seemed that 'the Eiffel Tower' would be the winner.

The structure required for the exhibition was almost certain to be a tower, of one sort or another; in the late nineteenth century, towers were becoming, at least in concept, all the rage. Engineers and entrepreneurs had been considering ways and means of erecting towers – usually characterised as 'the tallest building in the world' – for many years. They are still doing it today. Eiffel was eager to take up the challenge:

Without rebuilding the Tower of Babel, one can see that the idea of constructing a tower of very great height has for a long time haunted the imagination of mankind. This kind of victory over the terrible law of gravity which attaches man to the ground always appeared to him a symbol of the forces and the difficulties to be overcome. To speak only of our century, the thousand-feet tower which would exceed by twice the highest monuments it had been possible to hitherto construct, was a problem set down to be solved in the minds of English and American engineers. Besides, the new use of metals in the construction industry made it possible to approach it with chance of success.[7]

In the nineteenth century alone, there were several proposals for spectacular towers, the first of which, and the one most closely related to the Eiffel Tower, was that of the ingenious eccentric English mining and railway engineer Richard Trevithick. 'The father of the locomotive engine', Trevithick had carried passengers by a steam engine named *Catch-me-who-catch-can* at a shilling a ride on a circular track at Euston Square in London in 1808. He was an innovative inventor of steam engines for countless purposes; he was involved in an abortive Thames tunnel project; he lived in Peru for ten years, where he was fêted as a national hero for engineering the country's silver mines; he had adventures galore and energetically made and lost fortunes. In a letter to the *Morning Herald* of 11 July 1833 he proposed to build a 1,000ft open-lattice, cast-iron tower in London to commemorate the passage through parliament of the First Reform Bill which, despite opposition from the House of Lords, transformed parliamentary representation. The tower, resting on a 60ft masonry plinth, was to be 100ft in diameter at the base and 10ft wide at the top, surmounted by a 49ft-wide platform carrying a gigantic 38ft statue; twenty-five passengers at a time would be carried to the top by a compressed-air lift inside the column travelling at the speed of three feet per second. Trevithick intended that his tower should be assembled from 1,500 symmetrical 3-ton segments, each with internal flanges enabling them to be bolted together; each section was to be pierced by a large, circular opening to reduce both the weight and wind pressure; the total weight was to be 6,000 tons, and he envisaged construction lasting only six months and costing £80,000.[8] Sadly, nothing came of this typically inventive proposal; Trevithick was sixty-two years old when he published his plan, and he died later the same year with no practical progress having been made either in finding the money or building the tower.

Twenty years later, in 1852, came proposals by the architect Charles Burton for the demolition of Paxton's Crystal Palace and its reconstruction as a 1,000ft tower of forty-seven storeys, complete with elevators. This was no doubt a feasible project in principle, since the iron and glass parts of Paxton's building had been replicated thousands upon thousands of times, and the supply of accurately produced matching parts would no doubt have aided the construction of a tower. Whether Burton had enough experience in the more complicated and problematic areas of the strength, stability and aerodynamics of structures is doubtful:

> It is proposed to build an enormous tower of the materials of the glass palace, preserving as much as is consistent with the new design, all the features of that structure, with a view of perpetuating the great event of the year 1851, and forming a depository of every branch of art and manufacture our own kingdom produces, as well as a choice collection of exotics from the four quarters of the globe.[9]

Burton planned to rely on twenty-four columns (presumably of cast iron) springing from the foundations and running the full height of the tower. In depicting his project he also adopted the 'pile 'em up' comparison, offering the image of St Paul's Cathedral on top of St Peter's and surmounted by Nelson's Column. There is no evidence that the proposal was taken seriously, although he claimed the benefit of seeing London from the heights of the aeronaut Charles Green's enormous and world-famous 80ft balloon: '. . . I passed over London in the celebrated Nassau balloon, and can speak feelingly as to the wonderful appearance of the Great Metropolis and the lovely scenery surrounding it, from an elevation of 1,000 feet.' It is fair to assume that Sir Joseph Paxton firmly showed the door to Burton and his idea. (Paxton formed his own company to buy the Palace, and it was re-erected at Sydenham, where it remained, with mixed success, until destroyed by fire in 1936.)

In 1853, the celebrated American architect James Bogardus, who pioneered cast iron in buildings in the USA (leading directly to the first steel-framed skyscrapers), proposed a 300ft observatory tower for the main building at the New York World Fair. His idea was not accepted, and neither was that of one of his countrymen who devised a gigantic centrepiece for the Philadelphia Centennial Exposition of 1876. Ten years before Koechlin and Nouguier first began thinking about a tower for Paris, the American engineer David Reeves, president of the Phoenix Bridge Company, devised plans for a 1,000ft iron tower 'to highlight the progress of science and art across the ages'. The exhibition organisers rejected the proposal for what has been described as a glorified factory chimney, a truncated cone 148ft in diameter at the bottom and 40ft diameter at the top. The structure was to be in the form of hollow wrought-iron sections incorporating an iron tube 30ft wide to accommodate lifts and stairways. The Phoenix Bridge Company had a good record in devising wrought-iron members for use in bridge building, but in later years it suffered a catastrophic series of deaths and accidents – most notably the collapse of a bridge under construction at Quebec City, resulting in the deaths of seventy-five workmen. Recent examinations of the drawings for the proposed tower have suggested that it would probably have collapsed under wind pressure.[10]

The next plan for a 986ft tower came as a direct competitor to the Eiffel proposal. This was also one man's idea taken over by someone else, and it was to develop into a public skirmish as a battle between stone and iron. A young French electrical engineer named Sébillot had become enthusiastic while in the United States in 1881 over the idea of building a huge 'Tour Soleil'. This was to be a monumental Parisian lighthouse with a 165ft electric beacon, comprising 100 powerful lamps fitted with parabolic reflectors, providing eight times the amount of light needed to read a newspaper at midnight in parts of the city several miles away from its proposed site on the Esplanade des Invalides. The beacon was to be surmounted by a huge figurative statue representing Science. Sébillot's idea was taken up by the arch-traditionalist architect Jules Bourdais, one of the designers of the Trocadero Palace, who promoted the idea aggressively to the exhibition's commissioners. The granite tower, on a plinth 217ft high and 323 square feet in area, was to be built in five tiers of reducing diameter, each decorated with columns and ornamental stonework. Suites of rooms could be built at various levels, including an 'aero-therapy hospital' to enable patients to benefit from the pure air at the top of the tower. Although Bourdais's tower was to be clad in embossed copper, he insisted that its masonry was to be its crowning glory. Bourdais promoted himself vigorously while engaging in loud public condemnation of Eiffel's 'vulgar' iron structure.

Eiffel had a well-formed understanding of the engineering potential of all the principal building materials, and although he knew he wanted to use wrought iron, he gave a confident elucidation of the differences:

> The use of iron, as you know, is very old; but it was far from being the equal of wood or stone – materials that nature placed at the disposal of man to work according to his needs. The latter remained for a long time the only building materials,

while the difficulty in manufacturing iron in quantity and, with the limited resources available, giving it the required forms, restricted its use. It was only for small parts, which required a special elasticity, that it was possible, with difficulty, to forge it by hand. In our times, the progress of metallurgy and steam-power, which transform so many things, places almost unlimited resources at our disposal – the easier manufacture and working of iron, or the obtaining of metals with well defined properties and precisely known elasticity.

It goes without saying that iron will never entirely replace stone and wood, which have their particular qualities; but in recent years there has been a constant battle, and iron increasingly invaded the field of major construction, and today it is one of the principal materials. What are the advantages of metal? Primarily, its elasticity. From the point of view of the loads which one can safely support with one or other of the materials we know, for equal area, iron is ten times more elastic than wood and twenty times more elastic than stone. It is in large constructions especially that metal elasticity reveals its superiority over other materials. The actual weight of the work plays a considerable role; it limits the height and distance which one can reach. At the same time, the relative lightness of steel constructions makes it possible to decrease the importance of supports and foundations. To quote only one example, that of the exhibition's tower, I have astonished more than one person who worried about the load on the foundations by saying that it would be no greater than that of a Paris house.[11]

During the ensuing public debate on the merits of the two towers, serious questions were raised about the stability and structural integrity of the stone edifice (would not the sheer weight of stone crush the lower courses?), and Bourdais's response was to retreat into evasions and brusque assertions that his calculations ought to be accepted without question. But Eiffel insisted that Bourdais did not understand that only iron or steel could have the tensile strength to support such a high structure; that he had not prepared appropriate calculations of wind resistance; and what was more, Bourdais had no intention of providing any foundations whatsoever – the base was to rest directly on the ground. Eiffel attempted to establish the engineering and financial consequences of building such a high tower using masonry, compared to his own iron tower; he had to abandon even an approximate costing when the potential costs became astronomical. Even a theoretical projection of the engineering principles was unequivocal:

> Iron or steel seems therefore to us the only material capable of leading to the solution of the problem. Moreover, antiquity, the Middle Ages and the Renaissance pushed the use of stone to its extreme limits of boldness, and it seems hardly possible to go farther than our precursors with the same materials – especially as the art of construction hasn't made much progress for a long time in this field. This unusually high building, as proposed by us, therefore required an otherwise new material, but one that at least the industry had not made available to the engineers and architects who had preceded us. This material could not be cast iron that would stand up badly to simple compression, it would have to be exclusively wrought iron or steel, by the use of which the most difficult problems of construction are simply resolved, and with which we fluently construct frameworks or long-span bridges that would once have appeared oppressive.[12]

Bourdais' intended *coup de grâce* against Eiffel was that the offensive iron tower would cost seven times more than his own beautiful and aesthetic stone one. Eiffel responded, defending his tower, with a grand flourish of national pride:

> The tower would seem to be worthy of personifying the art of the modern engineer and the century of industry and science, for which the road was prepared by the Revolution of 1789, to which this monument will be erected as testimony of the gratitude of France.[13]

Lobbying continued for both the Eiffel and Bourdais proposals (and plans for towers by seven other competitors) through the spring and summer of 1886. The arguments were largely contained within professional circles, but as the protagonists and their supporters attempted to impress the various committees and their members, the issues were taken up in the press, some of whom adopted partisan positions. The journal *La France*, for example, particularly pleased Eiffel on Christmas Day 1884 when it publicised his own emphatic wish that his tower would be useful as well as simply an exhibition feature. Eiffel remained adamant that a tower of the required height could not be built in stone; the problems of foundations, integrity of mortar under pressure, and construction time all militated against such a project. At the time, the world's highest stone structure was the Washington Monument; this was only 555ft high and had taken thirty-six years to build, and Eiffel argued that to build a tower twice that height would require new materials and techniques.

Seven hundred initial project ideas became one hundred serious applications, which were further narrowed down to nine, including both the Eiffel and Bourdais towers. A committee to make the final decision was established in May under the chairmanship of Edouard Lockroy, aided by the presence of Charles Adolphe Alphand, the Paris Director of Works, and other substantial figures in engineering, design and public administration. Lockroy immediately made his announcement of the guidelines – guidelines modelled upon Eiffel's proposal – and on 12 June, the unanimous announcement came from the committee that:

> . . . the tower to be built for the 1889 exposition universelle should clearly have a distinctive character, and should be an original masterpiece of work in metal, and that only the Eiffel Tower seemed to satisfy these requirements fully.[14]

Subject to more detailed investigations into the questions of elevators and lightning protection, engineering had triumphed over the traditionalists. Perhaps; or maybe the decision to favour

Eiffel had been taken some time before. At any event, the supporters of Bourdais did not pack up their tents. One influential professional journal, *La Construction Moderne*, mounted a new attack on Eiffel on the very day that the announcement was made, concentrating on the alleged impossibility of providing lifts for the tower. Other malcontents were to join a campaign that would draw to a conclusion over the following eight months.

Whatever the opposition, Eiffel was going to build the most spectacular – and highest – structure in the world. He took some considerable time before rejecting the use of steel; it would be lighter than iron, but more costly, and its greater elasticity would produce too much sway in adverse wind conditions. The tower in iron was promised to weigh an incredibly light 7,000 tons, and cost 6,500,000 francs (it would in fact cost a million francs more). One rather unexpected benefit that Eiffel offered to the committee was the opportunity of his being able to dismantle an iron tower and remove it to another location, should that eventually be decided; there could be no such possibility with a masonry tower. The trouble for the otherwise elated Gustave Eiffel, however, was that the committee would only pay 1,500,000 francs, less than a quarter of the expected costs.

Eiffel embarked on a highly personal campaign to persuade the exhibition's organising committee of his tower's distinctive *usefulness*. This aspect of the affair was to become a great obsession for him; the Eiffel Tower was not to be thought of as a mere *attraction*. In effect, he increasingly thought of the tower as a glorified scientific instrument, to be used for experiment, measurement and analysis. This in itself was not a particularly new notion. Even the luckless Bourdais in designing the aborted 'Tour Soleil' planned that the huge column would be hollow, to permit gravity experiments with falling objects. In addition, there was to have been a basement over 200ft deep, with a museum celebrating the new marvels of electricity.[15] However, the concept of purposely designing buildings with such additional features and intentions has a much greater and older pedigree, and goes back to the period when astronomical solutions to the problem of calculating longitude were being avidly sought. Sir Christopher Wren (architect and Professor of Astronomy at Oxford University) and his friend and collaborator Robert Hooke (skilled surveyor and first Curator of Experiments to the Royal Society) together designed the Monument to the Great Fire of London. This 200ft stone column, completed in 1677, has a hollow core and a forgotten underground laboratory intended for experimentation on heights, using pendulums, barometers and other instruments; they intended the use of the Monument as a huge vertical zenith telescope capable of having lenses fitted inside the laboratory and at the top platform of the column.[16] This latter purpose was thwarted due to the fact that the column swayed in the wind, imperceptibly, but enough to invalidate measurement. Wren's biographer, Lisa Jardine, draws attention to the precision of the design and construction of individual elements of the Monument, such as stair risers and the positioning of various apertures, all of which confirm the clear intention that the Monument had a dual purpose. Wren, who had designed the Royal Observatory at Greenwich, was fascinated by many scientific issues, and discussed with Hooke the possibility of adapting designs for St Paul's Cathedral (Hooke had previously conducted scientific experiments in the derelict tower of the condemned church of Old St Paul's, destroyed in the Great Fire of London in 1666).[17] Other buildings they planned to design with scientific experiment in mind were the Royal College of Physicians in London and an aborted new home for the Royal Society.

Even before his tower rose from the drawing-board, Eiffel had plans for scientific observation and experiment, which he thought could extend into the realm of national defence. These ideas were not simply casual notions of vague possibilities, but were areas of personal interest that would develop into a lifelong practical passion. Following discussion with the directors of a range of eminent institutions, he summarised his concept:

Strategic operations: In case of war or siege it would be possible to watch the movements of an enemy within a radius of 45 miles, and to look far beyond the heights on which our new fortifications are built. It we had possessed the tower during the Siege of Paris in 1870, with its brilliant electric lights, who knows whether the issue of that conflict would not have been entirely changed?

Meteorological Observations: It will be a wonderful observatory in which may be studied the direction and force of atmospheric currents, the electrical state and chemical composition of the atmosphere, its hygrometry, etc.

Astronomical Observations: The purity of the air at such a height, the absence of mists which often cover the lower horizons in Paris, will allow many physical and astronomical observations to be made which would be impossible in our region.

Scientific experiments may be made, including the study of the fall of bodies in the air, resistance of the air according to speed, certain laws of elasticity, compression of gas and vapours, and, using a large-scale pendulum, the rotation of the earth. It will be an observatory and a laboratory such as has never before been placed at the disposal of scientists.[18]

Eiffel was successful in obtaining considerable influential support for his concept of using the tower for scientific purposes. Among many who were enthusiasts was the astronomer and Academician Pierre Jules Janssen:

It is incontestable that from a meteorological point of view the tower will render real services to science. One of the greatest difficulties in meteorological observations is the disturbing influences of the station in which the observations are made. How, for instance, is it possible to ascertain the true deviation of the wind if some local obstacle affects it? How can we arrive at the true temperature of the air if the thermometer is influenced by the radiation of surrounding objects? The meteorological elements of the great inhabited centres are usually taken from outside these centres, and even then it is always necessary to be at a certain height above the ground. The tower offers an immediate solution for these difficulties. I would also recommend the institution of a service of meteorological photography. A good series of photographs would give us the forms, the movements, the modifications to which the clouds are subject, and the atmospherical occurrences from sunrise to sunset.[19]

This was all some way ahead however. The funding of the project was still not agreed, and discussions had not yet even settled on a precise site. When it became clear that the committee would not increase its grant beyond 1½ million francs, Eiffel acted with typical imagination and shrewdness. In a move which would have been unthinkable for anyone other than a man of his self-confidence and experience, he decided to take extraordinary personal risk by floating a company to distribute 10,000 shares of 500 francs each. He planned to retain half the shares in his own name, and by astute estimation of attendance figures, he calculated the likely profit to be made by the other partners such as the company itself and the consortium of banks that showed interest. He confidently estimated that the annual dividend would amount to 80 per cent of the subscribed capital. Everything depended on whether or not the tower would be a success, and both the City of Paris and the French government gambled that Eiffel would carry a loss. As it happened, he covered his costs during the first year, and subsequent profits, and associated worldwide fame, made him extremely wealthy. But as contracts were designed and made ready for signature, no-one else was willing to make such a prediction, and the authorities were confident that they had positioned Eiffel to bear the brunt of the costs, and potential failure, of the most spectacular building project ever undertaken.

Eiffel's contracts with the exhibition's organisers allowed him the total income from the commercial exploitation of the tower (including entrance fees, revenues from restaurants, cafés, theatre and any other commercial business he chose to operate – including, crucially, the sale of images of the tower itself) during the course of the exhibition. After the first year, the tower would become the property of the city, although Eiffel would continue to receive all income generated during the following twenty years. (In 1910, the income was extended to the Eiffel company for another seventy years, although the arrangement was not renewed by the successor company itself when it expired in 1980.)[20]

The contract committed Gustave Eiffel himself, 'acting on his own behalf', not his company's, to accepting total and sole financial responsibility for the construction and operation of the tower. It was part of the original agreement that each level had to be provided with a room designated for appropriate institutions to conduct scientific or military experiments. Although confident of his intentions, Eiffel tried to gain some financial protection by seeking to build the exhibition's proposed Galerie des Machines on the Champ de Mars. He pleaded that this would compensate him for the huge financial risk he was accepting on the tower. His proposal, while apparently financially attractive, was rejected in favour of that of the engineers Dutert and Contamin, who went on to build the momentous iron gallery in which Thomas Edison would display his first phonograph. That refusal perhaps saved the tower; to be successful, Eiffel needed to keep his eye fixed on that project alone. Barely two years remained to construct the tallest building in the world, and still there was no decision as to precisely where it should stand.

Although the main exhibition site was to be the Champ de Mars, there were arguments against having the tower located there. Such a gigantic iron structure might overwhelm the entire exhibition; some suggested that it deserved its own site, perhaps on an elevated site or hill, at Chaillot for example, near the Trocadéro, where it would be even more dramatically outstanding. The composer Charles Gounod insisted that the tower should be built on another site:

My artistic feeling on this undertaking is unchanged. Yes, I admire engineer Eiffel, but I persist in declaring that the Eiffel Tower is not an artistic monument. What attracts the attention about it is its height. It is three hundred metres high! But a high monument ought to be built on a height. If this monument attains its importance only by being higher than others, it ought to be built on a summit to enhance its grandeur. But no, it has been placed on the banks of the Seine. And look! the misinterpretation is blatant. The first floor of the tower is higher than the monuments of Paris. That is what distinguishes it. But if the Tower had been constructed on Montmartre, this first floor would dominate the city even more, and would distinguish itself to a much greater extent.

The life of this monument ought to begin where that of the others finish. There lies (he tells us) the solution of the interesting problem of statics. Also, for me, the Tower is more interesting to examine than pleasant to look at. Even if it doesn't satisfy my artistic tastes, it delights me as metal construction, and I pay homage to the engineer.[21]

Countering this argument was the claim that the tower's financial future would be much more uncertain if it was separated from the exhibition as a whole. There was also resistance to the Champ de Mars site on the reasonable grounds that succeeding exhibitions would almost certainly be held there, and that the tower would inevitably be an obligatory imposition on every other exhibition, whether or not it matched the architectural and other considerations of the time. The tower was already recognised as the proposed centre-piece of the 1889 Exposition, and in the end the decision came down to either the Champ de Mars or the Trocadero across the Seine. In the end, it was thought that siting the tower near the Trocadero Palace might spoil the views and the architectural proportions; in addition, it was decided that if the tower was sited on the Champ de Mars then money could be saved by not designing a separate monumental entrance to the entire exhibition. The only condition was that the precise site should be far enough from the Seine to ensure that the necessary deep foundations could be constructed without unacceptable geological or financial problems. The foundations would in fact be a crucial factor. The slightest instability at foundation level would be greatly magnified at the top of the structure, causing catastrophic stress far beyond the calculated specifications.

Eiffel must have felt enormous euphoria and self-confidence as the plans for his huge undertaking were published. 'When it is finished, they will love it,' he is reported as having insisted.[22] In the event, his exhilaration received a rapid puncture. For many months there had been frivolous gossip, but as soon as work began on the foundations and the tower began to seem like a coming reality, a groundswell of scepticism arose. Those who lived in the vicinity of the projected tower complained about the enormity of the planned structure, of the potential for its collapse under wind pressure, and of the probable damage to themselves and their properties. But these practical objections paled into insignificance compared to the efforts of those who belittled the concept and used aesthetics as their weapon. *La mode* demanded affected pastoral imagery – whereas the tower was to be something decidedly modern and technological. The concept, the alleged physical monstrosity and the sheer permanence of the tower galvanised huge protest by largely self-obsessed guardians of discernment before the first iron beam appeared on-site.

A Committee of Three Hundred – one member for each metre of the tower's height – was formed from the most celebrated names of Parisian (and French) arts, music and letters. The great controversy of Art versus Industry was about to be reignited with a vengeance, characterised on this occasion by the subtext of architect versus engineer, or stone versus iron. It was soon to be reduced to the personalities of Charles Garnier and Gustave Eiffel, since the celebrated designer of the neo-baroque Paris Opera House, with whom Eiffel had happily worked on the Nice Observatory, was to be one of the principal instigators of the protest campaign. In Garnier's view, iron had its uses, but should never be part of any 'artistic' endeavour. Iron was pretentious, tasteless and vulgar – a means, never an end; it was an offensive material that was essentially alien to the classical beauty of a stone façade. He was one of those who often pointed to the conceptual parallels of the new craft of photography and painting; photography at best was merely a commonplace tool that replaced feeling with sterile precision. There was also an element of

94

professional snobbery at work. Engineers were often still regarded as backwoodsmen of little education (some had been, of course, like Richard Trevithick, a one-time circus wrestler), and establishment architects would have balked at seeing the exhibition's grand projects falling into the hands of mere artisans. Another reason for Garnier's new-found hostility could have been that he resented the possibility that the tower might eclipse his own project for the exhibition – his History of Housing of All Times and Peoples. This was a fine (and popular) idea, which replicated, along Les Invalides, human dwellings from the most primitive times to those of sixteenth-century Paris.

Other self-appointed taste-makers who joined Garnier's protest included the composers Charles Gounod and Jules Massenet, the writers Guy de Maupassant, Alexandre Dumas *fils*, François Coppée and Sully-Prudhomme, and artists such as Ernest Meissonier and Adolphe Bouguereau. Eventually, in February 1887, forty-seven of the most dogged and righteously offended signed (and published in *Le Temps*) a reactionary, pompous and sycophantic 'Protestation des Artistes' addressed to the exhibition's commissioner, and Minister of Public Works, Charles Adolphe Alphand:

Honoured compatriot – authors, painters, sculptors, architects, enthusiastic lovers of beauty, which has hitherto been respected in Paris – we wish to protest with all our energy, and with all the indignation of which we are capable, in the name of art and of French history now menaced, against the erection in the heart of our capital of the useless and monstrous Eiffel Tower, which public satire, often full of good sense and a spirit of justice, has already christened the 'Tower of Babel'. Without falling into extravagance we claim the right to assert that Paris stands without a rival in the world. Above its streets and boulevards, along its quays, amid its magnificent promenades, abound the most noble monuments which human has ever put into execution. The soul of France, creator of *chefs-d'oeuvre*, shines forth from this wealth of stone. Italy, Germany, Flanders, so justly proud of their artistic heritage, possess nothing comparable, and from all corners of the universe Paris commands admiration.

Are we then going to allow all this to be profaned? Is the city of Paris to permit itself to be deformed by monstrosities, by the mercantile dreams of a maker of machinery; to be disfigured forever and to be dishonoured? For the Eiffel Tower, which even the United States would not countenance, is surely going to dishonour Paris. Every one feels it, every one says so, every one is plunged into the deepest grief about it, and our voice is only a feeble echo of universal opinion, properly alarmed. When foreigners come to visit our exhibition, they will cry in astonishment, 'Is this the horror that Frenchmen have invented, intended to give us an idea of the taste of which they are so proud?!' And they will be right so to mock us, because the Paris of the sublime architects, the Paris of Jean Goujon, of Germain Pilon, of Puget, of Rude, of Barye, will have become the Paris of M. Eiffel.

Nothing further is wanting to prove the justice of what we say than to realise for an instant this tower dominating Paris like a gigantic, black factory chimney, crushing with its barbaric mass Notre-Dame, the Sainte Chapelle, the Tour Saint-Jacques, the Louvre, the dome of the Invalides, the Arc de Triomphe; all our monuments humiliated, all our architecture shrunken, and disappearing affrighted in this bewildering dream. And for twenty years we shall see, stretching over the entire city, still thrilling with the genius of so many centuries, we shall see stretching out like a black blot, the odious shadow of the odious column built up of riveted iron plates.

It is with you, sir, dear compatriot, who so dearly love Paris and have so greatly embellished her, who have so many times protected her against administrative devastations and the vandalism of industrial enterprises, it is with you that the honour rests to defend her once again. We entrust to you the care of pleading the cause of Paris, knowing that you will expend on it all the energy and eloquence which must be inspired in such an artist as yourself by the love of all that is beautiful, all that is great, and all that is right. And if our alarm call is unheeded, if your arguments go unheard, we shall at least have given voice to a protest which does us honour.[23]

After the formality of the Artists' Protest followed a cascade of satirical comment and insult from all and sundry; the religious writer Léon Bloy referred to 'this truly tragic street lamp'; to the poet François Coppée it was 'this mast of iron gymnasium apparatus, incomplete, confused and deformed'. The novelist Joris-Karl Huysmans described 'a half-built factory pipe, a carcass waiting to be fleshed out with freestone or brick, a funnel-shaped grille, a hole-riddled suppository', while Maupassant (who was to maintain his aggressive objection to the end) condemned 'this high and skinny pyramid of iron ladders, this giant ungainly skeleton upon a base that looks built to carry a colossal monument to Cyclops, but which just peters out into a ridiculous thin shape like a factory chimney'.

A surprised but philosophical Eiffel rejected the protestors' accusations of the tower's uselessness and ugliness with gentle sarcasm:

Nous parlerons de l'inutilité tout à l'heure. Ne nous occupons pour le moment que du mérite esthétique sur lequel les artistes sont plus particulièrement compétents. (We will speak of uselessness presently. We will deal for the moment only with the aesthetic merit in which the artists are more particularly qualified.)[24]

In general, he responded to vehement attacks with equanimity, questioning why Garnier was only now finding fault with the proposal, since for two years he had been one of the project commissioners, and pointing out that the foundations were already dug, the iron ordered, and that the sound and fury was all too late. He wondered how the objectors could know much about the tower since no one had seen more than one simple drawing. He insisted that engineers also understood beauty, and that the laws of nature with which engineers worked also conformed to the laws of harmony. He later admitted to being irritated at the protestors' disdainful tone and responded somewhat in kind:

Of the form of this *philippique*, I will say nothing: the great writers who signed it had however up to then given their readers a different idea of the French language. As far as content was concerned, the attack was wholly excessive, given that it was the views of the protesters on the aesthetic value of the work. The crime that the organisers of the exhibition were accused of, that of complicity with M. Eiffel, was in no respect black enough to dishonour Paris. Similar exaggerations can be excused on the part of the artists, painters, sculptors and even composers: for them, anything is allowed; they have the monopoly of taste; only they have feelings of beauty; their vocation is infallible; their oracles are indisputable. Perhaps the dramatists, the poets, the novelists and other signatories of the letter deserved less indulgence.[25]

Garnier, who had always complained of the height of the housing erected near his Opera House, was the recipient of a particular gibe; Eiffel condemned as invalid the argument that a high building was inevitably dominating:

Regardez si l'Opéra ne parâit pas plus écrasé par les maisons du voisinage qu'il les écrase lui-même. (See whether the Opera does not look more crushed by the houses in its neighbourhood than vice versa.)[26]

The controversy was picked up with enthusiasm in the USA, where one writer on contemporary life and thought in France wrote from New York of the 'Exposition des Incohérents' and similar buffoonery producing an era of self-indulgence:

A worse sign still is the Eiffel Tower – an iron tower some thousand feet high, ugly in itself and certain to make everything else look ugly in its neighbourhood, which the organisers of the Exhibition of 1889 are determined, in the face of all opposition, to set up in the very midst by way of a centre-piece. It will of course dwarf all the surrounding buildings; and it has not a single merit of its own except its immense proportions and the technical difficulty of making it. There is something in this craving for the extraordinary and monstrous instead of the beautiful which really does savour of a period of decadence.[27]

The protest letter to Alphand found its way to Edouard Lockroy, whose enthusiasms for the tower would not be thwarted. He saw the structure as a manifestation of a new democracy, with its unique cooperation between public and private ethics; it embodied the best attributes of current science and technology and it demonstrated to the world French innovation, economy, initiative and passion. In his view, it would (physically or emotionally) become a part of the life of every French citizen. Ostensibly responding to Alphand, but clearly expecting a more public readership, Lockroy exercised the potent weapon of controlled irony in his defence of the tower and in his contempt for the backward-looking protestors:

Judging by the stately swell of the rhythms, the beauty of the metaphors, the elegance of its delicate and precise style, one can tell without even looking at the signatures that this protest is the result of collaboration of the most famous writers and poets of our time. . . . But do not let yourself be impressed by its beautiful form, and note only the facts. The protest is already irrelevant. You will inform the senders that construction of the tower was decided upon a year ago and that the work site has been open for a month. They could have protested in time; they did not, and 'honourable' indignation unfortunately comes a bit late.

I am profoundly sorry about this. Not that I fear for Paris. Notre-Dame will remain Notre-Dame and the Arc de Triomphe will remain the Arc de Triomphe. But I could have saved the only part of this great city which is seriously in danger; that incomparable sand pile called the Champ de Mars, such an inspiration for our poets and so attractive to our landscape painters.

Please express my sorrow to these gentlemen. Above all do

not say that it is unfortunate that the exhibition is being attacked by those who should be defending it; that a protest signed by such illustrious names will echo throughout Europe and may be used as a pretext by some nations not to take part in our celebration; that it is bad to attempt to ridicule a peaceful undertaking that France is so attached to, especially now when she is so unjustly suspected abroad. Such petty considerations concern a cabinet minister, but they are meaningless for rarefied minds which are occupied above all with the interests of art and the love of the beautiful.

What I pray you do is to accept this protest and to keep it. It should be placed in a showcase at the exhibition. Such beautiful and noble prose cannot but interest the crowds, and perhaps even amaze them.[28]

Lockroy's sarcasm successfully punctured the bloated pomposity of the protestors, who as a group were never heard from again, although a few individuals such as Garnier and Maupassant maintained a relentless sniping against the tower for years; others, to their credit, became apologetic enthusiasts for the completed icon.

Apart from occasional skirmishes, Eiffel had essentially won his battle with Garnier, and it was the latter's petulant insistence on the innovative, artistic and cultural superiority of stone over iron that was exposed during the 1889 Exposition as false. In his self-defence in *Le Temps*, Gustave Eiffel, the educated graduate of France's celebrated engineering academy, moved the sterile argument away from Garnier's forced intellectualism:

There is an attraction and a charm inherent in the colossal that is not subject to ordinary theories of art. Does anyone pretend that the Pyramids have so forcefully gripped the imagination of men through their artistic value? What are they after all but artificial hillocks? And yet what visitor can stand without reaction in their presence? The tower will be the tallest edifice ever raised by man. Will it not therefore be imposing in its own way? It seems to me that the Eiffel Tower is worthy of being treated with respect, if only because it will show that we are not simply an amusing people, but also the country of engineers and builders who are called upon all over the world to construct bridges, viaducts, train stations and the great monuments of modern industry.[29]

Eugène Marie Melchior, marquis de Vogüé, the historian and writer, was a fierce enthusiast of the tower and wrote with shrewdness and insight on the 1889 Exposition; he imagined a dialogue between the Eiffel Tower and the older masonry pillars of Notre Dame; as searchlights played over the nocturnal scene, he gave the most potent words to Eiffel's tower:

Old abandoned towers, no one listens to you any more. Don't you see that the earth's poles have changed and that the world now rotates round my iron axis? I represent the power of the universe disciplined by calculation. Human thought runs along my members. My brow is encircled with rays stolen from the sources of light. You were ignorance; I am knowledge. You enslave man; I free him.[30]

SEVEN

The Tower Rises

The Champ de Mars, an unlikely stretch of originally rough sandy plain that ran from the Quai d'Orsay by the Seine to the Place de Fontenoy, had long been in the forefront of French history. It was used as the parade ground of the Ecole Militaire, built between 1769 and 1772 (and which still exists as the Ecole Supérieure de Guerre). The site was to witness the spillage of much French blood during the time of the Terror, but earlier on 27 August 1783, the Champ de Mars was chosen by Joseph and Etienne Montgolfier to demonstrate their unmanned 'trial balloon', taking advantage of the proximity of the Ecole to promote the military potential of their new device. The Montgolfier brothers were in the papermaking business, and their machine was in effect a huge paper bag filled with a 'gas' obtained from burning wet straw and chopped wool. As thousands of Parisians filled nearby streets, members of the French Academy hauled their telescopes and tripods to the roofs of Notre Dame and the Ecole Militaire.

A cannon shot signalled the release of the balloon, and within two minutes it had soared through a rain-shower to a height of 3,000ft, disappearing and reappearing through the cloud, accompanied by further frantic and unsynchronised cannon fire. The crowds, apparently spellbound by this wholly unnatural event, became even more puzzled when the balloon disappeared completely from sight, without sign that it would ever reach land again. When it finally did, in a village 12 miles away, it was received by farm-workers as a fearful monster and attacked with pitchforks. The government was prompted to issue a proclamation of guidance to the public:

A discovery has been made which the government deems it right to make known, so that alarm be not occasioned to the people. On calculating the different weights of inflammable and common air, it has been found that a balloon filled with inflammable air will rise towards heaven till it is in equilibrium with the surrounding air; which may not happen till it has attained a great height.

The same experiment has just been renewed at Paris (27 August, 5pm) in presence of a great crowd. A globe of taffetas, covered by elastic gum, 36ft in circumference, has risen from the Champ de Mars, and been lost to view in the clouds, being borne in a north-easterly direction; one cannot foresee where it will descend. It is proposed to repeat these experiments on a larger scale. Anyone who shall see in the sky such a globe (which resembles *la lune obscurie*) should be aware that, far from being an alarming phenomenon, it is only a machine, made of taffetas, or light canvas covered with paper, that cannot possibly cause any harm, and which will some day prove serviceable to the wants of Society.[1]

The government's decision to take up the issue was well judged, and it was only a matter of weeks before another flight was arranged, this time bearing a sheep, a cockerel and a duck (which all survived) and observed by Louis XVI and Marie Antoinette. These aerial events have a relevance to Eiffel's story that will become apparent later.

The Champ de Mars was soon in the news again, and this time the tone was not one of happy carnival celebration. Talleyrand, as president of the National Assembly, had conducted secular holidays such as the Feast of the Federation at an altar set in the middle of the Champ de Mars. But the mood of post-Revolution Paris was dangerous and unpredictable in 1791, with angry crowds regularly protesting about low wages, and others prowling around in search of counter-Revolutionary plots; just who was a patriot and who wasn't was never more uncertain. On 17 July a crowd on the Champ de Mars protested against the possible reinstatement of a traitorous king and encouraged the signing of a mass petition.

The excuse for what followed was the discovery by the crowd of two suspicious individuals, whom they set out to lynch. The mayor (a distinguished astronomer and politician who would later be guillotined in revenge on the same site) declared martial law, General Lafayette ordered in the National Guard, stones flew, and what became known as 'the Massacre of the Champ de Mars' was under way:

> One section of the troops entered at the far side of the military school, another came through the entrance somewhere lower down, and a third by the gate that opens on to the Grande rue de Chaillot, where the red flag was placed. The people at the altar, more than fifteen thousand strong, had hardly noticed the flag when shots were heard. 'Do not move, they are firing blanks. They must come here to post the law.' The troops advanced a second time. The composure of the faces of those who surrounded the altar did not change. But when a third volley mowed many of them down, the crowd fled, leaving a group of only a hundred people at the altar itself. Alas! They paid dearly for their courage and blind trust in the law. Men, women, even a child were massacred there.[2]

Fifty people were killed by the National Guard, and in the aftermath radical societies and newspapers were closed, leading citizens were arrested or went into hiding, and politically inspired executions continued apace.

Three years later, in June 1794, Robespierre led the inaugural Festival of the Supreme Being, an extraordinary attempt to create a kind of civil religion supposedly intended to unite the nation. A great deal of symbolism, including a statue of Wisdom, a Flame of Truth, the burning of an effigy of Atheism, a new 'Hymn of the Supreme Being' and of course 'the Marseillaise' were employed. The population was called to action at five o'clock in the morning, and was required to conform to a long series of instructions governing the course of the day. Led by a group of blind children singing a 'Hymn to Divinity', a long procession made its way to the Champ de Mars (renamed for the occasion the Champ de la Réunion), where the artist Jacques-Louis David had constructed a symbolic mountain of plaster and cardboard surmounted by a statue of Hercules (representing the French people) and holding a figure of Liberty. During this bizarrely didactic spectacle, Robespierre led the deputies of the Convention from the summit of the structure to address the gathered masses and bask in their tumultuous applause:

> The eternally happy day which the French people consecrates to the Supreme Being has finally arrived. Never has the world he created offered him a sight so worthy of his eyes. He has seen tyranny, crime, and deception reign on earth. At this moment, he sees an entire nation, at war with all the oppressors of the human race, suspend its heroic efforts in order to raise its thoughts and vows to the Great Being who gave it the mission to undertake these efforts and the strength to execute them. The author of Nature linked all mortals together in an immense chain of love and happiness. Perish the tyrants who have dared to break it![3]

With these and other similarly nauseating sentiments, Robespierre attempted to bind the nation against what he called 'the ungodly union of kings'; only a month later, with the pace of the guillotine becoming faster and faster, Robespierre himself went under its insatiable blade.

As time passed, the character of the Champ de Mars changed: after the triumphant Napoleon Bonaparte honoured his victorious troops there in 1804, its significance as a military venue waned, and the days when the Champ de Mars saw 10,000 troops displayed in battle formation became fewer and fewer. Horse-racing became the big attraction, until Longchamp was built in 1855; thereafter it became the perfect site for a succession of great international exhibitions. Today the Champ de Mars is quintessential chic Paris, with its tourists and manicured lawns.

When Gustave Eiffel took over 'ownership' of the site on 1 January 1887, it was bordered on one of its long boundaries by a scattering of houses, workshops and small factories, and on the other by the apartment blocks whose owners had shown such interest in pre-emptively complaining about the industrial structure soon to be built next to their properties. Initial test-bore samples obtained by a contractor told Eiffel that his immediate problem was to be geological rather than one of neighbourly consideration. The tower's four feet, corresponding precisely to the cardinal points of the compass, formed a 410ft square. The east and south feet would have foundations in firm ground, where the gravel was about 20ft thick, but the other two stood on distinctly unstable land nearer to the Seine. The main substructure of the area was thick dry clay resting on chalk, but near the river, the clay was wet and covered by compacted sand, mud and gravel mixed with all the permeable organic detritus that came from the river itself. Eiffel sank caissons to a depth of 53ft before feeling confident that he had reached a sufficiently solid bed of firm clay; the foundation blocks farthest from the river could be cast in concrete in the open air, complete with the huge anchoring bolts and pistons with which to adjust angles once the piers were fitted; on the side nearest the river, foundations would have to be constructed inside the caissons. Eiffel built sixteen massive caissons, four for each pier, each weighing 34 tons, to be sunk to a depth of 70ft (5ft below water level). Each caisson was 50ft in length by 20ft wide, and 10ft in depth. Workers entered by an air-lock into a 6ft work chamber lit by electricity; compressed air kept the working chamber free from flooding; the bottom of each caisson was wedge-shaped to enable it to sink further into the clay as material was progressively excavated.

Each of the four foundations required the excavation of 266,520cu.ft of earth, and comprised a base of cement 20ft deep topped by huge limestone boulders which were in turn capped by specially selected and extremely hard stone blocks from quarries at Château-Landon. Into this mass were inserted anchoring bolts 26ft in length and 4in in diameter. The load on each bolt was estimated at no more than 70lb per sq.in., while the crushing strength of the hard stone was 1,600lb per sq.in. These bolts were not vital to the tower's stability, but gave important benefits to later assembly; attached to each bolt was a cylindrical iron column which Eiffel designed as a hydraulic piston capable of acting with a force of 800 tons. This ingenious mechanism enabled the principal iron ribs to be precisely adjusted so that at each stage in the construction, accurate horizontal alignments could be guaranteed. The critical time would come when the four great curved quadrangular piers rising from the foundations reached the height of 189ft, the level of the first platform; significant misalignment at that stage would be catastrophic if continued to the top of the tower, but the hydraulic rams guaranteed perfect conjunction. As the leading French engineer Max Nansouty observed:

> Isn't it marvellous to see our constructors thereby adjusting in space, from heights of 80 metres, the position of such enormous weights of iron with as much ease as a careful land-surveyor delicately adjusts the supports of his precision instruments by hand?[4]

Apart from the piston arrangement, there was little especially notable about the foundations, other than their magnitude and the fact that they were completed without mishap in only five months.

Although work began on the actual building of the tower in July 1887, Eiffel and his designers had been perfecting thousands of drawings for many months. The precise actions of gravity and wind on every individual component of the structure had been calculated, and since those mathematical reckonings had to allow for imperceptibly varying curves and inclinations, each iron part was unique in its manufacture. In all there were 5,500 engineering drawings and over 18,000 parts:

> We established by the drawings of each isolated part, calculated with a rigour requiring the constant use of logarithms, the position of each different rivet-hole by which its relationship to its neighbouring part would be achieved. The spacing of the holes was calculated mathematically to a

tenth of a millimetre. Each part thus required a particular study and an individual drawing usually drawn to half size for the small parts and one-fifth size for larger parts.[5]

Eiffel's understanding of the significance of wind pressure enabled him to conduct the most rigorous calculations. He employed the concept of a wind of 148 miles per hour at the top of the tower, reducing to 105 miles per hour at the base; not only that, he assumed for the purposes of calculation that the structure was to be solid, instead of the open lattice that he intended; in addition, he made an allowance of 800 tons for the weight of visitors. In practice, Eiffel defeated the wind problem not by increasing the weight and solidity of the structure, but by reducing these factors and having a light, open design. His basic principle governing both design and construction was succinctly expressed by the journal *Engineering*:

. . . to give the angles of the tower such a curve that it should be capable of resisting the transverse effects of wind pressures, without necessitating the connection of the members forming these angles, by diagonal bracing. The Eiffel Tower, therefore, consists essentially of a pyramid composed of four great curved columns, independent of each other, and connected together only by belts of girders at the different stories, until the columns unite upwards towards the top of the tower, where they are connected by ordinary bracing.[6]

Following Eiffel's calculations, the drawing-office staff under Maurice Koechlin at Levallois-Perret produced a highly accurate drawing for each individual part. Under the engineering supervision of Emile Nouguier, the pieces were then produced and each rivet-hole carefully drilled. Related parts were then loosely pegged together for delivery by horse-drawn wagon to the Champ de Mars in the form of small sections of girders or trusses up to 16ft in length, ready for assembly under the direction of Jean Compagnon. The official who described the entire project observed in his *Rapport Général*:

In spite of the importance of the assembly work, we did not see on the building site as many teams as one might expect to find there; the number of the workmen does not exceed 250; not only the human workforce has been kept to a minimum, but also the number of operations ready to begin. The parts arrive from the Levallois-Perret workshops prepared to an extreme degree impossible at the Champ de Mars; there were no holes left to bore, no fitting to be done; the majority of the rivets were positioned; the structural components fitted one to another, without any final improvement. The assembly of the tower illustrated very well the major difference between the French method and the English method.[7]

As the tower progressed, the assembly workers replaced pegs with engineering bolts as assemblies were further linked together; next came teams of four riveters who removed the temporary bolts one by one and replaced them with white-hot rivets, which were hammered in position, cooled and contracted to form supremely tight joints. In contrast to 'the English method', no cutting or drilling or production of parts whatsoever was allowed to take part on the tower itself; the entire erection was carried out as if using a giant Meccano set. Max Nansouty, writing in the French professional journal *Génie Civil*, made the comparison with the Forth Bridge, then under construction in Scotland:

It is in the setting up that the real difference of method is seen. For the Forth Bridge, the workers are furnished with the plans of the fitting and with the parts referred to on the tracings; and some margin for discretion is left in their adjustment and completion. An opportunity is thus given for a certain amount of initiative, and there is need for the employment of a varied and complicated stock of tools requiring mechanical power. In the works on the Eiffel Tower, there are on the contrary no such complications. There is not a boring or a shaping machine on the spot. The pieces reach the tower complete in every way. Each piece is numbered, and fits on to the preceding piece with mathematical precision, and if the rivet-holes do not correspond, the foreman sends the pieces back to the factory. It is difficult *a priori*, to say which system gives the best results; but it is certain that M. Eiffel's method has the advantage of leaving nothing to the unforeseen.[8]

At the Eiffel Tower, the extending structure of the four piers, each inclined towards the position of the first platform at an angle of 54°, would eventually collapse inwards if left unsupported, and Eiffel calculated that this would happen before they had reached half the height required. This appears to have been spotted by his detractors for, when at this point construction work apparently stopped and Eiffel, Nouguier, Keochlin and Sauvestre disappeared from the site for a week, the headline-writers had a field day. 'Eiffel Suicide!' shouted one; 'Gustave Eiffel has gone mad: he has been locked up in an asylum,' claimed another; 'The Eiffel Tower will never pass 26 metres!' alleged another.[9] The truth was more mundane; the answer lay in the construction of twelve temporary wooden scaffolds 90ft high. In addition, Eiffel ordered a massive wooden framework to be positioned just below the extremities of the extending piers. Each scaffold was fitted with a series of small jacks and cylinders; the jacks could raise the ironwork slightly as it approached the level of the first platform, while releasing sand from the cylinders allowed it to drop slightly under its own weight. Eiffel and his collaborators had spent the week finalising the engineering of these arrangements and of small, highly versatile 12-ton 'creeper' cranes innovatively designed to operate inside the piers themselves. Each was capable of lifting 4 tons, and was designed to climb the structure using rails which would later become part of the tower's system of elevators.

However, the hysterical press attention agitated nearby residents, who again raised anxieties about the potential for the tower's collapse, with subsequent damage to their properties. These worried individuals were encouraged in their paranoia by a plethora of 'authoritative' scaremongers who predicted that the tower would inevitably collapse at one or other of a range of predicted heights; others stirred up anxieties about lightning conductors and the electrical effects of the tower during thunderstorms. When one individual threatened to begin court action, and work on the tower was again brought to a halt, Eiffel was forced to issue pacifying statements demonstrating his own confidence. The City of Paris was quick to point out that Eiffel had taken upon himself sole responsibility. With time at a premium, and aware of the potentially disastrous delays resulting from legal action, he publicly took full financial responsibility for any damage or other ill-effects on local residents. Despite his bold move, malicious reports continued in the press that the tower was in fact sinking and that construction ought to be stopped immediately. It was put about that the entire project was too difficult, dangerous and impossible, and impressionable heads nodded in agreement. Eiffel countered by setting out the great experience that he and his workmen had amassed during previous projects:

My workmen, who have worked out in the open air, and on the incline too, have never had any vertigo at all. Were these workmen specially trained? Not in the least, they were for the most part simple peasants who very quickly became accustomed to working at great heights, and amongst them were some very young men. All the engineers who are engaged in this branch, myself included, never experience any apprehension whatever. It is quite an error to suppose that the tendency to vertigo increases with the height; the contrary is the case; those who have been up in balloons, even in the captive balloon, are well aware of this; besides, on the tower the men will not work swinging in the air as they did on the viaducts I mentioned; they will be on a platform 49ft wide, where they will be as undisturbed as on the ground. In every way you see these fears are chimerical. Evidently people are uneasy because we are going to work at 820 or 986ft from the ground, but when they know we shall be on a floor 49ft wide, they will easily see that the men have never worked in greater safety.[10]

Public anxiety passed; along with the prefabrication of carefully designed parts, the ground-breaking small cranes gave the entire project a distinct sense of a new system of working. Eiffel had clearly developed a concept of a logically ordered method of design and construction that enabled him to build a complex structure without highly specialised components and equipment:

Like Turner before him [Richard Turner, engineer of the Palm House at Kew], Eiffel segregated issues to solve detail problems. Eiffel's kit-of-parts approach to construction influenced and simplified steel bridge and high-rise construction. It was even adopted by Meccano, an open-ended British engineering construction toy for boys in 1904. Meccano (known as Erector Set in the USA) embedded the concept of open-ended, standardised assembly kits in the minds of generations of future engineers and manufacturers. The toy both mirrored and reinforced the cultural implications of the open system.[11]

In Scotland, the builders of the Forth Bridge were also encountering a confusing variety of reactions, both to the viability of the project as a whole and to the aesthetic implications of such a vast steel structure. In his defence, Benjamin Baker attempted a side-swipe at the Eiffel Tower:

Occasionally it has been suggested that the appearance will not be as elegant as could be desired, but I retort, mentally, in Lord Bacon's words, 'Houses are built to live in, and not to look on; therefore let use be preferred before uniformity, except where both may be had.' We aim at getting both, and our granite faced piers, with their simple but bold mouldings, certainly look better than cluster-columned metallic piers, however scientific.[12]

When the four great piers of the Eiffel Tower reached 180ft, they were to be joined together by four massive 70-ton horizontal iron trusses running from pier to pier, like a 25ft deep iron skirt covering the top of the piers. This was a supremely critical stage, because the platform to be erected upon the structure at this point would be the base for the remaining 800ft of the tower; the alignments had to be perfect. Judicious use had been made of Eiffel's hydraulic jacks and sand-boxes, and he had arranged that each rib of each pier would be slightly nearer to the vertical than required so that each would require a slight lowering to meet its final position (by releasing sand from the appropriate box); the alternative of having to lift the ribs would have been considerably more troublesome, as the civil engineer Max Nansouty observed in 1889:

> . . . one saw a masterpiece whose progressive steps first of all seemed to spring randomly into space, then settled into their relative proportions, shrinking themselves to some extent in force and power to leave the eyes of the spectator finally filled with wonder . . . [13]

The whole process was completed without mishap or problem, and the four piers were integrated in perfect alignment at the end of March 1888. Parisians could now see that this was the huge base of an enormous tower, and Eiffel was aware that a critical hurdle had been cleared:

> Joined by the belt of girders, the piers formed a solid table with a wide base. The sight of it alone was enough to brush aside any fear of its overturning. We no longer had to worry about a major accident, and any minor ones that might occur now could not compromise completion of the structure.[14]

With the first platform of the tower successfully finished, the prospects for a rapid completion of the remainder were good. One of the first things Eiffel did was to construct a canteen for his workers on the new platform. This was no simple benevolent gesture:

> To urge the men to take their meals there, the quality of the food was well supervised. The prices were decreased by 20 per cent on ordinary prices; this difference was refunded to the canteen-keeper by the site office. This additional expenditure,

funded by the works, was compensated for by the reduction in the waste of time due to the workmen's descent and ascent, and by that in the resulting tiredness. The sale of and access to alcohol other than brandy and rum, apart from at mealtimes, was forbidden. The installation of a canteen in the middle of a building site would be seen as careless if the men's drinking during working hours had been tolerated, drinking to excess being the cause of the majority of accidents. This canteen was reinstalled on the second floor when that platform was completed. Despite its prohibitions, the canteen had very good results; it made it possible for the workmen to eat and rest quietly for an hour, while serving cheap, healthy food. Everyone benefited from it, and it was never necessary to intervene to ensure good order; disrupters were certain of immediate dismissal in the event of arguments.[15]

Eiffel's mid-air canteen was simply one of many examples of his highly responsible insistence on safety. Not one death occurred during the entire construction of the tower, with the exception of one worker who entered the closed site at night after work had finished and fatally attempted to show off to his girlfriend by climbing dangerously. This was a safety record which is remarkable when compared, for example, to the deaths of fifty-seven workers on the Forth Bridge in Scotland. Press interest began to be more positive:

I was standing at a height of about 200ft, among a maze of ironwork painted with red lead, drilled with holes and arranged in criss-cross fashion as far as the eye could see. Above a confused greyish mass of timber, and looking very small in such a grandiose setting, 250 workmen came and went in a perfectly orderly way, carrying long beams on their shoulders, climbing up and down through the latticed ironwork with surprising agility. The rapid hammer-blows of the riveters could be heard, and they worked with fire that burned with the clear trembling flame of will-o'-the-wisps. The four cranes – one for each pillar – which brought up the pieces for this vast metallic framework one by one, stood out against the sky with their great arms at the four corners of this lofty site. During short winter days, when night falls, the twenty rivet forges blaze in the high wind, casting a sinister glow over this tangle of girders until it acquires a fantastic aspect. The men work as late as possible and move about like shadows between these dark red smoky fires.[16]

In assembling the second stage, the four 'creeper' cranes were redeployed to the second-level struts; a large 10-horse-power steam crane was also mounted on the first-level platform. Materials were hoisted by crane to the platform and then distributed in trolleys to the appropriate creeper crane by a circular railway laid round the circumference of the platform. To help prevent vertigo, small wooden work platforms were also built out around the main vertical columns. The good working conditions did not prevent occasional demands from the workers for more money, backed up by the threat of strikes. Without doubt, the tower was a good high-profile target for industrial action; it was a very visible public project with a tight time-scale. The worst trouble came after completion of the first platform; hot weather, cold weather, dark days and vertigo were all used as justification for increased rates of pay. Eiffel resisted, but increased pay slightly and declared that every man who remained at work until the French flag flew from the top would receive a special bonus. Boldly, he transferred strike leaders from the higher levels and restricted them to working on the construction of the buildings for the first platform, thus exposing them to the ridicule of their peers. The second-level platform was reached in July 1888, and on Bastille Day, the 14th, a fireworks display was arranged at the new height of 380ft, while Eiffel hosted a celebratory banquet for journalists on the first-level platform. Claiming a greater ability in assembling iron than sentences, he made a flowery promotional speech, extolling the virtues of French science and engineering:

The beginnings were painful, and criticisms were addressed to me that were impassioned as much as premature. I did my best to head off the storm, thanks to the constant support of one of yourselves, M. Lockroy, then Minister of Commerce and Industry, and I tried, by the good progress of the works, to reconcile if not the opinion of the artists, at least that of the engineers and the scientists. I made a point of showing, in spite of my self-effacing personality, that France continued to hold one of the top places in the art of metal construction where, right from the start, its engineers were particularly distinguished and covered Europe with the product of their talents. You are indeed not unaware of the fact that almost all the great structures, in Austria, in Russia, in Italy, in Spain and Portugal are due to our French engineers and that it is with pride that, while travelling abroad, one finds traces of their activity and their science.

The 300 metre tower is, above all, a dramatic demonstration of our national genius in one of its most modern forms; there we have one of its principal *raisons d'être* . . . .

If I judge it by the interest that it inspires, both in France and abroad, I have grounds to think that my efforts will not have been sterile and that we will be able to make known to the world that France continues to remain at the forefront of Progress.[17]

One writer for the Boston magazine *Atlantic Monthly* was transfixed as the tower reached for the sky:

When one sees the workmen, in their baggy corduroy trousers, red caps, and red sashes, climbing up and down the stairways, though these men are by no means angels, as they showed in their repeated strikes in the air against Engineer Eiffel, one has perforce to recall that staircase in Jacob's dream, upon which the angels were ascending between heaven and earth. By no other work of man have heaven and earth been so closely connected. Along both the first and second platforms of the tower, the latter as high as the top of the dome of St Peter's at Rome, is a row of pavilions, each like a large hall in itself; and each side even of the second platform has apparently a stretch as great as that of a long New York city block. The eye is continually baffled, and continually returns in renewed wonderment at these vast dimensions; and I speak of the tower when it has yet 200ft to rise.[18]

Above the level of the second platform, the four converging quadrangular piers rapidly formed a single column, requiring some different assembly techniques. Eiffel made use of the fact that there were vertical columns rising through the upper levels of the tower on which the elevators were to be mounted. He suspended 50-ton mobile cranes back-to-back on these columns and was thus able to employ a different form of climbing cranes for the higher assembly levels. This system of using highly mobile cranes, deployed in a variety of modes, was one of the keys to erecting the tower so quickly; accounts suggest that a 3-ton girder could be raised into position in 20 minutes. As the tower began to soar above the second platform, the components to be assembled became smaller and lighter, and although working space was more restricted, progress was rapid.

As it neared completion, the tower attracted an increasing number of visitors, many of whom were journalists:

A thick cloud of tar and coal smoke seized the throat, and we were deafened by the din of metal screaming beneath the hammer. Over there they were still working on the bolts; workmen with their iron bludgeons, perched on a ledge just an inch or so wide, took turns at striking the bolts. One could have taken them for blacksmiths contentedly beating out a rhythm on an anvil in some village forge, except that these smiths were not striking up and down vertically, but horizontally, and as with each blow came a shower of sparks, these black figures, appearing larger than life against the background of the open sky, looked as if they were reaping lightning bolts in the clouds.[19]

Other visitors were given the VIP treatment. The journalist Hugues Le Roux rose on the morning of 24 February 1889 ready to take part in a special ascent led by Gustave Eiffel, only to be faced by appalling weather:

On rising, the first thing I do is to run to the window to see what the weather is doing. Devastation! The air is appreciably colder, the sky filled with cloud. Snow is falling intermittently. The thermometer shows one and a half degrees below zero.[20]

It must have been daunting indeed to contemplate climbing the tower in such conditions. However, they managed to ascend later in the afternoon and saw Paris as never before; and the weather, still decidedly inclement, gave Le Roux ample opportunity to display his descriptive talents:

Indian file, with M. Eiffel and the guide in the lead, we start up the staircase. At that moment the thermometer says 1 degree below zero. The weather is still ominous, but the snow has stopped. The 350 steps leading to the first platform are easy to climb. Just as well, as this staircase has been built for use by the public.

M. Eiffel advises me to imitate his gait. He climbs slowly, with his right hand on the railing. He swings his body from one hip to the other, using the momentum of the swing to negotiate each step. Here the incline is so gradual that we can chat as we climb, and no-one is winded when we reach the first platform.

Four pavilions rising inside the structure hid the views of Paris. These were the foundations of a Flemish brasserie, a Russian restaurant, an Anglo-American bar and a Louis XIV cabaret. They were building a night-club – 190ft up in space! At meal-times this vast terrace would hold 4,200 people – the population of a town.

The city already appears immobile. Life and movement cease. The silhouettes of passers-by and carriages are like little black spots of ink in the streets. Only the Seine seems still alive, ripples running across its muddy surface – the impression of a canvas agitated by a gust of wind.

To the south there is a fine view of the Exposition grounds, with the glass roof of the Machinery Hall looking like a lake of molten lead; the domes materialise like island peaks. And soon, lower down under the increasingly black cloud, this mirage changes in a trick of light, as if to the huge nave of a church that takes the Tower for its own. I peek through a crack in the wooden flooring and look straight down into the void. Far below, I can see very small ducks swimming in a half-frozen pond. A shiver runs down my spine at the thought of a possible fall from this height.

Continuing up the staircase, the cold iron railing hurts my fingers so much that I try to climb with my hands in my pockets, without holding the railing, but the wind buffets me and I am blinded by driving sleet. I had to grab the railing again and shield my face with my arm. For a quarter of an hour I.didn't even think of looking at the view. All I can see is M. Eiffel's coat ahead. There is no more chatting.

We reach the platform at 906ft. Here a dozen erectors are at work, lost in space. They do the best they can to shelter from the wind behind canvas. Today there is a wind of only 15 miles per hour, but it is enough to take my breath away. As we arrive, they are about to insert a rivet. The great pin is taken red-hot from its portable forge, positioned in the hole and struck with heavy hammers in a shower of sparks.

Below, the shadows descend on the streets. Night drowns everything. Paris seems to be sinking into the night like some fabled city descending to the bottom of the sea amid a murmur of men and church bells. We return to the second platform for hot drinks in the canteen. M. Eiffel says that congratulations are coming in from all over, even from some of the artists who signed the famous protest to the minister. 'There are only three or four stubborn writers still holding out,' he says. 'I really don't understand why.' Conversation is enchantingly slow. We are reluctant to leave the warmth of our shelter to go back into the wind which seems to weep with the sound of human sobs in these hundreds of feet of iron stretched from earth to the clouds like an aeolian harp.[21]

Not all the scribes were as well disposed; the reporter from the *New York Times* was scathing of the tower's entire concept, and concluded his report by stating that attendance figures predicted in *Le Figaro* could not be realistically approached unless his compatriots from 'the Big Republic' came in large numbers:

> If its great height does not make the shaft appear too spindling, and if the top has been designed with some attempt at art the result may not be so dreadful as it was supposed. The pictures of the tower as it will be when complete, however, bear a strong resemblance to the electric light tower at Hell Gate or the elevator tower at Coney Island. Imagine that framework of iron twice as high as the Washington Monument, of thick iron beams, and with its four corners flaring or 'battering' outward near the ground, and you have the Eiffel Tower. [M. Eiffel] thinks his tower by no means devoid of artistic worth, admires the way in which it seems to spring from the ground, and states that whatever may be the opinion of it as a thing of beauty, it is a useful work. In fine, M. Eiffel is charmed with his huge tower, and will be greatly disappointed if the big crowds of the big Republic do not vote his work the biggest thing in the Exposition.[22]

It was a journalist from the daily *Le Temps*, visiting the tower in March 1889, who first confessed to the suspicion (for a reporter, seemingly lacking in cynicism) that the tower had cast a spell on him:

> Was it simply the weather that day, or do visitors always feel it? Whichever the case, an indescribable melancholy, a feeling of intellectual prostration took hold of me. At a height of 350 feet, the earth is still a human spectacle; an ordinary scale of comparisons is still adequate to make sense of it. But at 1,000 feet, I felt completely beyond the normal conditions of experience. At 350 feet one can admire the fact that such a puny being as man has accomplished the marvellous work that this infinite city represents; at 1,000 feet one no longer understands why man went to the trouble.[23]

The tower was not of course the only attraction for such parties of invited guests. There was a rather frantic competition by other features and pavilions of the exhibition, and the associated factories and suppliers. Hoping for favourable publicity, in advance of the opening day and for weeks afterwards, they would regularly throw open their doors to groups of journalists and VIPs (indeed, such visits and excursions were arranged across the whole of France). For example, the delicate journalist contemplating with some degree of terror an ascent of the tower on foot in conditions of freezing wind could easily have chosen instead on the same day an alternative such as a visit to that stretch of the Paris sewers from the Place du Châtelet to the Place de la Madeleine, or to the Popp Compressed Air Supply Station at the Rue St Fageau. The more adventurous might take a trip by the Paris, Lyons and Mediterranean Railway to the works of M. Decauville at Corbeil, where the railways to be used at the exhibition had been built (in which case they would have been hauled by a locomotive named *Dumbarton* which was destined for the Denny Brothers shipyard in that West of Scotland town).[24]

Yet the tower soared above everything. Its 172sq.ft third platform was at a height of 906ft. Above this was a campanile incorporating a scientific laboratory, with a spiral staircase leading to an upper gallery 20ft in diameter surrounding a 22ft-high lantern with a powerful central lamp and a series of lenses in the national colours of France; under this light were installed two powerful projectors on tracks. The final total height of the tower was 986ft. (Later, a spire and communications antennae were added, bringing the total height to 1,053ft.) This unique tower, weighing 7,300 tons, was completed on 31 March 1889, having been built in two years, two months and five days, at a total cost of 7,799,401.31 francs.

It was an extraordinary achievement. Later engineers used such refinements as the telegraph, and a system of graphic bar-charts to ensure that contractors and workers could understand how progress in the different departments was related and interdependent, and in 1912 the telephone was first used in a major construction project, at the Langwies Viaduct in Switzerland. It is known that Eiffel used methods of prefabrication and pre-assembly, but he never clarified how he programmed these functions. His genius partly lay in managing the design and assembly, but we have no knowledge of how he ordered the logistics of making everything work as planned.

Soon after midday on 31 March 1889, Gustave Eiffel led a party of senior engineers and civic and state dignitaries, accompanied by the press, on foot to the top of the tower, to celebrate its completion. This was to have been his relatively private affair, but it became grander than he had intended:

> Right from the start, one deputy covered his eyes for the climb and groped his way up on the arm of his neighbour – an image of parliament both lively and blind. The climb was very slow, often delayed for explanation by M. Eiffel at each level, and took over an hour. In the distance, on the banks of the Seine, or in the streets around the Trocadero, the eyes of a curious crowd followed this hardly visible human anthill climbing imprisoned in the red mesh of this immense birdcage.[25]

Most dropped out at the first and second platforms, but Eiffel and a few others, including Emile Nouguier, Jean Compagnon and the president of the city council, reached the flagpole just after 2 p.m. The reporter's impression would have silenced Charles Gounod:

> The vista is superb. Mont-Valerien, Montmartre, Sannois seem small grey blots; the forest of Saint-Germain grows blurred in the blue clouds; the Seine becomes a quiet brook, furrowed by the boats of Lilliput, and Paris a cardboard model with its straightforward streets, its square roofs and its aligned frontages. Small black spots are the crowds. All, moreover, seems deprived of life, all except the greenery of woodland, because no movement is visible in this vastness.[26]

The man from *Le Monde Illustré* recorded the momentous event at the highest point in the man-made world:

> M. Eiffel was accompanied by ten gallant men when, at two-thirty-five he pulled the cord used to hoist the enormous

tricolour, which unfurled gracefully in the air, while the applause of his excited assistants and the cannon-fire thundered on the lower floors. It was a truly imposing spectacle, and revealed a curious fact which deserves to be reported. With cries of 'Vive Eiffel!' and 'Vive la France!' from every breast, everyone around the eminent engineer exchanged cordial handshakes, under the spontaneous influence of common admiration and powerful shared emotions.[27]

The *Illustrated London News* was also present, and noted the unexpected attendance of the prime minister:

. . . a salute of 25 guns was fired. M. Contamin, engineer-in-chief of the Exposition's metal constructions, then made a speech, and explained that the tower was a monument worthy of the grand date of 1789 which it commemorated. M. Berger, Municipal Councillor, drank the health of M. Eiffel, of the workmen of the tower, and of the Municipal Council. On descending, M. Tirard (the Prime Minister) accompanied by M. Alphand, Director of Public Works, was found awaiting the party.[28]

After refreshments on the descent, Eiffel addressed the assembled company at a small lunch, paying special attention to his own workmen:

My dear friends, I have just experienced a great satisfaction, that of flying our national flag on the highest building which man ever built. We are at the end of our task; but, to get there, we all made efforts, either by brain or by muscle! Steadfastness was ours – for me and my immediate collaborators, in preparing and co-ordinating the work, and for you in carrying it out in bad weather, in the cold and the wind which you so often braved on this high summit! But none of us engaged in this work could shrink from it; having promised to carry out a masterpiece often enough tried or dreamed of but still never achieved, we had to keep our word, under penalty of compromising the national honour.[29]

One of his workers, M. Rondel, spoke on behalf of his comrades:

> Mr Eiffel, I come in the name of my comrades and friends, the workmen of the 300-metres tower, to express to you all the sympathy and respect that we owe you for completing this great work. For two years, your name has resounded throughout the entire universe. The hour has now come for you to complete your imposing idea and to admire your masterpiece. We can repeat to the children of our grandchildren that we have worked on the most imposing monument in the world! Thank you to the Municipal Council for the honour that it gave us in helping to hoist our flag!
>
> Long live engineer Eiffel! Long live France! Long live the Republic![30]

Prime Minister Tirard eulogised the tower, apologised for having once opposed its construction, and concluded by announcing that Eiffel was to be made an Officer of the Légion d'Honneur. The poet Sully-Prudhomme, who had been such a vociferous member of the Artists' Protest two years earlier, made a long but witty and contrite apology for his opposition:

> It is with a quite natural timidity that, as a poet lost in a company of scientists by some stroke of fortune, I allow myself to speak at this banquet. But could I resign myself to silence? I signed the protest of the artists and writers against the creator of the gigantic building whom we celebrate this evening, and I am anxious that you are not unaware, members of *la Scientia*, of how concerned I am to associate my homage with yours. I would not have liked to let you fear that you had brought a traitor into the place, and I would have been too humiliated if you had judged me unable to share not only your work, but still your admiration.[31]

Although Eiffel had celebrated the achievement of his tower, been awarded the Légion d'Honneur, and the workers had been promised a silver commemorative medal by the City of Paris, there was much left to complete. There were buildings to be fitted out and prepared on both platforms, staircases to be provided and, most problematical of all, a series of elevators which had been in process of installation for some time were still a long way from being satisfactory. It was assumed that, while many visitors would be willing to ascend the 363 steps to the first platform, most would be unlikely to go further on foot (a total of 1,665 steps). Almost 2,000 people per hour would need to be lifted to the first platform; 455 per hour all the way to the top (in 7 minutes). The exhibition was due to open in two months' time, and both it and the tower had to be ready to face their demanding international public, who would subject it to the most rigorous of testing processes.

EIGHT

'Unique, strange and truly grandiose'

While the tower's upper reaches were being assembled, work was proceeding apace to complete the range of buildings and the fitting-out of services on the first and second platforms. At the first level, where it was expected most visitors would remain, there was an outer 9ft-wide promenade area with decorative arches on each side, totalling 900ft in length. This was where the public would stroll and get their first panoramic views of Paris. Around the central open void there was to be a Flemish brasserie, a Russian restaurant and an Anglo-American bar; these facilities were each able to cater for 500–600 people at a time. For the postprandial period there was a 250-seat cabaret theatre in which to relax at a show afterwards. There was also a variety of kiosks, souvenir stalls and hirers of deck-chairs and binoculars. On the second platform, the Paris daily *Le Figaro* installed a printing press and newspaper office where it produced special editions during the run of the exhibition; a patisserie and refreshment area also shared the space. The small octagonal third platform at a height of 906ft was entirely enclosed behind glass panels and provided the highest point to which the public was normally admitted. However, guests who were permitted to climb the short spiral staircase would reach another level, just below the campanile, which contained three small laboratories for the study of astronomy, physics, meteorology and biology, as well as a small furnished apartment reserved for Eiffel himself, intended for entertaining guests rather than as living accommodation. Outside on a surrounding balcony were installed tracks for the operation of two high-powered mobile spotlights with a range of 7 miles (the electric lamp on top of the campanile was visible from a distance of well over 100 miles). These were to be used to illuminate the city's monuments in evening performances, which were the precursors of today's sophisticated *son et lumière* events; this would be the year that Paris would adopt the lighting of public buildings on a grand scale. The tower's topmost features were eight lightning rods which were connected to 3in-thick conductors leading deep into the foundations.

Painters began the first of the continuing efforts to paint the tower (using a reddish-brown iridescent concoction called Barbados Bronze, applied saturated at the bottom, becoming progressively lighter near the top to enhance the impression of height); erectors, carpenters and electricians continued with the various buildings, and work began on the staircases and elevator systems. There were two staircases from the ground to the first platform, one each for up- and down-traffic; they were wide, easy to negotiate and were provided with numerous landings as the direction changed. Between the first and second platforms, two up and two down spiral staircases 2ft wide were provided; stairways from ground to second platform were designed to accommodate 2,000 people an hour. From the second platform to the peak a staff-only spiral staircase 196ft high was built. However, fast, safe and comfortable elevators were regarded as essential to the public success of the tower. This was an issue that was to prove extremely problematic; there were to be technical difficulties and contractual disputes, and the various systems would not be ready by opening day.

The science and practice of elevator technology were in the early stages of development, pushed forward by the popularity in the USA of 'elevator buildings'. The hydraulic passenger lift had been around for some time, but it wasn't until 1854 that E.G. Otis made it a safe prospect by devising a system of pawls which, if the rope failed, would engage with ratchets at the side of the lift-shaft and bring the cage to a stop. There were also steam-powered and helical screw systems, but both had practical drawbacks and a lack of speed which limited their use to freight or low-rise purposes. The hydraulic system, in which the passenger cage was moved by the action of a piston moved by water pressure, was widely in favour. Nevertheless, there were outstanding considerations. For safety reasons, European engineers would generally only accept a cage which was built directly onto the piston, as against the favoured American method of suspending the cage by rope; the former system would have required a piston-well hundreds of feet deep below the foundations of the tower. Apart from the great height to be travelled, the main problem in providing elevators for Eiffel's masterpiece was the fact that the second-level elevators would have to move within the piers on a varying curved trajectory, since the piers themselves arched at an angle of 78°.

From ground to first platform, there were to be two lifts by Roux-Combaluzier et Lepape and two by Otis Ascenseur et Cie (the French branch of the American Elevator Company). The tricky problem of providing two lifts to rise from first to second platforms was awarded to Otis (they were in fact extensions from the ground-level lifts); and the one lift from second level to campanile was awarded to the Leo Edoux Company. The use of foreign equipment in constructing the tower was against the Exposition's charter, and the Otis bid was initially rejected, but with time running out and no indigenous French offer in sight, the die was cast. The matter was the subject of considerable smugness in New York:

The cylinder operating one of the lower elevators in the Eiffel Tower in Paris has just been shipped by the makers, the well-known firm of Otis Bros & Co of this city. It is no small tribute to American ingenuity and enterprise that a leading French engineer should appeal to America when confronted with a new problem. The elevator starts from one of the legs of the tower, following an inclined path that varies its degree of inclination, until the landing, 489ft above the ground, is reached. The difficulty arose from the nature of the curve the car was to follow. No satisfactory offer could be obtained from French firms. After the 489ft landing is reached, the difficulty ends, and an ordinary elevator of French manufacture is used for the remainder of the distance.[1]

Although the innovative use of electricity had initially been mooted as the driving power for the elevators, there were objections on the grounds of complexity and noise, and all proposed systems were hydraulic. Water was pumped to tanks strategically placed at appropriate points on the tower, and supplied to the various systems as required. Eiffel almost certainly detested the fact that there were to be three completely different elevator designs being installed by three different companies. Neither he nor the exhibition's organising committee knew anything of lift technology; since he was forced to rely on the judgements and expertise of specialist engineers, his natural wish personally to plan and control logically could not be applied to this part of the undertaking. The apparently cumbersome business of having several different systems and companies involved seems on the face of it to have been self-defeating. None of the elevators was ready for use on the exhibition's opening day, 6 May (it would be another six weeks before they were open; indeed, the tower itself would not be open to the public until 15 May). However, despite the complexity of the technical arrangements, and the fact that everyone was working on the tallest building in the world, the outcome was impressive. The time specified to reach the top was only 7 minutes; 750 people per hour were to be enabled to make that elevator journey, and 2,350 per hour to the first and second platforms.

The Roux-Combaluzier et Lepape system used articulated, double-looped chains, made from a series of hinged bars, which moved on guide-pulleys driven by two hydraulic pistons with a diameter of 39in and a stroke of 16ft. The motion was transferred to the driving wheels by the chains passing over pulleys with a ratio of 1 to 13. The chains were fixed to the sides of the passenger compartment carrying 100 people at a speed of 200ft per minute; in the event of a break in either chain, the whole system was designed to become rigid and remain secured by the guides. In operation, the system proved highly unsatisfactory and was entirely replaced in time for the 1900 Exposition. Gustave Eiffel asserted his authority and became intimately involved in the design for the new hydraulic system, by Fives-Lille. This technology remained intact until 1987, when it was partially automated using high-pressure oil pumps. The modernisation was not entirely successful and was remodelled in 1992. Today, two-thirds of the original 1900 machinery remains operating reliably alongside some modern improvements.

The Otis system was seen as the simplest; it used a 36ft long cylinder with a 38in piston inclined parallel to the double-decked cabin's initial running angle. As water pushed the piston, the cabin, suspended from twelve pulleys by six steel cables, was pulled along rails that curved at the level of the first platform to accommodate the dynamics of the tower, before continuing to the second platform. The whole system was balanced by counterweights beneath the elevator path, and safety brakes with automatic clutches were fitted both to the cabin and the counterweight. The Otis elevators carried fifty passengers at 400ft per minute, but were so out-performed by the Five-Lille design that they were dismantled some time before 1909. A new north pier elevator by Schneider Creusot Loire was installed in 1964 and further modernised in 1995. The elevator in the South pier was replaced in 1983 by modern machinery specifically to serve the prestigious Jules Verne Restaurant on the second platform.

The Edoux elevator was a vertical piston system that was required to operate between the second platform and the top of the tower, a vertical distance of 525ft. This was done in a 'split-shift' as described by the journal *Engineering* in May 1889:

An intermediate stage constructed midway between the second storey and the upper platform is the starting point of the Edoux elevator. One cage is placed at the top of a pair of pistons, and travels from the intermediate stage to the upper platform, a distance of 262ft; the cage is connected by cables to a second cabin which acts as a counterweight and carried passengers from the second storey to the intermediate stage, also a distance of 262ft; the arrangement is such that when the elevator is at work the cages are travelling in opposite directions; at the intermediate stage the passengers change from one cage into the other, and in this way the whole journey is accomplished by one system.[2]

The 110-passenger cabin travelling from intermediate to top level rested on the pistons of two vertical hydraulic jacks 81 metres long. The counterbalancing cabin was suspended by four steel cables running over pulleys at the top of the tower. Although the maximum load at any time was 21 tons, the breaking strain of the cables was rated at over 893 tons; for the sake of the squeamish, automatic brakes were fitted. The final stage of the journey from the second platform could be completed in about 4 minutes, including the change of cabin in the middle (when passengers had to walk along a narrow gangway with an impressive vertical view!). The major drawback of this system was the huge volume of water required; this precluded the use of anti-freeze additives, and resulted in the system being closed every year from November to March. This Edoux system was completely replaced in 1983 with a system that enabled the journey from second platform to the top without requiring a change of cabin; the original spiral staircase was also replaced with a modern rectilinear structure.

Gustave Eiffel was very fussy during the later stages of the elevator saga; and, with time running out, he was nervous. He argued with the Otis company that rack-and-pinion safety devices were preferable to their proposed brakes shoes. Otis claimed that such a change would be noisy and compromise the achievable speed. A real stand-off developed, but Otis knew that time was on their side and essentially 'won' the dispute by simply doing nothing. Not, however, before Eiffel had manoeuvred the Otis company into conducting a hair-raising test:

The lift was fastened with ordinary ropes, and this done it was detached from the cables of steel wire with which it is worked. What was to be done was to cut the ropes and allow the lift to fall, so as to ascertain whether, if the steel cables were to give way, the brakes would work properly and support the lift. Two carpenters armed with great hatchets ascended to the lift and were ready to cut the cables; at a given signal, a blow cut the rope. The enormous machine began to fall. Everyone was startled, but in its downward course the lift began to move more slowly, it swayed for a moment from left to right, stuck on the brake, and stopped. There was a general cheering. Not a pane of glass in the lift had been broken or cracked, and the car stopped without shock at a height of ten metres above the ground.[3]

However, all was not well in the relationship. Eiffel had threatened to withhold payment to Otis when it was clear that the elevators would not be completed by the contracted date of 1 January 1889. This dispute ended with a furious reaction from Otis:

> After all else we have borne and suffered and achieved in your behalf, we regard this as a trifle too much; and we do not hesitate to declare, in the strongest terms possible to the English language, that we will not put up with it.[4]

Time being of the essence, the argument was again won by Otis, who simply waited while Eiffel raged impotently.

During the latter stages of assembly, Eiffel had maintained a rigorous observation of the tower and its verticality, anxious to assure himself that everything conformed to his expectations.

> These observations showed conclusively that the foundations had not yielded at all under their very moderate load, and that if any deviation from the vertical existed, it was so slight as to be scarcely appreciable with the most careful measurement. All the other calculations of M. Eiffel have been so complete and accurate, and his experience with high structures so exceptional, that his assurance may be taken with confidence that the oscillations of the Tower at the summit under the most unfavourable conditions of wind pressure will not exceed 6 inches, while the periods of vibration will be relatively slow; under ordinary conditions of weather, the tower will remain absolutely rigid.[5]

Apart from the graduated coating of paint, and the arcading of the first platform, the tower remained almost wholly undecorated. Eiffel did, however, turn the tower into a historical document by painting the names of the 199 permanent workmen on a prominent girder; this would not be his only commemorative gesture on the structure. Still anxious to dispel comment and accusation that the building was essentially a frivolous waste, he decorated the four sides of the first platform with a frieze on which he painted, in 2ft-high gilded lettering, the names of seventy-two French scientists who had distinguished the nation in the previous century.[6] He felt that it had been under their cultural influence that the tower had been built, and wanted public recognition of the homage he felt was their due. The names of such as the chemist Lavoisier, the physicist Ampère, the engineer de Dion, the astronomer Delaunay, and painter and physicist Daguerre and their dozens of illustrious fellows no doubt helped, at least in Eiffel's mind, to give the stark, brand-new and quintessentially technological tower a fitting nobility and provenance. Ironically, at some point in the early 1900s, the names were obliterated during the process of regular painting; happily however, the frieze was restored to its original glory in 1986.

The French airship designer, physicist and exponent of photography Gaston Tissandier (who had been one of those who ascended with Eiffel on 31 March, when he hoisted the tricolour at the top) published in 1889 his clearly 'authorised' book (including an autographed letter of approval from Gustave Eiffel), *Description of the Monument, its Construction, its Machinery, its Object and its Utility*:

If the tower of 300 metres is a grand scientific enterprise, it is also an admirable work of art, in the opinion of some of our greatest artists, even of some who opposed the enterprise at the outset. At the time of the recent banquet of the *Scientia* conference, the meeting at which M. Janssen made the speech we have quoted from, M. Sully-Prudhomme of the Académie Française raised his poet's voice in favour of the iron giant. The orator reminded his hearers, with the peculiar charm with which he knew how to invest everything that comes from his thoughts, that he had had to hesitate in daring to choose between his worship of grace and his veneration for genius when it fetters force. But the colossus appeared to him then 'as a witness in iron raised by man towards the azure to testify to man's immutable resolution to pass to there, and to establish himself there. Behold,' said M. Sully-Prudhomme in conclusion, 'the point of view which reconciled me to this monster, this conqueror of the sky. And when even in the face of its imperious grandeur I do not feel myself converted, assuredly I feel consoled by the proud joy common to all to see the French flag float higher than all the other flags in the world, if not as a sign of the warlike, at least as an emblem of the invincible aspirations of my country.'[7]

Sully-Prudhomme's retraction, made on the day of Eiffel's private opening ceremony in March, had been the first of many by signatories of the infamous Artists' Protest. Charles Gounod was another early guest, spotted having a meal by Eiffel and invited to join him. Gounod was delighted, and joined Eiffel and Thomas Edison in the private apartment under the campanile; later, he often entertained a select company far into the night in Eiffel's apartment at the top of the tower.[8] Many other celebrity visitors arrived during the exhibition. The symbolist poet Stéphane Mallarmé was sent to write an article and was lost for words, claiming that the tower had surpassed his wildest dreams. Paul Gauguin, the post-Impressionist painter thought that 'these engineer architects' had created a new decorative art.[9] One visitor alarmingly claimed that 'the very best moment was when the Eiffel Tower let us glimpse utterly unexpected female genitalia between her open legs'.[10] Yet another was amazed at '. . . the strange logic of the French language which will class such an enormous phallic symbol as feminine'.[11] It is hardly surprising that everyone had an opinion about this sensational structure, for the tower has consistently attracted comment throughout its life from writers, artists, poets, philosophers, engineers and people who had both preconceived impressions and none. What was very quickly certain was that, despite all the earlier mutterings and anxieties, the tower was going to be popular, even in 'smart society'. As the reporter from the *Illustrated London News* who attended the opening of the exhibition noted:

> Whatever may be the utility of the tower, its popularity cannot be contested; it may be only the most colossal scientific toy yet invented, but it will nevertheless reveal to average humanity a number of new sensations, and a striking vision of the sky, and of the grandiose panorama of one of the capitals of the world reduced to the dimensions of a mere brown, silent and leprous spot on the face of the globe, for such is the aspect of Paris from the upper platforms of the Eiffel Tower.[12]

The exhibition was to attract huge numbers of visitors from the USA, where interest was intense. The journal *Scientific American* was greatly impressed by Eiffel's ability to control the tower project:

> The remarkable regularity with which this erection has been accomplished, and the fact that no correction of any kind was ever required, is an ample proof of the precision with which the innumerable parts that compose the structure were turned out from the ateliers of Levallois-Perret. This achievement also shows how well the arrangements for the erection were combined, all having come to pass as had been foreseen, without error, without accident, and without delay.[13]

However, the journal expressed a jaundiced view, shared by many others, of the financial risks taken and of the prospects for the tower's future existence:

> No doubt during the period that this Exhibition is kept open the ample facilities thus provided for the public will not be found excessive, but it is scarcely reasonable to suppose that after all the buildings on the Champ de Mars have been swept away, and the vast column alone remains to suggest the glories of the departed centennial celebration, great numbers

of people will go so far out of Paris as the Champ de Mars to enjoy a sensation which by that time will have ceased to be novel. It is to be hoped that, by the time the Exhibition closes, the enterprising syndicate which has acquired the Eiffel Tower will find themselves repaid to a large extent. Otherwise there is reason to fear that their speculation may not turn out profitable, and that their twenty years' concession will scarcely suffice to make their speculation a satisfactory one.[14]

Visitors from all parts of the world thronged to Paris for the opening of the exhibition. The day before the opening, Sunday 5 May, saw an inauspicious start to the celebrations, with an assassination attempt against the French president Marie François Carnot on his way to the ceremony at Versailles to mark the centenary of the Revolution. No one was injured, and Perrin, the assailant, seems to have been a disgruntled loner complaining about a period of military imprisonment in Martinique; in the words of one newspaper, 'he seems not to be in the enjoyment of all his mental faculties'.[15] The editorial in *The Times* of London noted that the incident appeared to have galvanised the crowds into voicing their enthusiasm – even if that was perhaps less directly for the centenary of the Revolution:

The enthusiasm awakened by the Centenary of the Revolution has been undoubtedly much quickened by the more practical hopes associated with the event of today. The French in general and the Parisians in particular are in good humour because they look forward to a time of social gaiety, commercial activity, and handsome profits as soon as the Exhibition opens its doors.[16]

Indeed they did. Paris cabbies were first off the mark to exercise bitter industrial muscle to ensure they got what they thought was their share. Their strike enabled *The Times* correspondent to declare with some pleasure that he had been able to rescue Edouard Lockroy from the crowd, most of which had been unable to obtain transport back into central Paris:

M. Lockroy is the real author of the Exhibition. He stood out against his colleagues for the Eiffel Tower, the ugly but immense attraction of the Exhibition. He, too, arranged the guarantee fund, without which there could have been no Exhibition.[17]

There was also a panic about the tricolour flying from the tower, after some dirty tricks by scions of 'perfidious Albion':

The first flag that was hoisted to the summit of the Eiffel Tower had the saddest fate. Some Englishmen, armed with penknives, scissors and other cutting tools, cut it to pieces as souvenirs of the other side of the English Channel. For a few days, the Tower remained without a flag, but on May 5th, the national Centenary, the national colours flew again from the summit of the monument. The following day, at the inauguration of the Exposition, everyone was astonished to see that only a shred of blue fabric remained on the flagstaff. Everybody thought at first that the English had secretly climbed the tower again to add to their trophy, but it was nothing like that; only the wind was to blame, and its ferocity during the night had put the flag in its pitiable state. By eleven o'clock, the misfortune had been repaired and the tricolour was again flying from the flagpole.[18]

The events at Versailles seem to have passed off in high good spirits, but the opening of the exhibition at the Champ de Mars on the following day was a drearier affair. Some of the features that might have been thought vital to underlying concepts of international brotherhood were missing. Queen Victoria recalled Lord Lytton, her French ambassador to London, to prevent any unintended involvement in events in Paris. Similarly, other royal houses of Europe largely stayed away in protest at what was seen as rampant French propaganda, and not one of them, with the exception of that of Belgium, was represented by its ambassador; most diplomatic representation was decidedly reduced in status. In the same way, a number of the big French aristocratic families absented themselves, along with many of the still-noisy monarchists; such enemies of the French Republic regarded the exhibition as a vulgar celebration of evil. Following the destruction of the French monarchy, an unspoken fear in Britain was aired when the *Manchester Guardian* reported, 'The Exposition will be seen abroad as a visible sign of the extraordinary recovery of France.' Reports indicate that many exhibits were still unfinished, and that the half-million people who jostled their way through the twenty-two entrances were neither properly marshalled nor informed of what was happening, with the result that there was a great deal of confusion about where they ought to be at any given time. To make matters worse, most of the speeches were inaudible to the great majority of the people, 'so that the proceedings were dull indeed'. According to *The Times*, Prime Minister Pierre Tirard complimented Gustave Eiffel, but the paper noted that there were problems with the conditions under which he gave his speech, 'many passages of which were applauded by those within earshot'. Most accounts described a low-key event which 'drew few plaudits'.[19] The report in *The Times* was detailed, if decidedly partisan, and began with a downbeat confirmation of a rather tedious opening ceremony:

It was all matter-of-fact and nothing appealed to the imagination. All was on a large scale, indeed, but there was nothing romantic, and the ceremony could not meet the expectations of the multitudes of visitors, except as regards its good organisation and the picturesqueness of the arrangements, and even in this respect it fell short.[20]

President Carnot (who 'arrived through a dense but not very enthusiastic crowd') made the expected speech and formally declared the exhibition open. Despite a lack of passion in the opening ceremony, the tower was an immediate favourite with visitors. *Le Figaro* published a special edition of the newspaper on the first day of the exhibition, and was highly enthusiastic about the tower:

The Tower has been described as many times as there are pieces of iron its construction. After all that has been written, we can say only these two words to the public – Climb it!! We already anticipate that the number of those who will answer yes! is incalculable. At 10,000 per day, that makes one million 800,000 visitors during the Exposition. This figure is nothing extraordinary, since the elevators can carry twenty to twenty-five thousand people per day. You can lunch and dine on the Eiffel Tower's 1st level. How one eats at the Exposition! You can also see the writing, compositing and production of *Le Figaro de la Tour Eiffel*.[21]

Despite complaints about the opening ceremony, Paris was in the mood. The sheer scale of the exhibition and the grandeur of the architecture were exciting, and flags, bunting and, of course, the tricolour were abundant on all buildings and streets:

The public buildings have been lavishly illuminated, and the Place de la Concorde has had the usual festoons of lamps, while the private illuminations, of late years almost confined to the wine-shops, have been on an extensive scale. Not only the large hotels, but a multitude of shops have displayed lines of gas-jets and transparencies. All the principal streets, indeed, are ablaze with light, and all Paris is in the open-air. The weather has been fine all day, and tonight there is a pleasant breeze. Numbers of people are supping or dancing in the streets, and processions of young men with flags are singing the Marseillaise. Displays of fireworks have taken place at many points, and have attracted crowds of spectators. The bridges have been brilliantly decorated and illuminated, and there has been a kind of nocturnal regatta on the Seine, between Passy and Auteuil. Never, indeed, has Paris presented a gayer, a more brilliant spectacle.[22]

The floodlit *bateaux-mouches* on the Seine had orchestras playing on deck, and there were balloons, flares and firework displays and all sorts of events in streets and squares; and closed as it may have been, the tower's beacon sent out its red, white and blue message from the top, while the spotlights illuminated the city. From the start, the republican soubriquet of *'l'Exposition Tricolorée'* was appropriate. At the Comédie Française a new verse play, *The Song of the Century*, celebrated the exhibition, performed by two actors representing France and Poetry:

> Clear-eyed Science and active Industry
> Have erected, among the spacious palaces,
> An iron Tower leading to the heavens.
> Unique, strange and truly grandiose spectacle![23]

The Eiffel Tower was not, however, to be open to the public for another ten days. Needless to say, some adventurous visitors tried to climb onto the lower structure, but were driven off by workmen turning water-hoses on them. Nevertheless, the tower was soon the subject of speculation. Within a week of the exhibition's opening, people began to come up with theories about the tower. In particular, popular opinion noted that the weather had been poor for the previous month:

Persons interested in the matter who have watched the tower closely believe they have noticed that large quantities of heavy rain and thunder clouds gather round it, and then, as though deprived by the lightning conductors of parts of their electricity, they are blown further on and break in showers far away in quite another part of the town. Briefly, the Eiffel Tower is seriously charged with having changed the electrical condition of Paris, and this is the reason why there have been so many heavy storms, which do not, however, have the effect of clearing the air. M. Eiffel laughs at this theory, alleging that his tower is only doing on a larger scale what every lightning conductor does.[24]

Considerable excitement had been rife for months in the press over the potential danger of lightning strikes, and a special commission had been appointed to investigate. The engineer Edmond Becquerel reported:

The 300m tower will be able to play the part of an immense lightning conductor protecting a very broad space around it, provided that its metal mass is in perfect communication, using good conductors, with the underground aquifer. Thanks to these precautions, the interior of the structure, with any people who may be sheltered there, will be absolutely protected against any accident resulting from the frequent thunderbolts which will undoubtedly strike the sides of the tower at various heights.[25]

One of the commonest reactions to the opening, as in *The Times*, was a kind of bemused wonder that everything could have come together quite as it did:

It seems incredible that all these beautiful buildings should have sprung up in such a short time within that desert of mud and sand known as the Champ de Mars, and that this waste should in two years have been converted into an oasis of shady walks, flower beds and bright lawns, amid which fountains play in all directions, and give coolness and freshness to the air. The buildings are remarkable for their graceful lines, and they have been admirably distributed in the midst of the verdure. Even the Eiffel Tower does not seem out of place, thanks to its vast proportions, and when seen close at hand it produces an astounding effect on the visitor, illustrating as it does the wonders that may be achieved by new applications of the forces of nature.[26]

Elsewhere in the English press, there was a fair degree of Francophobia, as here expressed in *The Spectator*:

The weather is propitious, the people are at leisure or make leisure; it will be a protracted summer carnival, relieved from the dullness of carnivals by talk about novelties in science and art, and scenic displays such as the one of Tuesday, when the Eiffel Tower became, from its head among the clouds to its base among the people, a column bathed in rosy light, a spectacle quite artificial, if you will, and even operatic, but unlike any ever before seen in this world. That kind of thing, science employing its wide knowledge and its gigantic strength to produce an operatic scene, pleases the French as much as ever Samson pleased the Philistines. Then, also, the Parisians are vain, and they see in this marvellous Exhibition, this obedience of the nations to their summons, this thronging of all peoples; and all celebrities and all costumes in their streets, proof positive that their city, which they are as proud of as Americans of their forty states, is the pivot of the world's thought, the object that concentrates on itself at once the interest and admiration of the whole human race. That is the proper position for Paris in Frenchmen's eyes, and seeing it realised for a moment, Parisians grow almost benevolent, and think with a pitying kindness of all those to whom face has denied the privilege of belonging to such a city.[27]

For more than a week after the official opening, frustrated Parisians could look at the tower as much as they liked, but could not ascend. But nine days later, the last-minute details all fell into place, with the exception for the time being of the elevators, and on 15 May *Le Figaro* produced its next special edition from its cramped offices on the second platform. That morning, Gustave Eiffel made an entry in the newspaper's guest book: 'Ten minutes to twelve, 15 May 1889. The tower is opened to the public. At last!'[28]

Of course, the tower quickly became a magnet for the well-to-do and the uncrowned royalty of Europe and beyond, even if they were reduced for the time being to an ascent on foot. There were also scores of notables who appeared at the exhibition in their own right, celebrities such as Buffalo Bill (who hitched his horse to the tower as he toured the exhibition), Frédéric Auguste Bartholdi (who brought a message from Liberty), and Thomas Edison (whose phonograph was one of the spectacular inventions unveiled). Edison was an undoubted fan, and there is an account of a breakfast conversation on the terrace of the first platform when he reacted enthusiastically to the remark of a companion about the tower as the work of a simple bridge builder:

'No,' said Edison decisively. 'No. It is a great idea. The glory of Eiffel is in the magnitude of the conception and the nerve in the execution. That admitted, and the money found, the rest is, if you like, mere bridge-building.'[29]

Certainly, the Parisian press was in full flight in favour of the tower, and almost immediately began to try to articulate the 'new' emotions that the structure, and the views from its summit, evoked:

All these monuments emerge like islands. Without doubt, M. Eiffel has given Paris a mass of very new feelings for which it is necessary to acclimatise the heart, soul and spirit. At the foot of the tower, the Seine, like a shimmering silvery cord in motion is more brilliant and star-studded even than the sky which reflects back to the boats. In the middle of all that, gigantic and superb, with its three hundred metres dominating the immense black plain that forms the endless horizon, the tower rears up, its platforms suspended high in the air, with its principal bold, curved rafters, its strongly emphasised arches. The crowd, hardly perceptible to the eye, circulates below; increasingly more charmed and more moved by the multiple spectacle which is being offered to it.[30]

Ordinary mortals queued for hours to climb the structure. This after all was going to be the sensational star feature – the touchstone – of the entire exhibition. People flocked to climb, to promenade, eat, drink and buy souvenirs (the ubiquitous miniature Eiffel Towers were quickly available in apparently endless manifestations) and have their personal copy of *Le Figaro de la Tour Eiffel*. Even the high society snobs forgot their prejudices and wanted to say they had been on the tower – and been seen. They wanted to boast of having lunch in the sky, and to release balloons bearing messages into the Paris sky; above all else they wanted to see the spectacular views of the exhibition, of Paris and the surrounding countryside; on a clear day, visibility stretched as far as 50 miles. For the 1855 Exposition,

Napoleon III had commissioned an enormous panoramic painting of Paris depicted as from a balloon; now citizens could come themselves and, from the tower, select and absorb a whole series of real panoramic views. Although there was excitement at the ability to see over such vast distances, people were mostly intrigued by the familiar seen in an unfamiliar way – the Paris monuments and buildings, the streets and neighbourhoods of common, everyday acquaintance.

Two months after the opening, President Carnot visited the tower with his wife and their children. Gustave Eiffel summoned all the board members of his company to be present, and a large official party made the ascent and headed for Eiffel's apartment on the third platform, where a buffet was served by his daughters Claire and Laure.

This room, located at 200 metres and decorated with flowers, was much admired; a hundred people were accommodated easily and the President of the Republic did not suspect the size of this last platform. It was a very clear day and the panorama was imposing. The President of the Republic, filled with enthusiasm, wanted to continue with the climb, and with his two sons, and led by M. Eiffel and M. Salles, they entered the cylinder which dominates the third stage, visited the beacon-room and crossed the last platform to the flagpole. A half hour after, the descent started. At the second platform, the Head of State honoured the workshop of the little *Figaro de la Tour* with a visit. The presidential procession then went down again by the Otis elevator at the northern pier, which goes directly from the second stage on the ground; they went then to the pavilion of the Tower Company. At half past eleven, enchanted by their climb, M. and Mme Carnot returned to the Elysée, after having very cordially congratulated M. Eiffel on the success of his colossal work, which was contributing so much to the success of the Exposition.[31]

During the 176 days of the exhibition, just under 2 million visited. From Mondays to Saturdays, tickets cost two francs up to the first platform, three francs to the second, and five francs to the top; tickets were reduced to roughly half-price on Sundays from eleven in the morning until six in the evening (closing time was ten o'clock); whichever ticket was purchased allowed the use of elevators. A correspondent of a Cincinnati newspaper gave an account of the stairways:

> The stairs in the midst of such a colossal edifice look slender, but are quite strong and shrouded in oil cloth, to prevent those who venture on them from being affected by giddiness. Going down the stairs is rather more ticklish to the average head and foot than going up. It is trying to look off through the prodigious iron lattice work that rises into the skies and behold the great city at one's feet. There is a sensation as if one might possibly step out into the air and find even a sustaining cloud.[32]

It is worth noting that many of the visitors were well dressed for what might otherwise have been a promenade by a windy lakeside; climbing the giddy, forbidding spiral staircases, seemingly heading into the skies, were gentlemen with long, heavy motoring coats, top hats and walking canes, and ladies struggling with bonnets, parasols, furs and heavy, hooped skirts. Smart clothes shops produced the essential chic but practical clothing in which to make the ascent. New hotels were opened, and the Gare St-Lazare was completely rebuilt to accommodate the hundreds of thousands who were expected to cross Europe by train to pay homage to the new symbol of modern France.

Although the exhibition was enormously successful in attendance and financial terms, there were churlish voices to find fault, in this case – again – London's *Spectator* magazine:

> The Paris Exhibition, though still not complete, is sufficiently so for the critics who are daily publishing their impressions, sometimes, we fear, with a strong wish to conciliate individual exhibitors. Corrupt or honest, able or foolish, they all, however, concur in two judgements. One is

that the Exhibition is too big, that the variety of displays is too distracting, and that the visitors are bewildered by the difficulty of finding their way about. Even the crowds are too great, and with 370,000 visitors in one day, there may at some unlucky moment be a catastrophe. The second judgement is that the Exhibition contains nothing absolutely original, no new invention of moment, no entirely novel application of thought even to design. The best of everything is there, and of course educates those who observe closely; but there is nothing, not even a machine, which will forward the course of human progress. The huge show is, in fact, a museum for the things of the day, which may be useful, but is not stimulating. As a speculation, however, the affair will succeed, the crowds of persons with cheque-books drawn to Paris to enjoy themselves or to purchase being far beyond the highest expectation, and including not only peoples of Europe and America, but of Asia.[33]

Just as in the case of London's Great Exhibition of 1851, there were some petulant voices to be heard against the general mood of gaiety and celebration. The ill-natured Guy de Maupassant was one xenophobic 'refusenik':

Beginning in early morning the streets are already full, the pavements flowing with crowds like swollen streams. Everyone is heading for the Exposition or is coming back or returning again to it. In the streets, the carriages form an unbroken line like the coaches of an endless train. Not a single taxi is free, no driver will consent to drive you anywhere but to the Exposition. Besides, the only customers they want are the flashy foreigners. Impossible to find a table in a restaurant, and friends no longer dine at home or accept a dinner invitation at your home. When invited, they accept only on condition that it be for a banquet on the Eiffel Tower – they think it is gayer that way. As if obeying a general order, they invite you there every day of the week for either lunch or dinner.[34]

The Garabit Viaduct, Faverolles, 1885. *(Agence Roger-Viollet 10428-8)*

Maria Pia Bridge on the Douro, Portugal, 1877. *(Agence Roger-Viollet 1142–11)*

Nyugati station, Budapest, 1877. *(Agence Roger-Viollet 1102–12)*

A competition entry by Eiffel and Sauvestre for the 1889 Exhibition.
(Agence Roger-Viollet 5091–16)

Liberty under construction in Paris. *(US Library of Congress LC-USZ62-95350)*

Liberty on her plinth on Bedloe's Island. *(US Library of Congress LC-USZ62-2284)*

Poster for the 1949 film
L'homme de la Tour Eiffel.
(From Simenon Cinéma *by*
Serge Toubiana and Michel
Schepens, Editions Textuel,
Paris, courtesy Michel
Schepens)

Gustave Eiffel hoists the
tricolour on the tower, 31
March 1889. *(Agence Roger-*
Viollet 7516-8)

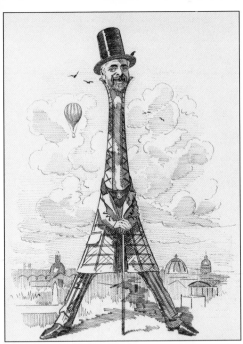

Eiffel depicted in the form of his tower, June 1889. *(US Library of Congress, LC-DIG-ppmsca-02294)*

Gustave Eiffel about the time of the construction of the tower. *(US Library of Congress, LC-USZ62-84681)*

Promenading on the first-stage platform of the Eiffel Tower in 1889.
(US Library of Congress, LC-USZ62-24984)

A view along the Seine from the first-stage platform, 1889.
(US Library of Congress, LC-USZ62-24983)

Photograph of the Eiffel Tower from a balloon, 1889, by Alphonse Liebert.
(US Library of Congress, LC-USZ62-94571)

The first transmission of 'TSF' (télégraphie sans fil) between Ernest Roger on the Eiffel Tower and Eugène Ducretet on the Pantheon, 29 July 1898. (Agence Roger-Viollet 2445-13)

The elevator and operator at the Eiffel Tower, during the 1889 Exhibition, photographed by Napoleon Dufeu. *(US Library of Congress LC-USZ62-11264)*

Gustave Eiffel, Drausin Salles, Mme A. Salles (Claire Eiffel), Adolphe Salles and M. Milon at the summit of the tower. *(US Library of Congress LC-USZ62-24985)*

Santos-Dumont's prize-winning flight around the Eiffel Tower, 19 October 1901. *(Smithsonian Institution, Washington, 85-3941)*

The Eiffel Tower looking towards the Trocadero, Paris Exhibition 1889. *(US Library of Congress, LC-USZC4-10733)*

Construction of the Rio Grande Dam, Panama, August 1888. *(From* Panama *by Philippe Bunau-Varilla; Trustees of the National Library of Scotland)*

Ferdinand de Lesseps. *(From* Panama *by Philippe Bunau-Varilla; Trustees of the National Library of Scotland)*

Eiffel's 'Appareil de Chute' for measuring air resistance at the tower. *(Glasgow University Library, Special Collections)*

Gustave Eiffel and colleagues at the base of the tower with measuring apparatus. *(Glasgow University Library, Special Collections)*

Gustave Eiffel and an assistant in the Auteuil Laboratory. *(Trustees of the National Library of Scotland)*

Eiffel's Auteuil Laboratory, opened in March 1912. *(Trustees of the National Library of Scotland)*

The wind tunnel at Auteuil. *(Trustees of the National Library of Scotland)*

Having been a sour observer of the Exposition as a whole, *The Spectator* also took aim at Gustave Eiffel and his tower:

It is not M. Eiffel who is to blame for his tower. Why were the government of France and the municipality of Paris willing to pay £160,000 in order that the Eiffel Tower should be put up? Nobody pretends that it is or will be of the slightest use. The tower has not even the grand claim of the Pyramids, that apparently endless durability which it is so difficult for the short-lived race of man to respect, and in some dim way to fear; for though M. Eiffel hopes for fifty years, no other observer, mindful of earthquake, of lightning, and of cyclones, will expect for it that longevity. Indeed, almost every observer who describes it suggests certain frightful consequences which might accompany its fall. Those who sanctioned and paid for the building can have been influenced only by the desire of putting up the tallest structure ever designed, and how is it that such a fancy pleases them? Their vanity is gratified? In what way?[35]

Transatlantic opinions, as expressed by the *Atlantic Monthly* were on the whole more lyrical:

Many beautiful designs are founded upon the tapering forms of flowers and leaves, as in the delicate tracery of frost-work. In building to secure safety from the action of the elements, M. Eiffel has perhaps unintentionally followed the methods of nature, and thus the architectural beauty of his work has the best possible confirmation.[36]

Another thoughtful Bostonian writer reviewed the century since the Revolution that the exhibition was celebrating. He considered that French society was still fractured, with an unsettled mix of republicans, monarchists, democrats and imperialists; and there was the impending prospect of a military adventurer, in the shape of the right-wing nationalist General Boulanger, threatening the Republic:

There is no enthusiasm for any existing institution or person. The reign of mediocrity has set in; and, as a friend observed to me, the only celebrity left for those great funeral honors France used to bestow is the aged Ferdinand de Lesseps.[37]

Considering, on the one hand, that the great men of France seemed to have disappeared, and that the state of French society after the Revolution, as depicted by Zola and others, deserved nothing other than a lament, the writer nevertheless concluded:

Is this all? Is this condemnatory verdict the last word we can utter? Then in that case we should say with the reactionists that the Revolution was a deplorable mistake, that we did not see with the philosophers that it was inevitable. But if the inevitable is also the wholly evil, then we must adopt the pessimist conclusions so general in Europe at the present time. In that case, instead of opening her magnificent Exposition and rearing her lofty Eiffel Tower, France should mourn in sackcloth and ashes, and the world should lament; for '89 was not of significance merely to France, but to all mankind. But to one who sits in the Exposition gardens in the soft warm air of the summer evening, and looks on at the thousand electric lights, the colored fountains, the great tower with its lights looming up in the deep blue sky, the gay throngs of men and women of all nations, there comes another idea of what the Revolution accomplished.[38]

Quite; after all, the city and the country had survived a century of war, revolution, civil war, *coup d'état* and siege. The exhibition was clearly setting France in a new direction, and one German observer was altogether very impressed by French determination:

. . . we are only too inclined, considering the division of the parties, to regard French industrial spirit as declining; a fatal error, as this Exposition strikingly shows us. I am strongly disinclined to want to make less of German successes in the commercial field, but that cannot diminish anything of the efforts made and the successes obtained by the French; the giant constructions on the Champ de Mars and l'Esplanade des Invalides, with their broad and rich glazed galleries, are living testimony; they are the proof that the diligent French spirit does not remain idle one moment and that it is firmly determined to preserve or to re-establish its dominance in the world market.[39]

But the tower was the thing. It was always going to be the main focus of interest, as a New York writer admitted:

So much had been said against it that a visitor to the Exposition might have been excusably surprised not to find the Eiffel Tower vulgar. But the unprejudiced visitor must have been still more surprised to find it a positively agreeable object. *A priori* objections to it were certainly reasonable enough. Everyone must have sympathised with the protest of the Paris artists made before the Tower was begun. The chances were entirely against the aesthetic success of something that was supposed to aim exclusively at height; though, after all, nowadays, since we have discovered that motive is of no importance in art, what does it matter if the motive of a work of art be height? Do we not all know – certainly, if we do not we are not 'modern' – that technique is what counts? If technique be generally competent and specifically admirable, the result must be successful. And technically the Tour Eiffel was superb. It may have been intended merely to be astonishing, but in reality it was in the highest degree impressive.[40]

Many commentators wrote of the impression that the tower made on them by night. Not only did it work a special magic in darkness, with intriguing floodlights at play, but descriptive abilities seemed enhanced:

. . . to a mind incapable of grasping the simplest principles of mechanics, the sight of the Eiffel Tower and the adjacent buildings was a pleasanter manifestation of human prowess. I found that they were most imposing by night. Then the vulgarity inseparable from an indiscriminate crowd, the trivial details, the clap-trap, the pasteboard aspect of huge temporary structures, were lost in a vaster and more comprehensive impression, at once more real and more fantastic.[41]

Human prowess was an appropriate phrase for the men who laboured in the sky to build the physical structure, and also for the one man who imagined it and who turned the imagery effortlessly into such unique reality. The tower was a triumph for Gustave Eiffel, achieved against all the natural apprehension and rather more spiteful objections that had plagued his intentions from the beginning. Contrary to all expectations, the project would be a spectacular financial success, and Eiffel himself would be wealthy for the rest of his life. He had astonished the engineering and artistic worlds with his superb, delicate parabolic arcs of Maria Pia and Garabit; now he had given them an incredibly light, lacework, spiked tower as the world's tallest structure.

The idea of 'building the highest' had been given an extraordinary boost, and already people were discussing even higher towers, and hoping to engage Eiffel in their contemplation. However, while he had developing interests in some quite different projects, such as a metro system for Paris, his immediate concern was to give full attention to proving the scientific value of his tower. But, it was to be a series of events on the other side of the world, and their bureaucratic consequences in Paris, that would determine his future path.

NINE

The Panama Plunder

The Paris Exposition Universelle of 1889 was planned to finish at the end of October, with the formal closing ceremony on Sunday 29 September, but popular demand kept everything open for an extra week before the demolishers moved in to dismantle and dispose of all the temporary grandeur. The fair had remained open until late each evening, thanks largely to the widespread use of electricity. Not only was electric lighting clean and efficient, but it enabled lighting to be more than just functional; thousands of multicoloured lamps and spotlights were an attraction in themselves, and gave the exhibition a distinctively different character at night. The exhibition had also stunned everyone by being a financial success; attendance had totalled 32½ million, and there was a profit of eight million francs.[1] The Eiffel Tower itself had attracted an average of just under 12,000 visitors per day over the seven-month period. Its income totalled 6½ million francs – one million short of the cost of construction; the difference was quickly made up after the exhibition closed. Contrary to the initial assumptions of administrators and others, Eiffel was in a position to recoup all his costs and repay bondholders within a year of the tower's opening; it has been in constant profit ever since.

The civil engineer Max Nansouty speculated on the possibility of building a tower higher than the Eiffel Tower. He also indulged in a prescient suggestion:

> If ever M. Eiffel was to build us a tower of 500 or 600 metres – not very likely, he informs us – here is probably how he would set about it. He would first of all build, on the ground,

four 250 metre towers, in the form of pillars; he would then connect their upper parts, in space, in order to constitute a rigid platform, a new ground, so to speak, and he would set out again from this platform to build a new monument of 250 or 300 metres height; at that stage the structure would be complete.

There is also the question of building, in France, on elevated points at various distances from Paris, a series of cheaply built iron pylons or Eiffel Towers approximately 100 metres high, which would be kept in communication with signals from the Eiffel Tower in Paris. This telegraphy would be absolutely ethereal, and after so many centuries it would be curious to see us return by the means of modern Science to a process of Gallic intercom-munication, like that of our fathers, i.e. by fires lit on the hilltops.[2]

The relationship between the tower and pure science, heavily promoted by Eiffel and hinted at by Nansouty, quickly began to be exploited. In August 1890, the Academician Louis Paul Cailletet (who had begun his research while working as a metallurgist in his father's ironworks) began working on a long series of experiments into the liquefaction of gases:

Advantage is being taken of the Eiffel Tower to obtain high pressure through a manometric tube (the height of the tower) containing mercury. M. Cailletet proposes to utilise the enormous pressure – about 400 atmospheres – for his researches on the liquefaction of gases, and interesting results may be looked for.[3]

The *Exposition Tricolorée* as a whole had been a cultural and political success. The fact that a general election the week before the closure had seen off the threat of a coup from the right-wing Boulangists seemed to convince the country that it really could sustain a viable republic. Somehow, the timing ensured that some of the political gloss rubbed off on the exhibition, and helped to sustain France's position in the world:

The most irresponsible loafer could not fail to pay a tribute of admiration to France for the magnificent scope of plan and completeness of execution which give this a place above former world's fairs. The achievement was not cosmopolitan, but French – a worldwide manifestation of French genius, to which the nations of the earth have lent helping hands. It is the outcome of her best qualities – method, organisation, executive ability, a liberal conception, exactness of detail, finish, industry, the desire for knowledge and for its diffusion, the love of art, and above all, taste.[4]

Paris began its reign at the centre of what the romantics called *la Belle Epoque* – the 'good old days' of artistic endeavour, physical and intellectual pleasure, elegant living, and the sense of man as master of his own fate. Certainly there was good living, and plenty of what might be called brash, playboy hedonism, but there was still no escape from social and political unrest and endless public controversies – the infamous Dreyfus Affair alone would be hugely momentous. The realists denied the sentimentality of the Belle Epoque, and referred instead to the *fin de siècle* – the end of the century that would be accompanied by social and moral degradation as the bleakness of industrial society replaced cultured civilisation.

The most spectacular and long-running public event in France was in fact to be a 1,448 million franc financial and political scandal that would involve hundreds of thousands of shareholders, dozens of financial institutions, scores of members of the National Assembly and many notable journalists and publishers; Gustave Eiffel was to find himself hauled ignominiously into court, with momentous personal consequences. In the mayhem, the future prime minister Georges Clemenceau would fight a duel over an accusation of treason in the Chamber of the National Assembly, and the government all but fell.

As preparatory work on the Garabit Viaduct was under way, events were taking place in Paris and New York that would in time have a critical effect on Gustave Eiffel. On 7 December 1880, public subscription opened for shares in the Compagnie

Universelle du Canal Interocéanique. Several hundred thousand individual shareholders, most of them French, besieged the company in a three-day stampede to obtain shares in what has been described as the most widely owned business in corporate history, and one which had the prospect of the greatest financial rewards.[5] The company's audacious proposal was to construct a 45-mile ship canal across the narrow isthmus of Panama, closely following the line of construction in 1855 of a railway line owned by the United States. This was a superficially intriguing landscape, whose penetration had been the object of intense speculation since the continent had been discovered by sixteenth-century Spanish and Portuguese adventurers. Orders had been given for the production of what we would today call feasibility studies for a much longer canal in Nicaragua, and the great Spanish conquistador Hernando Cortés produced the first plan for linking the two oceans.

In Panama, however, the prospect was even more intriguing. From a height on a clear day, a man could see both the Atlantic and Pacific Oceans. Geologically complex, the land was wet, mountainous and disease-ridden – a treacherous swamp-land that had already killed explorers, sailors and soldiers. Crucially, the route was subject to sudden landslides and torrential flooding. Although as many as 6,000 men may have died, largely from yellow fever, during the five-year construction of the railway in the 1850s, the lessons of geography, medicine and project management which might have been learned were ignored, and tens of thousands more would die during next twenty years. Nevertheless, a canal would halve the distance from Calais to California and be of huge interest to traders and travellers between the east and west coasts of North America. The commercial exploitation of this strip of unstable yellow-fever- and malaria-infested jungle was a dazzling prospect, and would bring into being one of the world's most strategic waterways.

Certainly no one appeared to have learned from the disaster that had befallen the 2,000 Scots adventurers, most of whom had died from disease in Panama between 1698 and 1701. The Company of Scotland Trading to Africa and the Indies established its initial base at Darien on the isthmus of Panama, anticipating the Panama Canal by 200 years. The dream had been to create New Caledonia as a fabulously wealthy international trading colony by linking the two great oceans by commerce, and making epic and dangerous sea voyages redundant. But the community was annihilated by political antagonism, internal squabbling, hunger, constant disease and attacks by native Indians. Half Scotland's wealth was lost, and the political result was the controversial Treaty of Union of 1707 between England and Scotland. Those who would construct a canal in such an unforgiving landscape faced a supreme physical challenge, and severe financial consequences.

The pioneering spirit who fatefully picked up the challenge was 78-year-old Ferdinand-Marie, vicomte de Lesseps, the charming and generous, but despotic and stubborn, French diplomat. It was he who had supervised the construction of the Suez Canal between 1859 and 1869 against opposition from the Turks, the British and his sceptical countrymen, and had proclaimed and wallowed in the triumph ever since. Lesseps the diplomat had served in Rome, Madrid, Barcelona, Lisbon, Tunis, Alexandria, Cairo and Rotterdam, but was reprimanded for exceeding his brief and left the diplomatic service in 1850. Although an old man, his energy and self-regard were boundless; in his late sixties he had married a teenage Creole girl who bore him nine children. Following numerous earlier failed attempts to canalise the isthmus, a meeting of the Congrès International d'Etudes du Canal Interocéanique met in Paris in 1879 to consider several proposals for an east-west link, including fourteen for a Panama route alone. Lesseps complained in an article published in New York that although the US government had in recent years spent 5 million dollars on exploratory surveys, they had kept the results secret.[6] It was certainly clear that the American government (which had greater interest in a Nicaraguan route) was keeping a distance from the French proposal, although at a later stage, for reasons of his own, Lesseps insisted that they were being very cooperative. For years, the USA, France, Holland and Britain had haggled over the isthmus, and locked diplomatic horns with each other and the governments of Colombia and Nicaragua, which controlled the area. The Paris Congress finally narrowed down their considerations to two options, an American-sponsored 77-mile route in Nicaragua, and the French Panama route at sea-level without locks.[7] Lesseps energetically used his international celebrity rather than any engineering knowledge to manipulate opinion in favour of the short Panama sea-level route, without locks but with some tunnelled sections, from the town of Colón on the Bay of Limon to the anchorage of Flamenco in the Bay of Panama. He seemed naively unappreciative of the fact that the terrain and weather conditions in Panama were completely different from what he had experienced at Suez, and that in attempting the project, human survival itself would be at great risk. On his return from inspecting the route, he boldly declared:

As for the salubrity of the climate of Panama, whither I accompanied the committee with my family, the perfect health whereof we presented living proof on our return to Europe shows how unjustly that beautiful climate has been condemned by those who know nothing of it – *omne ignotum horrendum*.[8]

Lesseps ignored the advice of expert engineers and surveyors who said that the canal would take twelve years to build at a cost of 1,200 million francs; he insisted that the canal could be built for progressively smaller sums, finally settling at 500 million francs, and that it would take no more than six years, with 8,000 labourers removing 1¾ million cubic feet of rock per day.[9] A principal opponent of the decision was Gustave Eiffel who, aware that the route had severe 400ft geophysical blockages and the difficulty of the torrential Chagres river, advocated the absolute necessity of a canal with locks and artificial lakes.[10] Eiffel was supported by seven other distinguished engineers, notably Adolphe Godin de Lépinay, chief engineer of the Ponts et Chaussées (the French Department of Bridges and Highways), who was both highly respected and experienced in engineering construction in tropical conditions. Lépinay, supported by Eiffel, introduced preliminary plans for an alternative canal with locks, which had the twin advantages of requiring much less excavation and avoiding the worst excesses of flooding. Despite walk-outs by members of the Technical Committee of the Congress at the voting stage, Lesseps' project was finally agreed by the full Congress, who voted 74 in favour to 8 (including Eiffel and Lépinay) against:

> The congress believes that the excavation of an interoceanic canal at sea-level, so desirable in the interests of commerce and navigation, is feasible; and that, in order to take advantage of the indispensable facilities for access and operation which a channel of this kind must offer above all, this canal should extend from the Gulf of Limon to the Bay of Panama.[11]

The ill-fated project was set in motion by Louis Napoleon Bonaparte Wyse, a cousin of Napoleon III, who had obtained a twelve-year option from the Colombian government. Lesseps was installed as president and his son Charles as vice-president. The frantic three-day scramble for shares in the company was in fact brought to an abrupt end when it was realised that despite the frenzied activity not nearly enough cash was to be forthcoming. This did not intimidate the megalomaniac vicomte de Lesseps; no more did the vitriolic denunciation of his character, his plans and his mind-set by the head of the US Bureau of Navigation, replying to Lesseps' article in *The North American Review*.[12] Lesseps boldly declared his insistence on getting his own way – an approach that hardly seemed likely to be an encouragement to potential investors:

> The parties who held the concession for the canal came to me, and said, 'We have the concession, but we can do nothing without you.' I replied to them, 'Gentlemen, I am very sorry, for I cannot take upon myself to organise such an enterprise in connection with other persons who might pledge credit on its behalf. I do not doubt that you are thoroughly honourable men; but, when I engage in such an undertaking as this, I can

not share the responsibility of it with anybody. I have my own ideas, which are not those of all the world; I must therefore retain my full liberty of action.'[13]

It would not be long before the first in a series of disasters struck: the financial burden soared to beyond 1,200 million francs and Gustave Eiffel, largely in spite of himself, became tragically ensnared in the débâcle.

Geographical conditions and disease had together ensured that by 1884 the main contracting company, Couvreux & Hersent (which had successfully undertaken the Suez Canal), opted out of their contract and the first director of works, Gaston Blanchet, died of yellow fever. His successor, Jules Dingler, the chief engineer of the Ponts et Chaussées, moved his family into a newly built house near the works site; within a month his wife, son, daughter and daughter's fiancé were all dead. *The Times* reported that:

. . . the Europeans who have lately arrived in connection with the canal scheme are apprehensive of the danger from the disease, and several of them are leaving the place.[14]

Apprehension was hardly enough; between April 1884 and March the following year, there were on average 96 deaths every month, with an October high of 163.[15] The company's business condition was no healthier, as a highly sceptical (and openly anti-Lesseps) report in *Scientific American* indicated:

. . . putting off the time of completion at least as far as 1892, the London *Financial News* puts the probable cost of the canal, including discounts, at £530,000,000. Whether M. de Lesseps has any charm by which he can manage to raise all this money among French investors, or whether anyone thinks the French government might eventually seek a controlling interest and complete the work, because the money now represents so many small subscriptions of Frenchmen, are questions we do not seek to pursue.[16]

The construction was now carried out by over twenty separate companies, rather than one, and both duplication of effort and inability to collaborate became major obstacles. As fast as the rocky Culebra range was excavated, the tropical rain and the torrential Chagres river washed away the workings and much of the equipment. Lesseps had disastrously underestimated the difficulty, danger and cost of the entire project. Because the American-owned Panama Railroad effectively had a monopoly of transport, the Canal Company was forced to buy it at a grossly inflated price at least three times its stock market value; in order to accommodate such a purchase, yet more bonds were floated. The project was being catastrophically mismanaged, and the route had become a constant cycle of deluge, collapse and re-excavation; even the ever-confident Ferdinand de Lesseps had become desperate. In six years, the Canal Company had already made four separate borrowing demands for a total of 615 million francs, and much more was to go the same way. Vast amounts of money were spent on 'public relations' and other dubious or unnecessary work, and Paris was soon awash with rumours of skulduggery. Numerous orders were placed around the world for equipment that proved to be wholly unsuitable, and a series of inter-contractor deals were struck, which effectively led to revolt on the site and the involvement of American troops.

During 1886–7 Lesseps tried to obtain support for a government-sponsored bond lottery to provide a further 600 million francs (at a time when he was letting contracts for 800 million francs). The lottery proposal was initially resisted, but eventually authorised by the French government subject to the design of the canal being changed to one using locks, as Gustave Eiffel had originally advised. Léon Boyer, with whom Eiffel had worked on the Garabit Viaduct when Boyer was state engineer, had already intervened. During a tragically brief tenure as director-general before succumbing to yellow fever, he proposed to Lesseps a system of huge boat lifts, similar to that at Anderton, near Northwich in Cheshire, which linked the Weaver Navigation with the Trent and Mersey Canal. On his deathbed, Boyer's last words were, 'Do not abandon Panama.'[17] Locks were now the order of the day; what had started as a sea-level waterway was now to become a 60ft-wide canal with locks, at an estimated three times the original cost; Lesseps was now recklessly promising that such a canal could be completed within three years.

In November 1887, he sent Baron Reinach, one of the company's most active financiers, to make preliminary contact with Gustave Eiffel, asking him to take over supervision of the project. Perhaps the stubborn and egotistical Lesseps had come to the conclusion that Eiffel was the only man to help save the project, despite their early and complete disagreement as to the route and the method. There is also little doubting that a cynical hope existed that the prestige conferred by the addition of Eiffel's name at this late stage would help generate desperately needed cash. Although Eiffel later said that he had felt out in the cold as far as the canal project was concerned, since the time of the decision of the International Congress eight years earlier, he had been quietly working with two other engineers, Pouchet and Sautereau. They perfected a characteristically innovative design for a system of massive locks capable of handling the huge difference in water-level of 70ft; Eiffel's professional curiosity had placed him in a unique position to deliver exactly what Lesseps now urgently needed.

Eiffel kept the demanding but fraught entrepreneur waiting for six weeks before he agreed terms 'in the national interest'.[18] On 10 December 1887, he signed a contract to construct ten huge hydraulically operated iron locks, each with a floor length of 584ft, width of 68ft and depth of 68ft, capable of handling the largest transatlantic liners then in use. The total height a vessel would be raised or lowered over the length of the canal would be 330ft. In order to avoid the earlier problems of delays and squabbles involving several different contractors, the agreement required not only construction of the locks and machinery, but all associated excavation of the sites, amounting to an estimated 13,417,720 cubic feet.[19] In an extraordinary coincidence of audacity and seemingly unlimited, and even unquantifiable, responsibilities, Eiffel signed this daunting contract in the critical week when the four great piers of his tower, still held by wooden frames and hydraulic rams, were about to meet at the level of the first platform.

Eiffel pushed ahead rapidly with his commitment to the project; the following month, he had 2,500 workmen on-site (by the following August it would be 6,000), and the excavation work went well. The great canal, the hope of centuries past, seemed at last destined to be proclaimed as a magnificent French success. This time, the heroic Gustave Eiffel was also involved, contracted to complete work worth 125 million francs.[20] For Eiffel this was, at fifteen times the cost of his tower, his biggest and riskiest contract. Since he had already completed most of the theoretical development of his proposed system of locks, the practical work of constructing the components, to be done in Brittany, was soon under way; he had decided to work on all ten locks simultaneously, to save time. He was very confident of his patented system, describing it as '. . . so simple that a child could set it in motion', and exhibited drawings in his company pavilion near the base of the tower during the exhibition.[21] However, Ferdinand de Lesseps had deluded himself and everyone else. He and his financial advisers had from the beginning almost certainly deliberately underestimated the vast costs involved, in an attempt to bolster the company and to attract additional funds. About one and a half billion francs essentially disappeared, and a year after Eiffel signed his Panama contract the end was in sight. A sixth and final bonds issue in June 1888 was destined to become a major feature in the final destruction of the entire project. The government had authorised the issue of bonds worth 720 million francs (probably sufficient to complete the canal) but the procedure was mismanaged, and the company failed to respond adequately to its detractors, who, at a critical financial moment, spread the false news throughout France that Ferdinand de Lesseps had died, causing the share price to plummet disastrously.[22]

Nevertheless, enthusiasm for the canal project in France, far from collapsing in humiliation, seems to have blossomed during its disastrous series of physical and financial reverses. A year after Eiffel signed his contract, and at a time when desperate attempts were being made to refinance the project under a new company, Lesseps addressed a meeting of thousands of shareholders on 11 December in the Panama Company offices in the Rue Caumartin in Paris; there were so many present that they stood on tables, and like the desperate gamblers they were, they were absolutely intent on continuing their financial support of the ageing vicomte, as reported in the journal *Engineering*:

> He was the hero of the hour, and his announcement that the existing company must be extinguished, and that present shareholders must be prepared to sacrifice all the money they had ventured, in order that the great national undertaking may be finished, was as enthusiastically applauded as if he had declared a 10 per cent dividend.[23]

Potential financiers were demanding an expert commission empowered to examine the entire project and to produce a report before they would make any financial commitment. Lesseps was as bullish as ever:

> As to the works, I will go myself and examine them; I will accompany this commission, not only to give its members all the information they may desire, but also, in your name, to shake hands with those noble workers, those heroes, who, over there, without allowing themselves to be discouraged, have defended, have saved your work, the work of France.[24]

The weeping vicomte assured them that the last bond issue had been a success:

> My friends, the subscription is safe! Our adversaries are confounded! We have no need for the help of financiers! You have saved yourselves by your own exertion! The canal is made![25]

There was general mutual celebration and insistence of support, and anyone who was in the slightest doubt was harshly treated by the euphoric crowd. The one member of his audience with the temerity to raise questions was promptly turned upon by his fellows, and objectors outside the meeting handing round copies of a tract entitled *Le Cataclysme Fatal du Panama* were chased for their lives. One reporter noted the sympathetic remarks of an elderly shareholder as conforming to the national sentiment: *'Il est vrai que notre argent est compromis, mais ce n'est pas sa faute, et le pauvre homme s'est donné tant de mal.'* (It is true that our money is at risk, but it isn't his fault, and the poor man has been to so much trouble.)[26] However, the following day, Lesseps' son Charles announced that the bond issue had not been successful, and that bankruptcy was looming. On 14 December, the company suspended payments and sought government authority for a three-month moratorium on meeting its commitments. The French National Assembly refused to allow a temporary reprieve for the company, and the directors resigned. Unbelievably, bondholders clamoured for Ferdinand de Lesseps, promising their hero that they would not press for repayments until the canal was completed, and insisting that a new company be established to complete the construction. However, some of the original subscribers rebelled and applied successfully to the Civil Tribunal, and on 4 February 1889 the Canal Company was formally dissolved and a liquidator appointed. Troops were posted along the route of the canal itself, and British, French and American warships took up station at sea in case of trouble. Some 800,000 individual French investors, many of them single women, pensioners and small traders, had bought shares and bonds in the canal, representing most of the 1½ billion francs borrowed.

These events unfolded as Eiffel's tower was in the final stages of preparation for opening. Eiffel himself was appalled to have fallen into this unaccustomed position, and shocked at the possibility of the government allowing the supposedly prestigious project to fail after such a long history of struggle. Anxious, in the meantime, to find a solution (and perhaps to justify advances that he had received), he insisted that all work under his control should proceed. Within a few months, the experienced and much respected receiver Joseph-Mathieu Brunet persuaded Eiffel to cease all works in Panama, and told him that there was no possibility of his being recompensed. He had completed a considerable proportion of the contracted work. At the end of August the previous year, he had already completed 16 million cubic feet of excavation out of a total of 44 million; two-thirds of the ironwork had been ordered out of a total of 37,000 tons (and 6,000 tons were already on site).[27] On 11 July 1889, Eiffel and Brunet signed an agreement by which they accepted various financial allocations between Eiffel as contractor and the Canal Company. Eiffel recovered 15 million francs due to him for works completed, and for injury suffered as a result of the cancellation. He returned equipment and materials to the Canal Company and paid back 3 million francs in respect of work which he had done after the bankruptcy was made official (and which he had been warned he could not expect to be paid for). This document was ratified by the Paris Civil Tribunal, and both parties relinquished all future claims on each other.[28] The stoppage was a huge disappointment to Eiffel; however, he must have thought that this legal procedure would at least represent the end of the matter. He was to be disastrously wrong. France was not prepared to allow the Panama scandal to slip away so quietly. Apart from anything else, there were bigger fish to fry than Gustave Eiffel.

In the spring of 1890, however, the *maître du fer* was in demand elsewhere. The Forth Bridge was nearing completion in Scotland, and Eiffel received an invitation to join the party of dignitaries to attend the official opening ceremony. The contract with Benjamin Baker and John Fowler, and contractors Tancred, Arrol & Co., had been signed in late December 1882 for a steel bridge built on three double cantilevers, rising 361ft above high water, each consisting of a central 12ft-diameter steel tower supported on four circular masonry piers. Each of the three cantilevers was to be lattice-braced, connected to each other by lattice girder spans, and the bridge – the longest in the world – would be 8,295ft 6in in length. This was the biggest, most complex construction project ever to have been undertaken. As one professional journal was to remark on the opening: 'In the Forth Bridge, Sir John Fowler and Benjamin Baker have created a monument of human contrivance the magnitude of which is unprecedented.'[29]

Nevertheless, the bridge had been attracting the kind of opprobrium in artistic circles that Eiffel would have recognised. While only forty years earlier, Joseph Paxton's Crystal Palace attracted wild public approval, William Morris wrote that 'every improvement in machinery [was] uglier and uglier until they reached the supremest specimen of all ugliness, the Forth Bridge.'[30] The bridge's co-designers, Benjamin Baker and John Fowler, responded initially with calm, if not especially well-illustrated, reason:

> Probably Mr Morris would judge the beauty of a design from the same standpoint, whether it was for a bridge a mile long or for a silver chimney ornament. It is impossible for anyone to pronounce authoritatively on the beauty of an object without knowing its functions. The marble columns of the Parthenon are beautiful where they stand, but if we took one and bored a hole through its axis and used it as a funnel for an Atlantic liner it would, to my mind, cease to be beautiful, but of course Mr Morris might think differently.[31]

In Britain, the argument between Baker and Morris was the equivalent of the dispute that would break out in France between Eiffel and the architect Charles Garnier. Both men were right, but both were blinded by self-righteousness. Morris insisted that what Baker and the engineers were doing was alienating man from his natural environment simply by considering the possibility of such structures. However, Baker and Fowler, for the first time in Britain, were following Eiffel and other European engineers by applying their theoretical understanding of structural behaviour to the determination of the form of the structure itself. Among the architectural establishment they had powerful and surprising supporters. Alfred Waterhouse, the leader of the Gothic revival movement and designer of Manchester Town Hall and London's Natural History Museum, wrote enthusiastically to John Fowler:

> One feature especially delights me – the absence of all ornament. Any architectural detail borrowed from any style

would have been out of place in such work. As it is, the bridge is a style unto itself; the simple directness of purpose with which it does its work is splendid and invests your vast monument with a kind of beauty of its own, differing though it does from all the beautiful things I have ever seen.[32]

Robert Roland Anderson, the founder of Scottish professional architectural education, and another exponent of the Gothic revival, was also an enthusiast for the new utilitarian concepts:

Who has looked down into the engine room of one of the great ocean steamers and not felt the impression of an irresistible power that rests not day or night? The designing of machinery, whether for peace or war, has now reached such a high standard of excellence in function, form and expression that one is justified in saying that these things are entitled to rank as works of art as much as a painting, a piece of sculpture, or a building.[33]

For over a year, the bridge had been attracting visiting parties of engineers and designers from all over the world, as the three huge cantilevers were assembled across the Firth of Forth. It was Baker who brilliantly and memorably illustrated the cantilever principle for a lecture to the Royal Institution in London, using two men sitting on chairs suspending a third man (the Japanese engineer Kaichi Watanabe) between them without the use of any supports; this surely counts as the clearest example of the power of a simple illustration in explaining a complex idea:

Two men sitting on chairs extend their arms, and support the same by grasping sticks which are butted against the chairs. There are thus two complete piers. The central girder is represented by a stick suspended or slung from the two inner hands of the men, while the anchorage provided by the counterpoise in the cantilever end piers is represented here by a pile of bricks at each end. When a load is put on the central girder by a person sitting on it, the men's arms and the anchorage ropes come into tension, and the men's bodies from the shoulders downwards and the stick come into compression. Imagine the chairs one third of a mile apart and the men's heads as high as the cross of St Paul's, their arms represented by huge lattice steel girders and the sticks by tubes 12ft in diameter at the base, and a very good notion of the structure is obtained.[34]

The Prince of Wales, who was to fix the ceremonial golden last rivet, accompanied by other members of the royal family, left London in early March on the *Flying Scotsman*, ensconced in a new saloon carriage specially built for the occasion by the Great Northern Railway Company. Events were described in *The Scotsman*:

In a separate saloon carriage were Monsieur Eiffel, the famous engineer, and about thirty other French gentlemen who have been invited to be present at the inauguration of the Forth Bridge. M. Eiffel was invited by the directors of the North Eastern Railway to a special dinner last night at the Royal Hotel. Sir Joseph W. Pease, Bart., occupied the chair. A couple of pipers marched round the dinner table playing the bagpipes and thereafter proceeded into an adjoining room where the other Frenchmen at the hotel were gathered, and in like manner entertained them.[35]

The ceremony itself the following day took place in the teeth of a howling gale, and many of those present were fearful of venturing out high onto the bridge. The Prince, shouting against the wind, said of the bridge that it 'harks to the triumph of science and engineering skill over obstacles of no ordinary kind'. There were popular comparisons made between the bridge and the Eiffel Tower – 5,280ft in length, built with 53,000 tons of steel, as against 1,000ft high and iron weighing 7,500 tons. When it came to driving the last rivet, the ferocious gale defeated the Prince, and William Arrol, the principal contractor, had to get down on his hands and knees to lend a hand.

The royal party, including Gustave Eiffel, made a hasty retreat to South Queensferry, where the drawing office and model room had been converted, with the addition of a massive oak chimneypiece, deer-heads, antlers, armour and Turkish carpets, into a baronial banqueting room capable of receiving the 500 guests. Eiffel was something of a centre of attraction during the day, and when asked for his autograph, penned the following inscription:

Monsieur G. Eiffel est très heureux d'avoir assisté à cette belle fête de l'inauguration du Pont du Forth, et très reconnaissant envers les ingénieurs anglais de leur aimable accueil. G. Eiffel 4 mars 1890.

During the lunch, Sir John Fowler (who later took a rather sour side-swipe at the unfortunate Thomas Bouch's reliance on the advice of Sir George Airey by pointing out, 'I do not believe in astronomy being a safe guide for practical engineering'[36]) replied to the Prince of Wales, and spoke of those who 'bad-mouthed' such great engineering projects:

When I was carrying out the Metropolitan Underground Railway I was told it could never be made; that if it was made it never could be worked; and that if it was worked no-one would travel by it (laughter). M. de Lesseps, of the Suez Canal, was warned that if the canal was made it would be quickly filled with desert sand, and the harbour of Port Said would be filled with Nile mud (laughter). And now we have a new and great engineering innovator, M. Eiffel (applause) whom we are all proud to have present with us on this occasion. He is a highly scientific and distinguished engineer, and has designed and carried out a very remarkable and original work, but he has not escaped the attacks of these good-natured people (laughter and applause).[37]

Fifty years after the coming of the railways, there was still a lingering latent fear of the dangers associated with machinery, speed and anything that smacked of big, new technology – the railways in particular were still regarded with suspicion by some people. In the middle of the night, just hours before the Forth Bridge was to be opened, an incident occurred that was to test corporate nerves. The ten-past-eight night express from London Euston to Glasgow was running half an hour late, and as it approached Carlisle Citadel station at three-thirty in the morning the driver discovered that the vacuum brakes had failed. The train roared through the station and crashed into the locomotive that was to have hauled the train to Glasgow. Two carriages were completely telescoped, four passengers were killed and many injured. Some newspaper reports went into particularly gory detail. The incident cast a further cloud over the stormy opening of the bridge later in the day, and it has been claimed that the tradition of throwing pennies from the carriage window for good luck as the train crosses the Forth Bridge originates with the unfortunate event at Carlisle.

In France, new popular outrage against Lesseps and the Panama affair was being agitated by the right-wing press, and in particular by Edouard Drumont, a blatant and highly dedicated racist who started an antisemitic newspaper and wrote virulent propagandist books and pamphlets. In one book, *La Dernière Bataille*, he denounced the (largely Jewish) promoters of the canal, and Ferdinand de Lesseps in particular, whom he described as:

> . . . this man who has lied so shamelessly, who has abused the public with false promises, who has squandered this money in the most disgraceful way, who used it in part to pay the newspapers told off to sing his praises.[38]

Two of the biggest advisers to the Canal Company were indeed Jews, a fact that sharpened the claws of the many antisemites. Baron Jacques de Reinach was an early director who went on to be a leading figure in the various attempts at refinancing. His associate was Cornelius Herz, a sometime quack doctor, electrical engineer, conman and alleged spy who had a Europe-wide reputation as a sharp operator. Both men were to be central in the many layers of bribery allegations. At the time, accusations against Lesseps may or may not have had more than a grain of truth about them, but the fascinating feature of the affair was that its increasingly long tentacles enveloped all areas of French society and became highly political in nature. In June 1890, it was decided that the Minister of Justice should examine the Panama affair. A full year passed without much activity, but in June 1891 an examining magistrate was appointed to investigate the directors of the Panama Company. On 7 September, the homes of Gustave Eiffel (who was not a director) and others were raided and documents seized. No incriminating evidence of criminal fraud was discovered and the magistrate advised against the instigation of proceedings. However, Drumont and others kept the issue alive, and for months every disparate political party and clique climbed on the bandwagon, and with mounting accounts of harrowing financial loss by many ordinary shareholders, the Panama scandal became one of the most talked-about issues in French public affairs.

Responding to political pressure from Attorney-General Quesnay de Beaurepaire, and regardless of the earlier advice from the examining magistrate, Prime Minister Emile Loubet instructed Minister of Justice Louis Ricard to start prosecutions. The engineer Philippe Bunau-Varilla wrote a book on the entire affair, and was scathing of the demands for prosecutions.[39]

He wrote of the Attorney-General's demand for prosecutions:

The author of such a letter deserves the most severe reproof from impartial minds. He had under his eyes an account of the facts that had been already deformed by the frantic pressure of baseless accusations. He deformed them still more under the pressure of his own desire of justifying a prosecution, when no breach of law, either civil or moral, could be shown. He reveals his whole frame of mind in the following sentence:

'The possible results, we mean by that, the dangers of a prosecution, are the following: An acquittal is possible. But what of that? The prosecuting magistrates will have done their duty, and if they do not succeed in convincing the courts they will have at least enlightened public opinion.' He thus implicitly states that there is no trace of the guilty actions which have been denounced, and which alone could justify a criminal prosecution. There is no trace of payments to the contractors outside of what was due on account of excavations made and of the stipulations contained in and provisions of the contracts. There is no trace of any fraudulent understanding between contractors and members of the Board. There is no trace of misappropriation of funds by the members of the Board or any other person belonging to the company's staff.[40]

On 21 November 1892, Ferdinand and Charles de Lesseps, Gustave Eiffel and two company directors, Henri Cottu and Marius Fontane, were indicted on charges of swindling and breach of trust. The first charge attracted a possible jail sentence on conviction of one to five years, and the second two months to two years. The offences fell under common law rather than public company law. The charges were:

. . . the use of fraudulent devices for creating belief in the existence of a chimerical event and of an imaginary credit, the squandering of sums accruing from issues handed to them for a fixed purpose and the swindling of others out of all or part of their fortunes.[41]

The same day, Jules Delahaye, a right-wing member of the National Assembly raised the stakes further by denouncing from the podium 150 members of the Assembly, who, he alleged, had accepted bribes to promote the affairs of the Panama Company. The floodgates of public and private accusation, denial and counter-accusation had been dramatically opened. Real sensation came when Baron Reinach, who was also to have been charged, was found dead in bed by his butler the morning before he was to have been indicted. Meanwhile, Cornelius Herz had fled to Britain. It later appeared that Herz had blackmailed Reinach for 2 million francs in return for not revealing what he knew about the company's corrupt practices. The London *Spectator* was cynical:

The consequences of the Panama scandal may be very grave, for there is, we fear, little hope that the public mind will be reassured by a series of triumphant acquittals. The death of Baron Reinach, the 'Patronage Whip' of the Canal, whether he died from worry and insomnia, or as half the public of Paris believes, committed suicide because a duplicate book of his letters had been stolen, sufficiently shows that there is much in the history of the Canal which will not bear light.[42]

Two separate proceedings were established: Eiffel and the others charged with fraud were to answer the charges in the Court of Appeal, and a parliamentary committee held a simultaneous inquiry into allegations of bribery by Lesseps and others, politicians, journalists and newspapers. *Le Temps* said ominously:

It was necessary at any price to get out of the shadows haunted by intangible yet menacing phantoms, where all suspicions seemed permissible. It was necessary to bring accusers and accused face to face, to let the light in upon this thick smoke, to define what was vague and fleeting, and to accomplish all this there was only the way which has been chosen. However, to the political point of view, the only thing that interests us here, is to wonder if the advantages promised by a parliamentary investigation will compensate for the inconveniences of it. It is, in the first place, a strange thing to see the matter brought simultaneously before the Court of Appeal and a Parliamentary Committee. To be sure the two inquiries are not directed at the same facts nor the same persons. But it will be sometimes a very difficult and delicate thing to draw the distinction between the obligations belonging to the first and those belonging to the second. A more disquieting aspect of the situation is the political consequences which all the noise and base passions which will be raised in this inquiry may have for the Republic and for the country. Legends are so easily created in the popular imagination and eradicated with so much difficulty. Either you want to discover the truth, the whole truth; or despite what one says, endorse the lie.[43]

The case in the Court of Appeal was temporarily thwarted when it was revealed that Ferdinand de Lesseps was neither physically or mentally capable of understanding the implications of the proceedings. He was to remain in bed at his country house in a state of frailty and mental confusion for the rest of his life. The bitter political nature of the separate parliamentary inquiry in particular was quickly illustrated when it came to selecting members of the committee; the process took several days, and was accompanied by acrimony, political posturing and walk-outs. *Le Temps* issued a note of advice to the commission of inquiry:

It will need the composure that appeared to everybody to be lacking a little at the hour of its birth. In particular, it should remember that, when one dares to take on the judge's role, it is also necessary to adopt the essential character of that responsibility on top of all the associated professional virtues, such as serenity, impartiality, self-possession and the faculty of discernment between the calumnies and the positive proofs. It will be necessary to hear the accusers, but it will be necessary at the same time to remind them that, while formulating their accusations they assume by the same token the duty to prove them, so that equal responsibilities apply on both sides. Finally, the commission will lead its work to a just conclusion so long as it never loses sight of the supreme interest of the Republic and the country.[44]

Philippe Bunau-Varilla was still in every sense – economic, patriotic, emotional and professional – a tireless promoter of French national interest in the canal. In describing the inflation of the political scandal, he uncompromisingly used terms such as national tragedy, calumny, cowardice, decadence and conspiracy. Of the treatment of Eiffel, he was scathing:

The law reports of the case only serve to exonerate the innocent and stamp the sentence as infamous. In order to condemn the contractor for the locks, M. Eiffel, President [of the court] Perivier resorted to an equally abominable subterfuge. He declared that as to part of his contract he was not a contractor but held a mandate from the company. The fact of a contractor being so transformed by the all-powerful will of President Perivier wholly changed the nature of his legal responsibilities. The innocent fact of a contractor having made a profit on this part of his contract was thereby transformed into a misdemeanour. His legitimate profit thus became money obtained under false pretences.[45]

It soon became clear that the scale of the alleged corruption was huge: the pay-offs to publishers, politicians and businessmen were enormous, and the term *chéquard* came into popular use to denote someone who had taken money from the company – a 'Panama plunderer'. Paul Déroulède, a nationalist member of the Assembly denounced Georges Clemenceau as Cornelius Herz's patron, mentor and collaborator, and the accusation in the Chamber led directly to a duel with pistols just before Christmas 1892. Although, during practice the day before the duel, Clemenceau had scored twenty successive bull's-eyes (and Déroulède on the other hand expected to be killed), when it came to the duel itself both men fired three shots, all of which missed, after which they wisely decided to go home. As rumours mounted that Reinach might have been murdered, orders were given for the exhumation of his body. In London, *The Spectator* ventured that '. . . our readers may imagine how Paris is bubbling with calumny and suspicion.'[46]

As the trials started in the Palais de Justice on Tuesday 10 January 1893, there were reports of dramatic security measures being taken: 'There was no demonstration, though extraordinary precautions were taken to prevent the rising threatened by the anarchists.'[47] Charles de Lesseps was questioned in court on why, when shares in the Panama Railway were quoted at 450 francs on the New York Stock Exchange, the Company had paid 1,250 francs per share, and why, in 1886, when they were seeking 600 million francs to finish the canal, they had let contracts for 783 million francs on current works. In answer to questions about the vast sums paid to publishers, he merely replied, 'Nearly all the papers were holding out their hands.' In the course of these questions, he made the sensational disclosure that high public officials had also been seeking bribes:

In 1886, when we were applying for the Lottery Loan Bill, M. Barhaut, Minister of Public Works, asked me for a million, one instalment to be paid on his introducing the Bill, and the second on its being passed. As it was not passed, I only gave him 375,000 francs.[48]

On 11 January 1893 came the turn of Gustave Eiffel to face questioning from the judge. His friend Pierre Waldeck-Rousseau acted as his principal lawyer. Waldeck-Rousseau was one of France's foremost jurists, former minister of the interior and future prime minister (1899–1902). The charges against Eiffel were that he had misused company funds and abused his position of trust and responsibility; his defence was that he was simply a contractor executing agreed works. But by this time, Eiffel was publicly perceived as having made a fortune from the doomed project, and when it was alleged that he had made 33 million francs (less 5 per cent paid in bribes) he was persuaded to agree that he had paid back 3 million francs, in the hope that this admission would pacify those who felt that he had been at fault:

G.E.: – M. de Lesseps applied to me in November 1887 to undertake the locks, the only system which I thought practicable, for the difficulties of a level canal from sea to sea were then obvious. Baron Reinach promised me financial cooperation, and I negotiated with M. Dingler, the company's engineer. I never sent the letter of 17 December 1887 to M. Hébrard, editor of *Le Temps*, in which I said, 'I reserve you 5 per cent commission, and you and your friends will be good enough to continue your support.' That letter was only a rough draft. I had known M. Hébrard for 20 years. He was a partner in a large building firm, and published the *Journal des Travaux Publics*.
Judge: – Is that why you gave him 1,750,000 francs?

G.E.: – He had the power of rendering great service by his journal and his business connections.

Judge: – M. Hébrard played an important role at the time of M. Rousseau's report, and you were entitled to give money to Reinach, but one does not see why you gave nearly 2 million to M. Hébrard, about as much to Reinach, and a like sum to a company. The prosecution will say that you paid for the cooperation of these persons in order to get the Panama contracts, which have yielded you a profit of 33 million.

G.E.: – It was necessary to ensure cooperation in so important an enterprise.

Here the judge went into figures to show that the defendant received 12 millions for materials amounting to only 2 millions in value, and he asked M. C. de Lesseps whether he would have knowingly signed such a contract.

M. C. de Lesseps: – I should probably have said, 'Let us discuss a little.'

The judge next asked M. Eiffel to explain his charge of 6 millions for transporting materials never delivered by him. The defendant, in a confused reply, was understood to admit the fact.[49]

There was further pressure on Charles de Lesseps; at the time when they were promising completion in three years, commissioners of inspection judged that ten years would be required. Lesseps simply responded to countless references to 'hush money' and bribes by saying that his duty was to carry on to the end. 'By squandering what was left?' asked the judge. 'No, by completing the canal,' replied the defendant. 'But the wasting of millions was not the way to do it,' rejoined the judge. During the course of the trial, with public opinion highly active against the defendants, the residents of the rue Panama in the 18th arrondissement in Paris (so named when the canal project looked like a huge national success) petitioned unsuccessfully for a change of name.

On 9 February came the judgment, accompanied, as was common, by a long preamble:

. . . if the defendants in 1888, after many disenchantments, still hoped to complete the lock canal, substituted for an original scheme unanimously condemned by all specialists who had visited the spot, they could not have seriously believed that this would be accomplished by 1890, that the future outlay would not exceed 600 millions, and that the immediate traffic could be estimated at seven million tons. From the very outset the defendants are declared to have constantly swelled or reduced the figures so as to justify the documents on which they appealed for subscriptions. To give more weight to his deliberate suppressions and untruthful allegations, M. de Lesseps is declared to have formed in 1888 the Reinach Syndicate, which, contrary to the usual practice, was an indirect method of procuring more or less improper co-operation in influencing the public.[50]

Ferdinand and Charles de Lesseps were sentenced to five years in prison and fined 3,000 francs; Gustave Eiffel was acquitted of swindling but found guilty of breach of trust and was sentenced to two years in prison and fined 20,000 francs, the verdicts suspended pending appeal. It may be that the excitable, supercritical atmosphere in Paris accounted for the harsh sentence on Eiffel, for there was never any suggestion that he had had a hand in the management of the Canal Company. If he had been knowingly sucked into an existing atmosphere in which large amounts of money were handed out for 'great service', it was hardly a circumstance of his own making. At any event, with little appearing in the press, he maintained his silence until the appeal process was completed. Three days after the verdicts, *The Times* reported the rather muted reaction in Paris:

The French papers say as little as possible about the severe sentences on the Panama directors. This silence, which is significant when contrasted with the painful feeling expressed throughout the world, is quite comprehensible. But apart from the newspapers the sentence continues to be the one topic of conversation, and it must be owned that, wherever men are not moved by the base passions of spite, or resentment, regret and pity are universal.[51]

Nevertheless, there was a degree of righteous justification:

M. Eiffel, the contractor who forgot to supply the goods he charged for, was exonerated from the charge of swindling, but sentenced to two years' imprisonment for breach of trust. The sentences are described as terribly severe; but there can be no doubt that the canal was latterly a colossal fraud, and that the condemned allowed, if they did not profit by, the misappropriation of enormous sums of money belonging to poor people.[52]

Eiffel appealed before the Cour de Cassation (the Supreme Court), and three months later his sentence was reversed, although this was on a technical violation by the lower court of the statutes of limitation (governing the passage of time between offence and sentence) and did not make any pronouncement on issues of guilt or innocence. Both Ferdinand and Charles de Lesseps had their sentences quashed on similar grounds. In the separate case of bribery, Charles was found guilty and jailed, although illness resulted in his spending a reduced period in hospital rather than in prison. One minister was sentenced to five years and served three. The principal architect of the bribery, Baron Reinach, had already died, possibly by suicide. Bunau-Varilla again castigated the trickery of the Court of Appeal:

The president of the court, Perivier . . . committed the most incredible breach of justice ever registered. For history this iniquity is an advantage. It bears testimony to the excessive desire to fling a victim to the excited mob. It bears testimony as well to the inability of justice to discover any reprehensible act in the defendants' technical management. When, in spite of every effort no misdemeanour could be discovered, a purely imaginary one had to be forged.[53]

The political fallout of the Panama scandal was extremely serious for the government and for the Republic itself. During the trial of Charles de Lesseps and nine others for bribery, detailed evidence was given proving that after the trial convicting Eiffel, the government wanted the whole affair hushed up. One of the imprisoned directors, Cottu, was to be released and the bribery case abandoned in exchange for his silence. As a result, two ministers in the Ministry of the Interior resigned immediately. The ramifications of these events were deep and long-lasting:

> The Panama trial is a Moloch – each day it claims and devours its victims. It has devoured M. Ricard, the dull unwitting minister who gave the signal for the trial; it has devoured M. Loubet, M. Rouvier, M. de Freycinet, M. Clemenceau, and how many others besides! Yesterday it devoured M. Bourgeois, Minister of Justice; and tomorrow or the day after it will most likely fasten its teeth in M. Ribot and the entire Cabinet. The tide goes on mounting higher; if the Republic itself is not swallowed up, it will be for reasons quite independent of this form of government and of Republicans.[54]

Surprisingly, after all this political and legal chicanery and the associated personal disgrace and upheaval, there were still many who wanted the Panama project to be completed. Even before the trial had reached a conclusion, on 15 January, a meeting of Panama 'victims' resolved to form a new company, and delegations were planned to the governments of Columbia and the USA. The *Times* correspondent in Paris wrote at the end of February:

> It would be a great mistake to imagine that recent events have discouraged those in France who dream of resuming the work of M. Ferdinand de Lesseps and of finishing the Panama Canal. It is impossible to conceive of France entirely giving up work once undertaken; and there are not a few who desire to see this great task carried through.[55]

There was a great deal of misinformation circulating, and it was popularly alleged that no works had in fact been begun in Panama. M. Georges Thiébaud, one of the promoters of a new company, gave a lecture to delegates representing potential investors:

> The speaker warmly denied the absurd assertion that nothing had really been done at Panama, and that the engineers had not even left Paris. He illustrated this portion of the lecture by limelight views of the works from photographs taken at Panama. More than 24 miles, he said, had already been completed by the company, the machinery and implements were still to be seen in existence, and could be made quickly ready for use at a slight cost.[56]

Thiébaud finished his lecture by showing pictures of Ferdinand de Lesseps being received by public acclaim on his return to France after his success in Suez; the meeting ended in rapturous excitement and applause. Quite whether the aged vicomte was regarded as a brilliant swindler or a clever entrepreneur suffering from ruinous self-deception is as hard to determine today as it probably was in 1893.

Yet the French government had not finished with the Panama Canal, and insisted on keeping the project alive with a devotion that defied reason. The receiver and a legal representative appointed to look after the rights of the dissolved Canal Company's bondholders were encouraged to form a new company. The rights to the Panama concessions were due to expire, and the French had no intention of either relinquishing or selling them. They embarked on attempts to find an initial 60 million francs, attracted by the suggestion that it might be possible to take legal action against contractors and underwriters of the original company on the grounds of making excess profits. The first case against a promoter was successful, and it was suggested that Gustave Eiffel, as the principal contractor, would be a good target. Under these pressures, Eiffel and several other contractors subscribed to shares in the Compagnie Nouvelle du

Canal de Panama in October 1894 – in Eiffel's case, to the extent of 10 million francs.[57] Ferdinand de Lesseps had lain in his bed since before the beginning of the court cases, senile and often unconscious, and on 7 December 1894, two months after the formation of the new company, he died at the age of eighty-nine, unaware of the events that had recently unfolded.

After four years of reviewing proposed new routes and the existing workings, and trying to raise the necessary funds, it became clear that the resurrected canal project had no chance of being completed. The French public had finally lost faith, and it was made clear that government funds would not be available. In 1899, the directors decided to sell the rights to the canal to the only likely buyer, the United States of America. Negotiations took five years to conclude, and the US government finally paid 40 million dollars in May 1904 for the rights to build the Panama Canal. The canal took ten years to complete, and was opened in August 1914. Now owned and operated by the Republic of Panama, it carries 15,000 ships each year, earning the country nearly 800 million dollars.

In the wake of the 1893 verdict, however, Gustave Eiffel faced further investigation of his conduct. The administrators of the Légion d'Honneur were persuaded that it should examine the allegation against its celebrated member. A committee of inquiry was opened by the Grand Chancellor, and Gustave Eiffel was summonsed to give an account of his behaviour in the Panama affair. The inquiry concluded that he had done nothing dishonourable, and that no action would be taken against him. However, the French National Assembly tried to interfere by attempting to persuade the Légion to re-examine its decision in the light of earlier legal decisions against Eiffel. The implication was that since he had been exonerated under provisions that took no account of guilt or innocence, there was still an issue to be settled. Officials of the Légion pointed out that he had been cleared by the Court of Appeal, the highest court in the country, and that the Légion had satisfied itself on the question of guilt. The reply from the Légion was accompanied by letters of resignation from many of its high-ranking members, including the honorary president of the very Court of Appeal that had examined Eiffel. The resignations were rejected, the entire matter dropped, and Gustave Eiffel was finally free of all the complications of the most disastrous contract of his life.

As part of his fight to clear his name, Eiffel wrote and had printed an account of his *Transactions with the Panama Liquidation* in November 1894, in which he explained and justified his decisions and actions; this document was presented to the French Society of Civil Engineers:

Since the beginning of the deplorable lawsuits which stirred up the business of Panama, I was the object of most odious calumnies. I have judged it worthier to remain silent, voluntarily avoiding all polemics, until justice had decided definitively and the means had been provided to me of responding by indisputable facts and documents. I have also thought that it was more useful to limit myself to attempting the protection of the body of my work than to contribute to the agitation of passions, which could only be disastrous. Today, justice pronounced the final word in this business, as far as it concerns me; a completion Company has been definitively formed and has resumed work in the building sites at the Isthmus.[58]

He pointed out the legal strength of his agreement with the Canal Company's liquidator, and the fact that the Court of Appeal had acted incorrectly:

We know that the strange decree declared by the first hearing of the Paris Court of Appeal of 9 February 1893 was quashed and anulled by the Supreme Court of Appeal on 15 June of the same year. The Supreme Court, going to the limit of its powers, since it could not judge the fundamentals, stated that 'in fact, Gustave Eiffel, contractor of a part of the Canal building work, and the liquidator of the Company, concluded, on July 11, 1889, a compromise settlement of their respective accounts which were mutually arranged to be discharged, fully and entirely, next 23 August.' Regarding the decree, it declared, 'That the Court of Appeal had FORMALLY violated the provisions of the laws.'[59]

Eiffel's self-justification contained much detailed financial and legal information from the various court hearings relating to the original Panama Company, its liquidation and the proposals for the Compagnie Nouvelle. The last series of hearings had been concluded on 8 August 1894, and considering all the earlier evidence in the context of the various codes of civil procedure, concluded that the case against Eiffel was badly founded, and the court declared that their judgement in Eiffel's favour '. . . is absolutely final and closes any debate'.[60] Eiffel insisted in his final comment that 'Here thus finally, for all men of good faith, the business receives its fundamental judgement, and light is only denied to those that will deliberately refuse to see.'[61]

The aftermath of the multitude of hearings and verdicts of February 1893 had been extremely difficult for Eiffel. At the end of 1889, Gustave Eiffel et Cie had become the Compagnie des Etablissements Eiffel, and Gustave began to relinquish control to his son-in-law, Adolphe Salles, husband of his favourite daughter, Claire. Almost immediately after the court case, on St Valentine's Day 1893, a meeting of the company was convened for the purposes of considering a further change of name. This move had been instigated by Eiffel before the trial began, when he made it clear that he intended to resign. At the age of sixty-one, he seems to have had enough of being a businessman, and his last move seems designed to protect the company's future in the event of his being found guilty:

I have absolutely decided to refrain from taking part in any industrial business affair; I have seen too much of the dangers therein, and even knowing that I would be sheltered from blame, I could see the possibility of being at risk again in the future. I specifically wish that my name is removed from the company's title, as I shall remove myself from the company itself.[62]

The successful business that had so proudly borne his name was reduced to the Société Anonyme des Ateliers de Construction de Levallois-Perret, with Maurice Koechlin as president. This was the most dramatic punctuation mark imaginable in the life of France's greatest living structural engineer and designer, who was never again to embark on another engineering project. Despite the appeal court decision, his public reputation had been tarnished, rather more by association than directly. Although his dignity remained intact, it would forever be true that, despite the reversal of his conviction, his absolute innocence had not been explicitly and publicly proven. He did not, however, withdraw from life, but simply changed direction. In today's parlance, he reinvented himself, at the age of sixty-two, to the extent that his new contribution was to be as energetic, as unique and as significant as anything that had gone before. It seems certain that he subjected his personal situation to considerable self-analysis, because he so clearly turned his back on his life as Europe's foremost constructional engineer and devoted his restless genius to a new life as a pioneering practical scientist. This would be no wealthy, retired amateur indulging himself in his declining years; his prodigious mathematical abilities were to be redirected in two particular directions. The surprising scientific instrument in his new future would be the most spectacular and enduring product of his now-rejected previous life – the Eiffel Tower.

TEN

New Directions

Eiffel continued to pursue a number of important projects, none of which achieved fulfilment, in the years between the completion of the tower and his decision to resign from his company, a period which must have been emotionally stressful for him. In 1890, Paris had well-developed municipal utilities. Gas lighting had been introduced forty-five years earlier, and thanks to the Exposition Universelle, the installation of electricity supplies was well under way. Commentators were predicting that, given Parisian taste and skill in municipal management, and the general zeal for 'the appliances of the electric age', Paris would be the best-lighted city in the world within two years. But unlike most of the world's greatest cities, there was still no underground system, apart from a small *Chemin de Fer de Ceinture*, which partly followed the city perimeter. It was Gustave Eiffel who proposed the first electric line to circle the centre of the city. Although planned to be only 6 miles long, it would have linked the main-line railway stations, grand boulevards, the rue de Rivoli and the quais of the left bank. Construction, partly underground and partly overground on viaducts, would have been financed jointly by his own company and the established railway company, the Compagnie du Nord, without the need for public funding.

It may be that the nature of Paris's urban development was the reason for the city's tardiness in constructing an under-ground railway system. At a time when London covered 120 square miles, Paris was only 30 square miles in extent; the distance from the centre to the circumference was only 3 miles. Throughout the compact city, the population of 2½ million was distributed in close proximity to shops and businesses; many shopkeepers, businessmen and even factory-owners lived literally 'above the shop'. There was no great need, as there was in many big cities, to transport huge numbers of workers to and from businesses and factories situated far from residential areas. In 1871, a licence had been granted for a cross-city line from the Bastille to the Bois de Boulogne, but nothing had been constructed. One well-informed American commentator wrote:

> The Compagnie du Nord proposes to build underground lines connecting its central station and the girdle line with the Halles Centrales on the one hand and with the Madeleine Quarter on the other; and M. Eiffel proposes, in continuation, to construct an inner circle that shall follow in general the grand boulevards and shall pass under the Seine. The lines will be below the sewers and conduits, will be operated by electricity, brightly lighted, of course, with electric lights, and reached from the frequent stations on the streets by large passenger elevators.[1]

The cost of the system, which was promoted as being capable of extension at any time, was estimated at over 100 million francs; the correspondent of New York's *The Century* looked enthusiastically forward:

> Paris seems now to be destined to resume her place in the forefront of progressive municipalities by securing the *Nord-Eiffel réseau* [network] of underground lines.[2]

Competing proposals and indecision ensured that this project came to nothing. It was to be another ten years before the first 6-mile underground line was opened, using a unique construction system by the engineer Fulgence Bienvenue and graced with art nouveau entrances by the architect Hector Guimard. Still known as Line No. 1, it ran across the city centre from Porte de Vincennes in the east to Porte Maillot by the Seine.

The second major project, on which Eiffel worked at the same time, addressed the age-old conundrum of what to do about the English Channel. This problem had been continually wrestled with by generations of politicians and engineers on both sides of the Channel. Eiffel's proposal was for a scheme which he called an 'underwater bridge to cross the English Channel'. Ironically, this project was being studied by Eiffel at the same time the French engineers Schneider and Hersent, working with Baker and Fowler, the engineers of the Forth Railway Bridge, were actively promoting an enormous steel bridge. Eiffel favoured a project much less dangerous for navigation, which would also be much easier and cheaper to construct – a 24-mile tunnel formed of 23ft-diameter sectional cement tubes encased in cast iron, costing 493 million francs. The system was intended to maintain equilibrium: essentially it was to float at a safe and convenient level below the surface. However, both these schemes failed, as did most others, partly because there were so many competing ideas and because there were passionate disagreements over issues that affected navigation and national security.

The one Eiffel project from this period that was at least begun was the construction of an astronomical observatory on Mont Blanc – at 15,770ft, the highest mountain in Europe. Eiffel had been approached by his friend, the celebrated astronomer Jules Janssen, founding director of the Observatoire de Meudon near Paris. Janssen still retains today a brilliant reputation for his work in using photography in the study of solar spectra, and in 1890 he persuaded Eiffel to design and build an observatory on the summit of Mont Blanc, where interference from oxygen, water vapour and other atmospheric pollutants would be greatly reduced. Eiffel was immediately attracted by the proposal, since he had become interested in astronomy after his work at Nice. On Mont Blanc, he planned to construct a metal building with an astronomical cupola, but insisted that there had to be rock foundations less than 40ft under the ice. He faced enormous physical problems as soon as he began work on the mountain; the wind, cold and surprising depth of the layers of packed snow were cumulatively almost insurmountable, and it quickly appeared certain that normal constructional techniques would be impracticable. Only three weeks after starting work, half-way through the drilling of two 75ft horizontal tunnels through snow and ice, one of Eiffel's workmen was killed in an accident, and it was decided to abandon the project. A wooden observatory built by carpenters from Meudon was eventually opened in September 1893 without Eiffel's further involvement; this observatory was crushed by ice movement and abandoned in 1909, two years after Janssen's death.[3]

At this time of great upheaval in his life, Eiffel made a significant change in his family situation. He had already established himself as a paterfamilias, the patriarch of a large and mutually loving family on whom he doted. He was determined to move from the rue Prony, and with the wealth that came to him from the financial success of the tower, purchased a large and opulent *hôtel* on the rue Rabelais, at the corner with Avenue Matignon, near the Champs-Elysées and the Elysée Palace. He was to be right in the heart of wealthy, sumptuous Paris, in a luxurious mansion that could have passed as one of the more important ministries of state. Here he installed his extended family – a movable feast of visitors who came and stayed, departed and came again. His daughter Claire, who had married the civil engineer Adolphe Salles in 1883, remained with him permanently to run his household, while Adolphe was his constant business advisor.

Despite his failure to carry through any of the three major projects with which he had been involved, Eiffel was applying himself to the scientific future of his tower with an enthusiasm and diligence uncommon in a man in his sixties whose wealth was sufficient to keep him in supreme comfort for the rest of his life. This new vocation was a natural progression of his increasing interest in the effects of wind on structures:

> During the course of my career as engineer and on account of the exceptional scale of the construction works that filled it, wind was always an absorbing subject for me. It was an enemy against which I had to anticipate a constant battle, either during the building or afterwards.[4]

Much as the effect of wind exercised his scientific curiosity as a structural engineer, Eiffel at the same time realised the urgent necessity to understand wind effects in aviation. Although flying was still the preserve of the playboy, the popularity of ballooning showed that aviation would be the new century's phenomenon. To begin with, he supervised the installation of batteries of meteorological instruments on behalf of the French Central Weather Bureau on the tiny 5ft-wide platform right at the top of the tower.

Right from the start of construction, in 1889, an extremely important meteorology service was carefully installed under the direction of M.E. Mascart, member of the Institute and director of the French central weather bureau. The measuring instruments are on the small 5ft-diameter platform which terminates the tower 300m from the ground; using a cable, they electrically transmit their readings to recorders located on the ground floor of the central weather bureau, which is nearby.[5]

There were maximum and minimum thermometers and a hygrometer, and further self-regulating thermometers, a hygrometer and a rain-gauge in a protected casing; there were also self-regulating and automatically recording thermometers, and wind-gauges and anemometers separately measured the horizontal and vertical wind speeds. For emergencies, at this highest-possible point of the tower, a telephone was provided:

All observations are taken every hour; wind-speed and direction, temperature, atmospheric pressure, the hygrometrical state, etc. are entered in the registers of the weather bureau and figure in the summary bulletin published daily. These observations are centralized by M. Alfred Angot, doctor of sciences and meteorologist of the central bureau, who has analysed the results comparatively with observations made in his office.[6]

For the first time, scientists had the exciting prospect of daily comparisons of a multiplicity of readings taken at precise heights. Eiffel was now also able to have proof of his calculations of static electrical effects and the tower's movements – a five-inch sway at the top in strong wind, and seven inches expansion in hot weather. He also conducted experiments with Foucault's pendulum on the rotation of the earth. His brother-in-law, Dr Albert Hénocque, director of physical biology at the School of Higher Studies of the Collège de France, was invited to perform physiological tests to define the reactions of the human body to an ascent of the tower; in particular he was interested in measuring the effect of altitude on the absorption of oxygen by haemoglobin. The result was a rather overstated account of the 'psychic excitement' to be experienced, together with the sensations of increased appetite and lack of awareness of the passing of time. Hénocque made comparisons with physiological data obtained from funicular railways and mountain ascents:

At the top of the Tower, one would be in the kind of climate comparable with that of much higher mountains; and besides, the meteorological observations show variations of ventilation, temperature, radiation and wind direction, just as for the electrical tension of the atmosphere, a similar analogy with the variations observed on very high mountains.

The opinion, expressed by several doctors, that one could remain on the 3rd platform with a therapeutic purpose, i.e. to manage a kind of altitude cure, was reasonable. Indeed, the staff, and in particular women employed in the shops on the various platforms, and even patients or convalescents, notice a very significant improvement of the general condition, in particular an increase in appetite and the regularization of nutrition in general.[7]

While he knew that the tower would continue to provide him with a handsome income for the rest of his life, these experimental activities were Eiffel's first moves in a long campaign to ensure the tower's continuing future. Despite a vocal minority who still canvassed for its demolition, there was now substantial public enthusiasm, even if some visiting correspondents could still refer caustically to '. . . that monstrous plaything of humanity'.[8] It seemed that everyone was learning to reach their own conclusion about the structure, and it soon attracted the first of many public spectacles enacted by self-publicists intent on defying accepted public sensibility. On 9 September 1891, a baker from south-west France climbed the 347 steps to the first platform on stilts (apparently in rehearsal for a stilt-walking attempt from Paris to Moscow).

Eiffel had been interested in practical meteorology long before he began experimenting on the tower, and also undertook rigorous observations at the Château des Bruyères, his house in Sèvres, the historic centre of ceramics manufacture a few miles south-west of Paris, near Versailles:

> The observations were started in December 1891 and were continued regularly; they have related for this period to the temperature and the relative humidity of the air, the mean velocity and the direction of the wind; from December 1896 rainfall was measured and the principal weather phenomena noted: rain, snow, hail, fog, mist, etc.[9]

He installed an array of thermometers, hygrometers, barometers, anemometers, rain-gauges and recording equipment to enable detailed readings to be retained. In 1904 he published detailed results of these experiments, and like all his published scientific work, it was comprehensive, comprising relatively little text but vast amounts of calculation and tabulated results and analyses.

> The operation of these various instruments was checked once or twice per week. The corrections to be made to the indications of the recording thermometer were established by means of simultaneous readings of all the thermometers at each examination, and of the observations of the maximum thermometers made almost every morning about 9.30 a.m. The indications of the hygrograph-recorder were compared at each visit with those of the hygrometer. The maximum and minimum thermometers and the hygrometer were checked

with the Central Weather Office, and their various corrections applied to the readings made by these instruments. The readings of the various instruments were recorded on the curves of the recorders at seven in the morning, midday and nine o'clock in the evening. We chose these times because it would appear from experience that, for the Paris area, readings at such times are very close to true averages obtained over eight observations per day.[10]

Over the years, his meteorological station at Sèvres was followed by others at his properties, at Beaulieu-sur-Mer by Cap Ferrat near Nice; at the painters' and writers' colony of Ploumanach on the Brittany coast; and at the château at Vacquey near Bordeaux (latterly his son Edouard's house, now an old people's home). His main residence continued to be in the Rue Rabelais in Paris, but he frequently visited his other homes with members of his family. He eventually extended his personal researches into wind speed, direction and velocity, air temperature, humidity and weather conditions to encompass research at a network of twenty-five weather stations which he established all over France. Initially, he funded much of this work himself, until the state gradually absorbed his contributions within a national system. He was determined to change the cultural milieu of French meteorologists, who operated within a tradition of sometimes using precise measurement and at others estimation, without any concept of understanding how to quantify the information imaginatively in a way that would provide a 'big picture'. He established new criteria for instrument-making, and began a regular series of publications of meteorological results and analyses which led to several important volumes on the mathematics of his particular obsession, wind resistance.

By the time of the Paris Exhibition of 1900, the future of the Eiffel Tower was a matter of public agitation again, and various ideas were promoted for the tower's modification. The most notable of these was probably the idea (never proceeded with) for its conversion to a Palace of Electricity and Engineering, which envisaged the addition of a huge iron-and-glass hall around the base of the building, with its apex at the level of the first platform. However, it had been agreed three years earlier that the tower was to be assimilated into the general plans for the exhibition, and Eiffel was asked to ensure that it was illuminated each evening. But with the 1909 date for the ending of Eiffel's concessions on the horizon, the detractors were girding their loins for another battle. In addition, the public appeared to regard the tower as yesterday's attraction and stayed away; although total attendance at the exhibition was 50 per cent higher than in 1889, the total ascending the tower was 50 per cent fewer. The novelty value had no doubt dissipated to some extent in the previous eleven years, but Eiffel himself was convinced the entire 1900 Exposition was far too big, with too many competing attractions and unnecessarily restricted opening hours. The debate on the tower's future rumbled on until late 1903, with intellectuals and learned bodies taking up conflicting stances on the old Art versus Industry dispute. Both the French Association for the Advancement of Science and the Society of Civil Engineers were motivated publicly to denounce those who were promoting the tower's demolition. The prevailing attitude in the end seemed to be that, since the building was there, it should remain, since to destroy it would be thought barbaric.[11] Eiffel knew the tower was secure until at least 1909, and devoted himself further to his attempts to demonstrate its unique usefulness.

The same new iconic status of the tower that had attracted the stilt-walking baker also appealed to those exploring the new science of aviation. A wealthy Dutch entrepreneur and oil tycoon named Henri Deutsch de La Meurthe, president of the Aéro Club of France, sponsored a balloon race. He offered a large cash prize for the first balloon to take off under its own power from Saint-Cloud, the magnificent hill park to the west of Paris, circle the Eiffel Tower 3½ miles away, and return without landing within 30 minutes, the flight to take place between 1 May 1900 and 1 October 1903. His challenge was taken up by the extraordinary 27-year-old Alberto Santos-Dumont, heir to a Brazilian coffee dynasty, who had been living in Paris for the previous ten years. Santos-Dumont, at only 5ft 1in tall, was something of a dandy, who apparently had the world's first wristwatch designed for him by Louis-François Cartier, the Parisian designer of exotic jewellery. But the young Brazilian was no womanising playboy; his obsession lay elsewhere. He had first made a balloon flight in 1898, and quickly began to construct his own hydrogen-filled dirigibles powered by petrol engine. He had, in fact, flown his dirigible No. 3 around the Eiffel Tower already, but not following the Deutsch course and not within the stated time constraints. In July 1901, he flew round the course in 40 minutes, not a good enough time to win the prize, but becoming the first recorded dirigible flight on a prearranged course. The following month, he tried again, but after circling the tower the balloon began to deflate and a cable became entangled in the propeller. The dirigible crashed into the Grand Hôtel du Trocadéro and the dapper aviator jumped at a height of 100ft from the basket on to a sixth-storey window, from where he was rescued with just enough time to spare to dress for his usual dinner in the city.

Santos-Dumont immediately built a new machine, No. 6, 108ft in length and with a capacity of 22,000 cubic feet. The Paris correspondent of *The Times* produced a detailed and quite excitable account of the next attempt, and the controversy that followed:

At 2.40 pm a telephone message from the third platform of the Eiffel Tower advised me to go on my balcony, which commands a view extending from far beyond St Cloud up to the Eiffel Tower, which is a few hundred yards distant. There were with me at the time a statesman who had arrived from abroad, an enlightened French politician, and several other persons attracted by the prospect commanded by the balcony. On receiving the message, we stepped out and found a rather stiff breeze blowing. I learned from the Meteorological Bureau that the rate was 12 or 13 miles an hour. We looked towards the slopes of St. Cloud. Suddenly, at 2.43, we saw the Santos Dumont emerge from the verdure of those slopes and mount straight upwards, the prow turned towards us. After an instant's hesitation, it took its direction in an almost straight line, and leaning a little to the left, appeared in the space within our view, of which the Eiffel Tower formed the extreme point. Never have I seen a finer spectacle. The balloon was then at right angles to us, the slight and almost transparent car hanging steadily from the centre. In the free space and lit up by a radiant sun, the fantastic creature advanced as in a dream, apparently without motion, and yet moving through space with striking rapidity. At this moment, 6½ minutes after its first appearance on the horizon, the balloon, moving at the rate of 30 miles an hour, was rapidly approaching one of the angles of the tower. We felt a thrill of terror. At the distance at which we were stationed we were convinced that it would dash against the tower, but with amazing docility it veered slightly to the left, almost grazed the side of the tower, and then, through the interstices of the tower, we saw it, with a grand movement, turn towards the centre of the Champ de Mars. There, with graceful hesitation, it sought its mathematical line, retraced its steps, and this time slowly and with certain effort passed into the exact axis of the Trocadero turrets and resumed the route to St Cloud.[12]

The balcony party, thinking that the balloon was slowing down, and reaching the conclusion that it must have failed in the attempt, turned its attention to the behaviour of the crowd:

From all directions crowds of men and women had rushed towards the Place du Trocadero. Motors and other vehicles hastened up. Looking down on the square filled with an excited crowd, all heads looking up at the balloon, the sight was a strange one. At every movement of the balloon there was a movement of this compact mass of faces, for tramcars and cabs had been taken by storm and had disappeared under a sea of heads. From all the streets leading to the square, moreover, people were excitedly running up in order to see the balloon before it disappeared. Then when it had gone, the 50,000 people collected from the Eiffel Tower to the extremities of the Place du Trocadero raised a cry which sounded as though a fleet had fired all its guns. The name of Santos Dumont was vociferously shouted.[13]

Santos-Dumont had expressed misgivings about the rules governing what constituted the exact moments of start and finish; he was reluctant to have his record attempt compromised by clumsy rope handling by unknown men on the ground. He was right to be concerned. He arrived above the finish point at Saint-Cloud 29½ minutes after departure, but due to some fumbling with mooring ropes, the committee announced that he had taken 40 seconds more than was allowed:

> When M. de Dion expressed to M. Santos Dumont the regret of the committee at their inability to award him the prize there was a loud and unanimous outcry. M. Deutsch, himself much touched, came up and told M. Santos Dumont that in his view he had gained the prize. The committee, however, held out. It was evidently unpalatable to them to give such a prize to a Brazilian named Santos Dumont.[14]

Santos-Dumont returned to Paris, saying that he would make no further attempts; meanwhile, the committee agreed to consider the matter further. On the Sunday, while waiting to hear the result of the deliberations, Gustave Eiffel invited Santos-Dumont to lunch in his apartment at the top of the tower.[15] Eventually, the committee relented, claiming that they had been on the 'blind side' of events thanks to a large shed that had obscured their view.

Santos-Dumont was presented with a gold medal, depicting the flight around the tower, from the Société de la Tour Eiffel, and the 100,000 francs Deutsch prize, which he distributed equally among his workers and the poor of Paris. Santos continued developing dirigibles before progressing in 1906 to become the first man in Europe to fly a heavier-than-air machine *using its own means of propulsion*; he never patented any of his designs, believing that they should be freely available. He gave up flying in 1910 because of illness, but maintained a lifelong interest in aviation. In 1913, not long after unveiling a statue of Icarus at Saint-Cloud to commemorate his flight, he was accused of being a spy by an officious police officer; in anger, he destroyed all his notes and records of his exploits and inventions and left France for ever. In 1928, he returned to his native Brazil, where he is still celebrated as a national hero and 'the father of aviation'. A generous idealist with a powerful sense of social justice, Santos-Dumont became deeply depressed by the way aviation was being misused for military purposes. This was no capricious worry: when Wilbur Wright was asked in 1905 what the purpose of flying machines was, he replied simply, 'war'. In Brazil itself, where there had been a revolt against the country's dictator, the situation was enough to drive the anguished Santos-Dumont to hang himself in July 1932, using two red ties from his Paris flying days. However, his momentous flight in 1901 made a prescient link with Gustave Eiffel, who at the age of seventy was as enthusiastic from his own perspective about the new science of aviation as had been the much younger Brazilian.[16]

Eiffel's work in meteorology soon extended into the practical study of air resistance, and in 1903 he set up a small laboratory on the tower's second platform in which he based his free-fall apparatus. He was motivated to carry out experiments on bodies at speeds between 50 and 130ft per second – the higher ranges of which had not before been attempted anywhere:

Even for low speeds, and in spite of the many experimenters who endeavoured to resolve these questions, the results obtained sometimes deviate greatly; it is enough to recall that the values given as coefficients of the resistance of the air varies between 0.07 and 0.13. Such deviations are explained as much by the diversity of the methods employed as by the difficulties presented by particular applications, such as rotating arms. It would indeed be useful to be definitively certain about low speeds, but it would be more necessary still to have unquestionable results for the higher ones. However, the experiments which relate to them do not exist, except some tests which were made using railway trains, but under rather badly inexact conditions, or using rotating arms, in which swirls of violent air distorted the results. As the Eiffel Tower makes it easily possible to carry out rectilinear motions which reach a speed of 130ft a second, I have naturally considered using the favorable conditions that it presented.[17]

He fixed a guide wire from the laboratory to the ground 377ft below, and began a long series of experiments in which a large variety of objects of differing weights, compositions and construction were dropped in free fall. Each object trailed an electrical connection to an array of measuring instruments in his laboratory, with the intention of discovering the relationships between air pressure and surface area, and the effects of air pressure on oblique planes. A typical experiment was described by a correspondent of *The Times* in January 1908:

A very heavy body is caused to fall from a certain height. The resistance offered by the atmosphere to the descent of this body is very slight. This body propels in front of it a plate on which the air pressure exerts itself. This plate is attached to the falling weight by means of a graduated spring, and the tension on the spring is clearly the result of air pressure. When the weight of the apparatus, together with its speed at any given instant, is known, as also the tension on the spring, it is easy to calculate the atmospheric pressure. In order to determine readily the speed of the apparatus and the tension of the spring at each instant of time, M. Eiffel has furnished his apparatus with a registering arrangement. It consists of a tuning-fork vibrating 100 times to the second and arranged as an integral part of the spring. The variations in the tension on the spring thus lead to displacements of the tuning-fork in a vertical direction, and these displacements are inscribed on an upright registering cylinder. In this way a diagram is produced which consists of finely toothed lines; the ordinates of this diagram represent the tension on the spring, as it varies from instant to instant. The marks due to the vibration of the tuning-fork render it possible to calculate the time. Furthermore, by means of a very simple device the speed of revolution of the registering cylinder is caused to be proportional to the rapidity of the fall so that the abscissae of this diagram are proportional to the distance traversed. The diagram thus contains all the elements needed to carry out the calculation.[18]

Eiffel concluded his first series of experiments with a significant finding:

We have verified that within the limits of our measurements, i.e. for speeds ranging between 58 and 130ft per second, the resistance of the air is very appreciably proportional to the square of the speed.[19]

These experiments were conducted with the help of several assistants including M. Lapresle, who later became the director of the Eiffel Laboratories, and who wrote in *l'Aéronautique* the day after Eiffel's death:

M. Eiffel was more than seventy years old when he began his first experimental research at Champ de Mars, releasing a long vertical cable from the second platform of the Tower; this was a very clever recording instrument, noting the surface under test and recording the airspeed at every moment. Speed limits thus reached 40 metres per second, a speed that had never been reached in these areas of research. These first experiments continued for three years, and elucidated many obscure points. They fixed the essential laws of normal air resistance and established that this varied by the square of airspeed.[20]

Eiffel's contribution was a notable improvement on earlier work carried out by numerous workers in the field including Samuel Pierpont Langley, director of the Smithsonian Institution in Washington who, since 1886, had used a technique which involved whirling objects at the end of a rotating arm 60ft in length, driven by a 10-horse-power engine. Langley approved of Eiffel's work, and confirmed that measurements of free-falling objects were superior to his own calculations, on which generally accepted formulae were based at the time.

In 1898, Eiffel began actively to encourage yet another field of scientific research. Radio had not yet become the popular term for what was still known as wireless telegraphy, but Eiffel recognised that his magnificent tower would have a significant role to play in future communications techniques. In 1865, the Scottish mathematician James Clerk Maxwell had proved the existence of electromagnetic waves, and on that theoretical work were based the practical researches of Gustav Hertz, Aleksandr Popov, Edouard Branly and Guglielmo Marconi. It was in 1896 that Marconi first successfully transmitted telegraphic signals without the use of wires over a distance of about a hundred yards, from the roof of the General Post Office in London. Marconi patented his apparatus, and the following year he succeeded in transmitting from England to France, and in December 1901 made the first transatlantic transmission from Cornwall.

Eiffel encouraged the French pioneer Eugène Ducretet to set up a transmitter system on the third platform of the tower, from where in October 1898 he and the Russian Popov successfully transmitted a signal to the Pantheon, 2½ miles away, as he described in a note of 7 November:

The transmission tests between the Eiffel Tower and the Pantheon, which I began on 26 October, have continued since then. The distance covered is 2½ miles and is filled with a large number of high constructions; the signals received in the Pantheon were always very distinct, even in a rather thick fog; it is thus possible to affirm that with the same apparatus this distance could be appreciably increased.

The 'receiving apparatus' was installed in the Pantheon, on the terrace above the colonnades. While under these inverse conditions, the Pantheon becomes 'transmitter' and the Eiffel Tower the 'receiver', and no signal reception was obtained; the immediate vicinity of the metal tower and the vertical collecting wire cancels the effect of the waves which should act on the radio conductor.[21]

Eiffel was very reluctant to accept that explanation, citing the fact that telegraphy had been successfully achieved on battleships despite the presence of masses of metal. He had for a long time considered that the tower would have an important part to play in military communications and, aware that the French Corps of Engineers was conducting telegraphy experiments using tethered balloons, he contacted the military authorities to offer the use of the tower.

Captain Gustave Ferrié, the young engineer in charge of these underfunded experiments, was delighted, and the tower became the army's principal wireless telegraphy laboratory, its activities subsidised by Eiffel. The first antenna, consisting of four cables from the top of the tower to the ground on the south-west side of the building (and thus arrayed approximately parallel to the Seine) was built in 1903, providing communication with military bases around Paris. Two years later, regular contact was established across France. In 1908, an even larger antenna using six massive cables (which would remain in place for almost twenty years) was constructed at right angles to the river, on the south-east side of the tower, with the transmission facilities buried under the Champ de Mars. This system enabled communication with Berlin, Algiers, Casablanca and North America, allowing the army for the first time to intercept enemy messages. In the summer of 1914, a message was intercepted at the tower from the German cavalry commander advancing on Paris; the message informed his superiors that the advance would have to be halted as he had exhausted the foodstuff for his horses. The result was that an opportune French counter-attack was successfully mounted on the German forces at the River Marne. Communications were also established with aircraft deployed in the protection of Paris; and in the summer of 1915 came the first transatlantic communication, between the Eiffel Tower and Arlington, Virginia. Perhaps most colourfully, the infamous sensuous dancer Margarete Gertrude Zelle, who had performed to rapturous crowds on the tower's first-level theatre was identified and convicted as the German spy Mata Hari, after a message was intercepted at the tower between Berlin and Spain arranging the payment of money to her from Germany at a

Paris bank. When she attempted to obtain the cash, she was arrested, tried and shot as a spy.

Since 1911, regular time signals had been transmitted for shipping, and an international organisation was established to determine accurate time zones and to confirm precise calculation of longitude. In the lead-up to the First World War, the promoted General Ferrié ensured not only that wireless telegraphy would play a significant part in the coming hostilities, but that the Eiffel Tower would remain a crucial feature of future developments in radio, television and even later forms of electronic data transmission. In the spring of 1913, on the occasion of the visit of the British Institution of Electrical Engineers to Paris for a joint meeting with their French counterparts, *The Times* correspondent reported:

> A good deal of experimental work evidently goes on at the Eiffel Tower Wireless Station. Communication was established recently from the Tower over a distance of 9,000 miles. A new *regime* will, it is hoped, be inaugurated in the transmission of time signals in a few weeks' time, when the Tower will co-operate with several other stations scattered about the world in emitting signals at fixed periods of the day, so that not only will those of different stations not run the risk of clashing, but a large number of them will be available throughout the whole 24 hours.[22]

By the time of the First World War, the availability of Morse-coded radio signals of various kinds began to appeal to a curious public, although there was virtually no provision of equipment for public purchase or use. A small personal telegraphy receiver was promoted in Paris around this time, but until the Eiffel Tower transmitted the human voice, in December 1921, and commercial receivers became common, some eccentric do-it-yourself solutions were offered:

> The large wireless stations, such as the Eiffel Tower in Paris, are now sending out time signals very regularly each day, and even

weather signals, but up to the present the need of a more or less complicated receiver has prevented the general public taking advantage of these signals on as large a scale as is hoped for in the future.

An open umbrella makes a good enough antenna when within 30 miles of Paris, and all that is done is to connect one of the metal clips through a flexible cord to the umbrella and connect the second clip to the ground. With a larger metal object, such as a bicycle or automobile, the signals can be heard as far as 120 miles from the Eiffel Tower, so that the tourist can stop anywhere out on the road in order to ascertain the exact time and set his watch. Other metal objects, such as a stove, wire fence or grating, bedstead and the like can be used, and for long distances, such as 300 miles, a good plan is to use a telephone circuit as an antenna, by connecting on to any existing telephone apparatus. Within the city of Paris, a double antenna wire of 80ft mounted on the roof allows of hearing the German and English wireless stations, even though numberless zinc roofs are in the way.[23]

Eiffel decided to continue with his experiments in aerodynamics. He now knew research could only be carried out in still weather conditions, so he determined to build a wind tunnel on the Champ de Mars, at the foot of the tower:

I began my research on the resistance of the air by using the apparatus which functioned at the Eiffel Tower from 1903 to 1906. It is represented here by its belfry, which was installed on the second platform of the tower, and by its movable rig, which was caused to fall to the ground. In the majority of cases, this apparatus provided excellent results and made it possible to establish with confidence the resistance of orthogonally struck surfaces, of which the coefficients still presented a degree of uncertainty. However, during these tests, aviation started to develop, and this apparatus did not lend itself to the research that this development required. That is what led me to install an aerodynamics laboratory at the Champ de Mars in 1909, in which the principle of the tests is very different.[24]

The early aeronautics investigators quickly realised that their experiments could basically take two forms: either to fly the experimental craft (which might be very dangerous, and would inevitably leave scientific measurement as a secondary objective), or to hold the aircraft part (or a carefully scaled model) static and blow air over it in a controlled manner. The whirling arm, or 'ballistic pendulum', which was invented by the brilliant eighteenth-century English mathematician, military engineer and pamphleteer Benjamin Robins,[25] and used and developed by Samuel Langley and others, was the 'third way' that proved wholly inadequate. Wind tunnels today have developed into extremely sophisticated machines, at least as complex as the aircraft to be tested, but when the first one was built in London in 1871 by Frank Herbert Wenham (who also designed the first successful stereo microscope) it was little more than a 12ft-long box, 18in square, fitted with a feeble fan at one end. Such characteristics as airflow velocity, friction temperature, pressure and humidity were largely disregarded. After Wenham's efforts, other pioneering wind tunnels were built in Washington, London, Rome, Moscow and Göttingen.[26]

In August 1909, about the same time that ownership of the Eiffel Tower passed as planned from Gustave Eiffel to the City of Paris (which is still its owner through the operating company La Société Nouvelle d'exploitation de la Tour Eiffel), Gustave Eiffel's first wind tunnel was ready for use. The building was 66ft by 40ft, with a large air reservoir, test chamber and fan room. The test chamber was 4½ft in diameter and 11ft in length, and the suction fan was driven by a belt from a 70-horse-power engine supplied by a generator on the tower. The airflow could be regulated at speeds up to 65ft per second, and since air pressure in the test chamber was often below that of the atmosphere, an air-lock was provided so that the chamber could be entered during experiments without having to stop the fan. Eiffel used the tunnel to confirm all his earlier experiments using free-fall, and conducted more sophisticated experiments using his own design of highly sensitive balances to measure the aerodynamics of scale-model aircraft surfaces, the efficiency of propellers, and the airflow in the vicinity of test-pieces. In these areas of research, Eiffel reached two important conclusions which had great significance for aircraft design. He showed that aircraft lift was largely achieved by airflow *over* the wing surface rather than *under* it; and he devised a new law governing propeller design. In two and a half years, he conducted over 5,000 experiments, but was eventually halted in December 1911, when influential residents in the increasingly sought-after quarter of the Champ de Mars complained to the city authorities about noise. Eiffel was informed that his activities would in future be regarded as intolerable; a new laboratory would be needed.

I have had reason to be satisfied with the results obtained at the Champ de Mars laboratory, and already, certain of these experiments have become classic and are included in the courses given by M. Marchis at the Sorbonne, by Colonel Espitallier of l'Ecole Supérieure d'Aéronautique and l'Ecole Spéciale de Travaux Publics, by Commandant Paul Renard, also professor of aerodynamics at l'Ecole Supérieure d'Aéronautique, and by many others. I have also been pleased to discover that the most recent textbooks use the wing diagrams given by me as a basis for the study of aeroplane construction and operation. However, I regretted to see our velocities limited to 58ft/sec, or 40 miles per hour, when the speeds actually attained in aviation were much in excess of this figure. Also, the diameter of our tunnel, 4½ft, limited us to experiments on rather small models. Therefore, when circumstances forced my leaving the Champ de Mars site, and I was urged to continue these experiments elsewhere, I decided to provide the new laboratory with larger and more powerful equipment.[27]

Eiffel began work on the establishment of a new laboratory at 67 Rue Boileau in Auteuil, in the 16th arrondissement, to the west of the city. He reinstalled his wind tunnel from the Champ de Mars, and built a bigger one with a test chamber 6ft in diameter, capable of wind speeds of up to 105ft per second. The smaller of the two in fact became the fastest tunnel then built, being capable of up to 130ft per second.

The new laboratory was inaugurated on 19 March 1912. At Auteuil, Eiffel conducted the first wind-tunnel experiments on complete aircraft configurations in model form – wings, fuselage, tail and landing gear. For many years, a concentration on military problems ensured that much sophisticated, systematic work was done on a wide range of French military aircraft designs, and the Auteuil Laboratory has been credited with contributing significantly to the outstanding performance of French aircraft during the First World War. In 1912, Eiffel wrote:

I take great satisfaction in announcing a result of the greatest importance. Following the lead of [various officers], the Laboratoire Aéronautique Militaire de Chalais-Mendon built an aeroplane laboratory in which Lt Saunier succeeded in making a number of experimental flights in a straight line through still air. His aeroplane was provided with recording devices to measure, either directly or photographically, all the elements of flight. By the pressure of a single button at a favourable time the following were recorded simultaneously:

1. the thrust of the propeller
2. the revolutions per second of the propeller
3. the relative velocity of the aeroplane with respect to the air, assumed still
4. the angle of inclination.

The total weight was known in advance and was equal to the sustentation, the fifth element. I was much impressed by the precision of the results obtained in this manner and requested Colonel Bouttieaux and Commandant Dorand to make me a small model of this aeroplane, to be given comparative tests in my laboratory. This model was most carefully constructed to a scale of 1:14.5. The mean discrepancy between the results of our model tests and the aeroplane flights is about 1 per cent.

Such a remarkable concordance breaks down the objection often offered to laboratory tests, that the actual conditions of flight are not simulated, because the model is stationary in moving air or because the model is too small to be comparable. I have always maintained that from model tests one may predict the conditions of aeroplane flight as regards sustentation and head resistance, and I now consider these tests a striking and complete confirmation of this assertion.[28]

Other military work at Auteuil related to the design of artillery missiles and the best methods of releasing bombs. Eiffel's wind tunnel designs were brought into use in Holland, the USA and Japan, and when his huge technical work, *The Resistance of the Air and Aviation*, appeared in translation in the USA in 1913, Eiffel was presented with the prestigious Langley Gold Medal of Washington's Smithsonian Institution. Making the presentation to the French Ambassador, Alexander Graham Bell said:

This eminent engineer, the constructor of the Eiffel Tower, though more than eighty years of age, still continues his studies in his chosen field of labor with all the enthusiasm of youth, and his writings upon the subject of resistance of the air have already become classical. His researches, published in 1907 and 1911, on the resistance of the air in connection with aviation, are especially important and valuable. They have given engineers the data for designing and constructing flying machines upon sound, scientific principles.[29]

By 1917, Eiffel had completed plans for a new and advanced fighter plane, the designs of which he refused to patent, preferring instead to allow them to be published and used by others. Two of the aircraft were built by Louis Bréguet, the famous designer and manufacturer of French military aircraft (whose Compagnie des Messageries Aériennes eventually evolved into Air France). When Eiffel presented a paper on the mathematics of his design to specialist journalists in 1911, the *Times* engineering correspondent was highly enthusiastic:

There is so much useless abstract theorising and, at the same time, so much diffidence in scientific investigations, that it is gratifying to notice such valuable work is being done by the eminent French engineer, M. G. Eiffel, of Eiffel Tower fame, in connection with aeronautics. The work to which he has paid so much attention during the last few years is no idle excursion into the realms of mathematical probabilities, but a treasure of practical information gathered from a large number of results co-ordinated with complete mastery of modern scientific methods. It is now possible to design aeroplanes with fair accuracy; the time for guesswork is past, and the sooner this is realised the better.[30]

One of the two Eiffel aeroplanes crashed during trials in 1918, and although the cause was officially found to be pilot error, it appears that the project was abandoned.

In 1920, at the age of eighty-eight, Eiffel finally decided to retire from his hugely productive, practical life, donating his laboratory at Auteuil to the state. It had been the first laboratory to establish the laws of aerodynamics and to give the new science of aviation its founding principles; Eiffel received a grateful letter of thanks from the under-secretary of state in the Department of Aeronautics and Transport:

Paris, 30 December 1920
Sir,
At this time of the transfer to the Aeronautics Service of the aeronautic laboratory that you created and directed, it is a pleasure once again for me to express to you the very high regard in which French aeronautics holds the work that you undertook to such good ends. Your research has been the basis of the study of the general laws which have enabled Aeronautics to leave the empiricism of its beginnings and to transform itself into a rational and unquestioned science. Creator of the first aerodynamics laboratory in France, you have undoubtedly played the greatest part in this happy evolution. I am happy to testify to you officially in this respect the recognition of the Government of the Republic.[31]

The laboratory continued under the Chambre Syndicale des Industries Aéronautiques as a principal research facility for the aviation industry until the time came when it could no longer offer the speeds required in modern aeronautical testing. Diversified experimental work continued, however, as the wind tunnel began to undertake sophisticated testing for the road vehicle industry, and later in 1945 the construction industry became its principal client, conducting stability testing on a wide variety of structures. Today, in a fine testimony to the significance the young Gustave Eiffel gave to the matter of wind force, the Auteuil Laboratory is operated jointly by the French Centre Scientifique et Technique du Bâtiment and the private company Aérodynamique Eiffel, offering research and testing facilities to architects and engineers in the study of weather effects on structures.[32]

In his retirement, Gustave Eiffel was seemingly as busy as ever at his large Paris mansion on the Rue Rabelais, working on a collection of private memoirs intended for his family rather than publication. However, he also refined a large number of scientific papers, monographs and books covering the great range of his engineering and scientific interests. The suspicion and bitterness generated by the Panama affair had long gone and, in addition to honours in France and the USA, he basked in the glory of the national honours of Greece, Japan, Serbia, Russia, Italy, Hungary, Austria, Portugal, Spain, Cambodia and Vietnam. His final years were spent firmly in the heart of his large, affectionate family of five children, their spouses and offspring. While enjoying his Paris mansion, he also made frequent visits, with as many of his family as he could persuade to accompany him, to his sumptuous steam yacht La Walkyrie on the Riviera, or to his properties at Vevey on Lake Geneva, Brittany, Bordeaux or Sèvres.[33] Extremely wealthy, comfortable and in full possession of his faculties, he was, at the end of his life, in a characteristically modest way, satisfied. He was able to understand and quantify his life's work in international engineering, and his family were successful in their own right. His grandson Georges Salles was to become a Director of French Museums, another became a successful motor vehicle engineer and his son-in-law Adolphe and grandson André were much involved in ensuring the increasing popularity and success of the Eiffel Tower.[34]

The innovative and self-effacing man who became known as '*le magicien du fer*' died peacefully at his mansion on the rue Rabelais on 27 December 1923, at the age of ninety-one. Surprisingly, for a city that has so proudly marked its famous sons and daughters with squares, avenues and underground stations bearing their names, his death was largely ignored by the national and municipal administrations in Paris. There may still have been vestiges of the more vindictive influences from the wake of the Panama affair, and it was to be twenty-six years before even the simplest bust of Eiffel was unveiled at the foot of the tower. Inscribed simply 'Eiffel 1832–1923', this late and modest commemoration was installed at the instigation of General Gustave Ferrié, who had forgotten neither Eiffel's personal friendship nor his national contribution.

ELEVEN

The International Icon

No other building in history has achieved the national and international recognition and status of the Eiffel Tower. From its inception, it incorporated all the features of a building, rather than a simple tower – rooms, offices, elevators, shops, cinema – and every day it still plays host to thousands of people both going about their business and visiting. There are, of course, many other iconic buildings and structures that evoke a national character, but none, with the possible exception of the Forth Railway Bridge, is so obviously a work of pure engineering, and certainly no other is so uniquely linked with the name of its builder. Yet it always had its detractors. The infamous Artists' Protest before construction began was the first point at which the future of the tower was in question, although most of those involved later became supporters. As we saw, Sully-Prudhomme recanted; so did Charles Gounod. On the other hand, the French composer Erik Satie, the man who devised 'furniture music' (later increasingly commercially represented as 'elevator music' or 'musak') had no need to recant – he was an immediate enthusiast.[1] Satie was an early visitor to the completed tower, and was so overcome with the atmosphere that he was inspired to compose 'Gnossiennes', an elegant and ethereal work. Another composer, the forgotten Adolphe David, composed his Opus 63, the Eiffel Tower Symphony, as a sequence of stark, physical images:

The arrival of the engineers and workmen at the Champ de Mars (*lento*)
Beginning of the Tower's foundation works (*moderato*)

Sounds of iron (*moderato e martellato*)
The ironsmiths (*allegro and cheerfully*)
Tumult and trouble among the workers (*allegro agitato*)
First platform (*andante cantabile*)
Second stage, the tower mounts
Higher, the top (*andante cantabile*)
The crowd climbs up (*moderato accelerando e crescendo al fine*)
Hymn to the French flag (*lento e grandioso*)[2]

As polkas and waltzes celebrating the tower proliferated in the streets of Paris, the most vociferous of the dwindling band of critics, Guy de Maupassant, maintained his lifelong antipathy to the tower and all it represented. He saw it as the 'headlight of an international bazaar' and, according to the philosopher and critic Roland Barthes, often took lunch in the second-level restaurant on the grounds that it was the one place in Paris where he could be guaranteed not to see the tower. This may have been an entirely apocryphal story, which has in fact been attributed to some of the other detractors opposed to the decadence of the new industrial culture, such as the writer Alphonse Daudet. Maupassant's alleged dining habit was not enough to assuage his feelings, however, as he asserted in his short story *La Vie Errante*, first published in 1890:

I left Paris and even France because of the Eiffel Tower. Not only is it visible from every point in the city, but it is to be found everywhere, made of every known material, exhibited in every shop window, an unavoidable and tormenting nightmare. I wonder what will be thought of our generation if, in some future riot, we do not unbolt this tall, skinny pyramid of iron ladders, this giant and disgraceful skeleton with a base that seems made to support a formidable monument of Cyclops and which aborts into the thin, ridiculous profile of a factory chimney.[3]

Until Eiffel proved the tower's scientific credentials before the First World War, there were indeed willing 'unbolters'. Some were undoubtedly Eiffel's cultural enemies, but in the wake of all the great international exhibitions, there has in fact always been a busy and entirely responsible trade in the recycling of buildings, those of Eiffel included. For the 1889 Exposition, the Eiffel Company had speculatively constructed iron buildings, for display and advertising purposes, intended as suitable for use by European civil servants in the African colonies. At the close, one of the exhibits was bought by Baca Diez, a South American rubber-baron who had it dismantled and shipped to Iquitos in Peru, where it was reassembled. When he discovered that it was too big for his purposes, he had it divided, and sold one half for shipment to a remote part of southern Peru, where it languished at the mercy of the most unsuitable weather conditions before being sold for scrap.[4] The other half remained in the Plaza de Armas in the centre of Iquitos, where it endured several owners and uses before being rescued in 1985: Eiffel's Casa de Fierro is now a fine restaurant run by a man from Wigan in Lancashire, who also happens to be the local British Consul. A similar iron building, allegedly by Eiffel, forms part of the National Archive in Maputo, Mozambique. This Casa de Ferro, also from the 1889 Exposition, was apparently brought from Paris by a Portuguese delegation anxious to mollify the colonial governor in Maputo, who had been complaining of inferior accommodation. However, the effect of the hot sun on the iron sheets of the Casa de Ferro ensured that the complainant quickly readopted his previous lodgings.

In the lead-up to the exhibition of 1900, there was a campaign demanding the removal of the tower. Maupassant was joined by the gloomy Catholic writer and social reformer Léon Bloy, who was a bitter observer and commentator on life:

I feel Paris threatened by this truly tragic lamp-post to which it has given birth and which will be seen at night from twenty leagues as a distress signal of shipwreck and despair.[5]

Yet again, around the time of the transfer of the tower into the ownership of the City of Paris in 1909, questions about its permanence arose, prompted by the inevitable band of self-appointed aesthetes who insisted on their right to determine public taste. By then, Gustave Eiffel was well launched on his, and the tower's, new career in aerodynamics and wireless telegraphy, and by the time of the art-deco-dominated Paris Exposition of 1925, its importance would be celebrated by the Swiss-born French architect Le Corbusier (whose Purist manifesto examined the correlations between modern machine forms and contemporary architecture).[6] Le Corbusier described the tower 'Rising above the plaster palaces with their twisted décor, it looks as pure as a crystal.'[7] By then the tower had become part of the skyline and the character of Paris, and its popularity with the citizens of both Paris and France was assured. As we shall see, it was to become an inspiration to film-makers, painters and writers in ways that could not have been conceived by the protesters of 1887. Later still, it would become a rich source of metaphor and meaning for a generation of philosophers and intellectuals. Such symbolic concepts have also been used to explain its popularity with would-be suicides, several hundred of whom have, unhappily, been successful. Inevitably, while continuing and expanding its career in telecommunications, the tower would also attract self-publicists, advertisers, producers of kitsch souvenirs, bomb threats and swindlers. More mundanely, the Eiffel Tower has endured the production of a succession of copies in various parts of the world, some decently respectful but many verging on the brash and tasteless, and almost all predictably pointless.

From the beginning, the Eiffel Tower was unashamedly a commercial enterprise. Indeed, the exhibitions – in particular that of 1900 – were intended to encourage consumerism. As Maupassant complained in *La Vie Errante*, as early as 1890 images of the Eiffel Tower flooded the market and were soon available everywhere, in a proliferation of forms. Gustave Eiffel attempted to exert personal control of the burgeoning souvenir business. In constructing the tower, he had inevitably become the creator of complex interrelated legal agreements and contracts with layer upon layer of contractors and sub-contractors the length and breadth of France, but even that considerable expertise was not enough to prevent him burning his fingers when it came to the banality of knick-knacks. As early as November 1887, Eiffel had signed an agreement with the department store Printemps and its founder and director, Jules Jaluzot, under which Eiffel undertook to supply iron scraps and waste from the tower's construction at a cost of eight francs per 100 kilos. These materials were to be used for the manufacture of souvenir trinkets of the tower bearing the legend 'exclusive dealers of materials from the Eiffel Tower' in return for a royalty to Eiffel of 35 per cent of the cost of manufacture. He had not reckoned on the bitter response of the large number of small independent artisans and shopkeepers, who could recognise a monopoly arranged by Jaluzot when they saw it. They were furious to think that their chance of cashing in on the windfall that the popularity of the tower represented might be snatched from under their noses.

Under some pressure, and perhaps blinded by his passion for his own creation, Eiffel wrote to Jaluzot in February 1889, insisting that, despite their agreement, he still retained the rights to reproductions of his work, and wished to end Jaluzot's monopoly:

> As I now clearly understand, a great number of small and large manufacturers were set up for the Exposition of 1889 in the hopes of the success of my creation, and I believe I would be lacking gratitude towards them and the Parisian population, which did not spare me its goodwill, if I did not propose to you the pure and simple cancellation of our contract, with regard to the reproduction rights of the Tower.[8]

Jaluzot had already established a factory to produce paperweights, and had entered into agreements with over thirty separate manufacturers, many of whom had themselves made financial commitments to the venture. The entire matter eventually went before the Court of the Seine, which decided that Eiffel had not secured reproduction rights, and that any manufacturer could make reproductions without risk of infringing copyright, which belonged to the City of Paris. Jaluzot, while claiming great admiration for Eiffel, insisted that he had been concerned for the health of French industry, and illustrated his agreement on royalties:

> I take only three centimes on the thirteen franc knives which a Thiers cutler manufactures. On this sum, I give naturally, following our conventions, one and a half centimes to M. Eiffel. One cannot thus show me abusing the situation. I will say even more: the treaty which binds me to M. Eiffel is a guarantee to the Parisian trade, for the French manufacturer. The day when this agreement would be cancelled, there would be a true crash in small national industry because foreigners, who have for months clandestinely manufactured Eiffel Tower articles, will flood us with their products.[9]

In the end, Eiffel and Jaluzot mutually agreed to give up their claims of monopoly rights in favour of the freedom of the small manufacturers of Paris. The business to be generated over the years was to prove of sufficiently gigantic proportions as to allow everyone a generous share. It would be easy to underestimate both the range and value of the reproduction of the imagery of the Eiffel Tower, and the multiplicity of objects has far surpassed the wildest dreams of those early manufacturers who objected to Eiffel's agreement with Jaluzot.

There had been considerable use made of photography during the tower's construction, and apart from rather formal engineering records, there are many sequences showing the advancing construction taken from precisely fixed camera positions. The great French architectural photographer Louis-Emile Durandelle, who with his partner Hyacinthe-César Delmaet had photographed the construction of Charles Garnier's Paris Opera and the basilica of Sacré-Coeur in Montmartre, also undertook a long series of painstaking, large-format photographs of the building of the Eiffel Tower. These photographs were masterpieces of the difficult nineteenth-century wet collodion process, and certainly did not constitute popular or commercial exploitation. Another series of similar photographs was published by Henri Rivière, whose considerable reputation was in the fields of impressionist wood engraving and lithography. Durandelle's photographs in particular reignited the claims for the tower's beauty in a way that natural human observation somehow didn't, and helped ensure that the controversy over the tower's presence and its aesthetic qualities would be brought to an end.

Soon, however, artistic and photographic reproductions and small metal or wooden models were commonplace, and Paris fervently adopted the image with pleasure, gratitude and the ringing of tills. Sometimes, Parisian enthusiasm for their new-found symbol, even in its least offensive forms, was an irritant, as Maupassant complained when he observed that it was 'to be found everywhere, made of every known material'. When the brilliant English crystallographer Rosalind Franklin was working in the city in 1947, she wrote home to London asking for some items to be sent to her, including plain postcards, 'an invention unknown to the French who only have them covered with the Eiffel Tower'.[10] Without doubt, the power of the photographic image resulted in an explosion of the forms of reproduction. Today, the Internet offers us websites devoted to the sale of nothing but objects either made in the shape of the tower, or bearing its image. One site boasting a shop in Paris, a warehouse in Sacramento and prices in American dollars shamelessly offers at least 600 different items, ranging from the mundane to the ordinary, and on through the absurd to the downright tacky. There are Eiffel Tower snow-globes featuring Santas, teddy bears, lovers and bâteaux-mouches, accompanied by a selection of music, music boxes, models, from three inches to three feet in height, made of various metals, glass, 'crystal' and plastic; fridge magnets, pencil-sharpeners, puzzles, picture-frames, mouse-mats and keyrings galore; T-shirts, playing cards, night-lights and all manner of nightwear, soft furnishings, jewellery, umbrellas, ties, cigar cutters, bags, bottles, backpacks and perfume; clocks, watches, pipes, paperweights, toys and lapel pins. There are candles, glassware, charms and medallions, tableware, candlesticks, table lamps, floor lamps and items for 'the home office', including telephones; Christmas-tree ornaments, crockery, porcelain trinkets and boxes. For the true enthusiast there are plant holders, coffee tables and patio furniture up to seven feet in height. The majority of these items are manufactured, in whole or in part, in the shape of the tower; others make do with unsubtle applied imagery of the tower or of Gustave Eiffel. At the end of the scale come wedding stationery, music, food and drink, and categories labelled 'others'. One hundred and thirty years after the Parisian artisans fought their corner, many people continue to make a great deal of money from the image, including the company that owns the tower on behalf of the City of Paris: La Société d'exploitation de la Tour Eiffel earned over 1 million euros in royalties during 2002.

In addition to the tasteless trinkets and the bewildering variety of everyday models of the tower that were soon on the market, there later appeared more-eccentric, individual 'scale models' lovingly toiled over by obsessed perfectionists. The 8ft model built of 11,000 toothpicks in the 1930s by an enthusiastic New York dental student was only surpassed thirty years later by one constructed by an Argentinean whose innovation was to use toothpicks collected from fifty-seven countries. These two were nevertheless outdone by the most extraordinary effort expended by the family of a French watchmaker who spent 8,000 hours in producing a one-tenth-scale model made with 2½ million matchsticks and 2,000ft of electrical wiring. This prodigious effort included working elevators, electric lighting and details down to a perfect scale model of Gustave Eiffel's bed in his private apartment on the third-level platform. Similar fetishists could be found across the world, including the US state of Ohio, where another fanatic built a scale model using over 700 separate hand-cut pieces of aluminium sheet, based on accurate drawings supplied from Paris.[11]

Moving up the scale, there is a long list of direct copies and imitators of the Eiffel Tower, from Shenzhen to Berlin to Las Vegas; none of the same size, but all offering an extraordinary homage to the original. Setting aside the many small representations – similar to the US Boy Scouts' copies of the Statue of Liberty – and the inevitably transient 200ft model of the tower built of ice in 1890 in St Petersburg, there are several that merit mention. The first to appear was a 200ft copy on Petrin Hill in Prague, which was built in thirty-one days for the Czech Jubilee Exhibition of 1891 using scrapped railway parts. This tower has recently undergone a two-year reconstruction, including a new lift and other facilities for visitors.

The first of several British copies also began construction in 1891. The foundation stone of the Blackpool Eiffel Tower, as it was originally to be known, was laid by Sir Matthew Ridley on 29 September 1891, and a phonograph recording of his speech was placed under the stone, along with other topical mementoes; it was opened in 1894, by which time the word 'Eiffel' had been dropped. Erected by Maxwell & Tuke, Blackpool Tower, at 518ft, is half the height of the original, but it still manages to dominate the surrounding landscape. Its base is not open but incorporates a number of associated buildings, the whole attraction including an aquarium, a menagerie, an aviary, bear-pits, an Old English Village, a ballroom (with Mighty Wurlitzer) and roof gardens. One authoritative observer notes that 'the Tower Ballroom is one of the great sights of northern Europe, a must to see both for the decoration and for the ritual dancing.'[12] The present children's adventure area at the top of the tower was where an earlier roof garden complete with waterfalls and fountains was located; before that, it had been the site of the original menagerie. Blackpool Tower has achieved its own unique niche in English culture, along with such potent symbols as the saucy seaside postcards of Donald McGill, to the adventures of Dick Barton, the 1940s radio secret agent, who featured in a 1947 film, tackling foreign spies firing deadly ray guns from the top of the tower.[13] The construction employed 5 million bricks, 2,500 tons of steel and 93 tons of cast iron, and the cost was £42,000. For decades, Blackpool Tower, assaulted by the salt atmosphere of the Irish Sea, was poorly maintained and there were calls for its demolition, but the entire structure was subjected to either replacement or renovation between 1921 and 1924. One of the tower's commercial rivals, the Blackpool Winter Gardens Company, at one time proposed to build a second steel tower, twice as high as the first and equal to the height of the Eiffel Tower; it was never attempted.

The second British imitator, 'Watkin's Folly' as it became known, was started in 1892 to the north of London. Sir Edward Watkin was chairman of the Metropolitan Railway Company. He resolved to build a tower bigger and better than the Eiffel Tower, and, being no slacker, he formed the Tower Company Ltd in 1889, with the intention of building a 'Great Tower of London' on a rural site near the River Brent; it was so far out on the fringe of the Metropolitan Railway that it didn't even merit a station. Gustave Eiffel, asked to build the new tower, refused, so Watkin turned to Sir Benjamin Baker, designer of the Forth Bridge, with whom he had been collaborating on plans for a Channel Tunnel.[14] An international design competition was announced, with a prize of 500 guineas, which within the three-month deadline attracted sixty-nine entrants from around the world, including, for example, the Thames Ironwork Company, which was owned by West Ham Football Club. Most submissions were heavily influenced by the Eiffel Tower, and included designs in cast iron, concrete, glass, granite and steel, with theatres, sanatoria, chapels and even, in one case, a spiral steam railway. Gustave Eiffel was delighted to include in his two-volume account of the construction of his own tower the remarks on the London submissions that were made in the English professional journals:

> To be fair to the candidates, it is however advisable to add that the existence of the Eiffel Tower and the desire to avoid imitations increased the difficulties of the problem considerably, because the Eiffel Tower brings together the most rational and most obvious means to combine a monument presenting an architectural aspect with an economic construction.[15]

The winning designers, with a 1,200ft-high octagonal steel tower with eight legs, and offering two platforms, a summit viewing platform, restaurants, theatres, an exhibition area, a ballroom and Turkish baths, was the Scottish firm of Stewart, MacLaren and Dunn. The journal *Nature* was doubtful of the outcome:

> . . . if the tower is to pay, it must be provided with some attractions to bring the people again and again; and if these attractions could be raised 200 feet or 500 feet above the smoke, they would be immensely increased. The country cousin and the conscientious sight-seer would go to the summit, but the first stage would detain the bulk of the visitors.[16]

Watkin's public subscription appeal was not as successful as he had hoped, and the project was quickly reduced to a tower of four rather than eight legs. Work began in June 1893, but finance was not the only problem; the ground proved unexpectedly marshy and the foundations became unstable. Building stopped in September 1895 at the first-platform level of 155ft. By this time, Watkin had surrounded the site with associated attractions such as sports fields, pleasure gardens, an artificial lake, a funfair, bandstands and a tea pagoda, and decided to open the base of the tower to the huge crowds that he was convinced would come to the newly opened railway station nearby. But no one came, and the tower languished and rusted; the Tower Construction Company went into liquidation and Watkin retired through ill health. In about 1902, not long after Watkin's death, the tower was declared unsafe and closed to the public; two years later it was demolished, and in 1907 the foundations were blown up and the scrap steel sold to Italy. In 1924, the site became home to the Empire Exhibition, and the anonymous patch of Middlesex turf that had played host to the high hopes of Watkin's Folly set out on a rather more popular and favourable future as Wembley Stadium[17], now itself being reconstructed.

The last British copy of the Eiffel Tower was New Brighton Tower, on the Wirral peninsula across the Mersey from Liverpool. Built of steel, this 544ft tower was started in June 1896 and opened by the New Brighton Tower and Recreation Company in 1900 at a cost of £120,000; it boasted a ballroom, assembly hall, billiard saloon, winter gardens and refreshment rooms. Within the steel-and-brick base the ballroom was one of the world's largest, and above it were a monkey house, aviary and shooting gallery. Four lifts carried sightseers to the top, from where fine views of the Welsh mountains and the Lake District were obtained. The surrounding gardens offered a fairground, a 3,500-seat theatre, an athletics ground, a roller-skating rink, cycle track and stadium. For military reasons, the tower was closed to the public during the First World War and never reopened, because of its poor condition. The top of the tower was demolished by 1921, leaving the ballroom and theatre intact. However, a fire in 1969 destroyed the remaining disused buildings and the entire area was cleared for redevelopment.

In other countries, a couple of towers were built, serving more essentially as radio antennae, but nevertheless modelled loosely on the Eiffel Tower; one of 450ft in 1926 in Berlin, and another of 1,000ft in Tokyo in the mid-1950s. The Berlin example, inaugurated by Albert Einstein, boasted a two-storey restaurant at 150ft and an observation platform near the top. Berliners apparently referred to the tower as 'Langer Lulatsch' (Longlegs) and between these legs was established the German Radio Museum. In about 1972, a 340ft replica was built in Ohio as part of an amusement park, and a small, 65ft version, topped with a red cowboy hat, exists in the Texan town of Paris. It is perhaps inevitable that it was in the Nevadan gambling centre of Las Vegas that a 540ft half-scale replica of the Eiffel Tower was opened in 1999, in front of the Paris Hotel and Casino. This is a welded steel structure (but boasting 300,000 fake rivet-heads) and is the centrepiece of an 800-million-dollar resort known as Paris Las Vegas, owned by the Park Place Entertainment Corporation. Also replicated are other Parisian architectural landmarks, such as the Louvre, the Arc de Triomphe and the Paris Opera; 'Parisian-themed lounges', 'quaint' cafés and a working French *boulangerie* provide more popular detail. At the inaugural event, when the French actress Catherine Deneuve threw the switch illuminating the tower, a former chairman of the Nevada Gaming Commission was reported as saying 'Wow!', while the mayor of Las Vegas was so overcome that he declared he would rather be there than in the real Paris.[18] The replica tower was apparently constructed using modified copies of the original Eiffel Tower plans, and the designers have at least recognised that 'no other structure in the world represents the glory of sheer structural engineering know-how.'[19] The replica certainly appears to be an accurate copy, down to the use of the same paint, although some aspects cannot actually be half-scale for practical or regulatory reasons.

The lure of the Eiffel Tower has not been restricted to either engineering devotees or to those obsessives who indulged their solitary vices with glue, toothpick and boxwood. The antics of Silvain Dornon, the stilt-walking baker who climbed the tower as early as 1891, set an attractive precedent for all manner of publicity-seekers and the hangers-on and rubber-necks whom they encouraged. In November 1905, the newspaper *Le Sport* promoted a Stair Climbing Championship, which attracted 227 competitors in various classes. The winner reached the first platform in only 3 minutes and 12 seconds, although one crazed aficionado over-excelled himself and everyone else in sight by heading for the second platform, which he reached in 8 minutes, with the wholly voluntary burden of 100 pounds of cement on his back. It was this mystifying necessity to carry an amusing or entertaining stunt to eccentric or dangerous lengths that characterised a succession of exhibitionists. Parachutists continued to be fascinated by the tower; they normally hid on the structure after closing time and took to the air during the night or very early in the morning. The modern phenomenon of bungee jumping is said to have become a recognised 'extreme sport' after its New Zealand pioneer, A.J. Hacket, in early 1987, hid on the tower overnight and leapt down through the hollow centre next morning.

In June 1923, Pierre Labric, a journalist at *Le Petit Parisien* and future mayor of Montmartre, cycled around the first platform before heading bumpily down the stairs to meet his waiting friends – and the local police. Despite the potential attraction of the antics of cyclists, it was to be twenty-five years before

Labric's attempt on the tower was challenged, by a professional stuntman from Saint-Tropez named Coin-Coin, who tackled the structure on a unicycle. The use of aeroplanes also intrigued some adventurers, despite the tragic consequences of the first attempt to fly a light plane between the tower's legs. In November 1926, a young Frenchman, Léon Collot, was blinded during his approach by the morning sun rising over the Ecole Militaire; the plane veered, a wing struck one of the tower's radio antennae, and the plane crashed, killing Collot. Shortly after the Allies retook Paris in 1944, a US Army Air Corps Flying Fortress allegedly succeeded in completing the manoeuvre that had eluded Collot. Inevitably, the activities of solo exhibitionists gave way to groups of people climbing all over the structure, some of them dressed, undressed or re-dressed for the occasion. Others were experienced climbers, who gave added value to their demonstration by adopting a particular 'trick' or daredevil exploit; by about 1970, 'streaking' was the feature most often providing the added value. As the possibilities of publicity increased, such events became more focused on particular social or political campaigns, from issues like the Cuban revolution, the Vietnam War, and the Algerian War to more prosaic, strictly Parisian concerns. The tower was simply the best means known to man for getting publicity – a truism that would soon be recognised by the princes of commerce.

Some of the attempted stunts resulted in casualties. It is a grim reflection of the dark side of the human psyche that the tower (perhaps rather obviously) seems to have held a fascination for those despairing souls who wanted to end their own lives deliberately and violently, mostly, but oddly enough not always, by jumping. The first of a seemingly endless succession of suicides (statistics are not officially maintained, but the total is probably approaching 500) was in August 1891. A young printer's mechanic climbed 50ft up into the north pier, undressed, left a note leaving his clothes to Gustave Eiffel, and very deliberately hanged himself.[20] Perhaps the most poignant story is that of the Parisian tailor named Reichelt, who in 1911, having heard that a fellow inventor had recently jumped successfully from the first platform to test a parachute, negotiated with the distinctly reluctant authorities to allow him to repeat the escapade in order to prove the viability of his own spring-loaded, bat-winged cape. He submitted to the pages of official disclaimers and waivers and arrived early in the morning to be confronted by photographers and an eager crowd of 'well-wishers'. At the last minute, he lost the last vestige of his courage, but, jeered on by the merciless spectators around him, he stepped out into the air; with his mechanical contraption fluttering ineffectually about him, he died from heart failure before his body hit the ground.[21] From the internet, the ghoulish can download film of his fatal leap, ending with the gendarmerie measuring the crater he left.

In addition to one murder, in which a woman was pushed to her death from the second platform by her husband, there is a catalogue of stories of suicide attempts, successful and otherwise, among which are accounts of particularly grisly incidents, miraculous escapes, and last-minute changes of heart. Perhaps the oddest concerned a middle-aged man who was grabbed by a member of staff as he went over the railing of the first platform. He was taken to the restaurant and given a free lunch, which so cheered him up that he bought champagne for everyone. To make sure that he got home in good order, he was driven to his house in the suburbs. Next morning, he was found drowned in a duck-pond near the tower. It seemed that he had gone back late at night to repeat his attempt, and, having found the tower locked, nevertheless achieved his desperate wish as nearby as possible.[22]

There were occasional outcries demanding preventative measures, but the authorities always relied on the excuse that the erection of high railings or barriers would impair or even completely block the spectacular views, and attach to the tower a rather too visibly sinister aspect. In any case, the argument went, a determined would-be suicide need only head for one of the many easily available public alternatives, such as the Seine or the Metro. Eventually, in the 1960s, safety barriers were erected, but determined suicides still occasionally succeed. What outraged Parisians more than either the suicides or the official attempts to thwart them with ugly and intrusive barriers, was the removal in the summer of 1957 of the flagstaff carrying the tricolour.

Despite the fact that it was replaced by a television antenna that increased the tower's height by a further 66ft, popular opinion and national pride was offended by the officious action.[23]

The tower had been hijacked for advertising purposes as early as 1925 by a single-minded Frenchman who managed to obtain a virtual monopoly on its use as a blatant advertising gimmick. André Gustave Citroën had watched the Eiffel Tower being built as a child, and realised then that he wanted to become an engineer. In 1925, as head of his own huge car company, he reached a unique deal with the tower's management, which had been seeking a spectacular project for the structure. The Italian lighting engineer Fernand Jacopozzi wanted to construct a gigantic lighting scheme based on animated shooting stars, comets, zodiac imagery, fountains and water cascades. The authorities were enthusiastic, but balked at the enormous cost. The wily Citroën recognised an opportunity to achieve matchless promotion for his company, and agreed to fund the cost in exchange for having the Citroën name and logo in lights 98ft high. A staggering 375,000 bulbs in six colours, connected by 800 miles of wiring, constituted the crude mechanics behind an extremely sophisticated system, the effect of which was visible from a distance of 24 miles. The world's biggest clock, with a face 50ft in diameter, was added in 1933, enhanced the following year by Jacopozzi's final project, a massive thermometer of electric lights that reached from the second platform to the top of the tower. There was considerable criticism of what was regarded as rampant commercialisation of the tower, and when Citroën's contract expired in 1936, nothing like it was ever agreed again. In 1937, however, as part of the Exposition Internationale des Arts et Techniques dans la Vie Moderne, the largest chandelier in the world was suspended under the first platform by the architect André Grasset; 6 miles of multicoloured fluorescent tubes were connected to 30 heavy-duty projectors to bathe the tower in spectacular changing light patterns. Lighting the tower has remained a potent area of public interest and concern, and has engendered considerable innovation encompassing gas, incandescent, neon, sodium and xenon technologies. When special lighting was dismantled after the spectacular millennium celebrations in 2001, there was such an outcry that the company had rapidly to spend 5 million euros on a new, permanent display using 20,000 high-technology bulbs installed by 25 mountain climbers.

The tower has also been the subject of numerous scams and scares alleging its removal, sale or modification. In some cases, April Fool stunts were in play: one declared that the tower was to be moved to straddle the Seine, with two feet on the Left Bank and two on the Right; another year's ploy was to suggest that the entire tower was to be dismantled and loaned as a gesture of goodwill to Greece. In the 1960s, the City of Montreal wanted to 'borrow' the tower for the 1967 Expo and when that scheme was quickly rebuffed, attempted to persuade the City of Paris to part-fund the construction of an even taller structure for Montreal; unsurprisingly, this proposal too was rejected.[24] In 1969, there was a serious but unsuccessful proposal to construct an artificial ski-slope from the first platform to the ground, giving a 600ft run to a fake Alpine centre with chalets and skating-rink.[25] One particularly crazed proposal, apparently based on a misunderstanding, occurred in 1974 when a property dealer from South Carolina tried to get planning permission to erect a 1,000ft tower at his local airport. He claimed he had heard an official guide in Paris say that the Eiffel Tower was for sale and reacted as would be expected of any rich American.[26]

These examples represent essentially misguided attempts to cash in on the extraordinary *cachet* of the Eiffel Tower, but there have also been a number of malicious attempts to use the tower in outright swindles. There was a fraud attempt as early as 1891, involving a ludicrous proposal to protect the tower by manufacturing a huge canvas sheath. Later confidence tricks involved 'special' paint, and various instances of attempts to 'recycle' often large parts of the tower's structure. The most spectacular attempted swindle involved an apparently high-ranking state official selling the building for scrap – not once, but twice. 'Count' Victor Lustig (one of his forty aliases) was born in Bohemia in 1890. As a young man, he earned his money as something of a sharp operator in various gambling operations.

He took to the high seas, plying his glib trade among the world's wealthy cruising fraternities, before migrating to the USA during the Prohibition, when he further honed his techniques in a number of lucrative frauds. Moving to Paris in the early 1920s, Lustig became aware of one of the periodic ripples of public concern about the physical condition of the Eiffel Tower. Posing as the deputy director-general of the Ministry of Posts and Telegraphs, he and his associate, 'Dapper Dan' Collins, complete with forged government credentials, arranged a meeting with six leading salvage companies at the sumptuous Hôtel de Crillon on the Place de la Concorde, a popular venue with diplomats and senior government ministers. He opened discussions on the contract for the demolition of the Eiffel Tower – negotiations which, he insisted, would have to be discreet in order to avoid unwelcome public outcry. There was, of course, no attempt to sell the tower; Lustig simply wanted to identify a victim. In this case, André Poisson had hoped for publicity for his business by winning such an important government contract, but ended up by paying several million francs. To compound the fraud, Lustig privately 'confessed' to Poisson that as a government official he was significantly underpaid, and required additional income to support his lifestyle. In addition to the huge contract fee, Poisson was now pressurised to deliver some hefty bribes to Lustig, who immediately left for Austria. By the time the unfortunate Poisson realised what was happening, he also understood that he could not afford the embarrassment of making his situation public. Lustig was so impressed by the simplicity of his scheme that he immediately returned to Paris and repeated the trick with another five companies. This time, the victim contacted the police, but Lustig and Collins escaped and headed back to the USA. In 1935, Lustig was eventually arrested for complicity in a counterfeiting swindle and sentenced to twenty years in Alcatraz. He died there of pneumonia in 1947; in final mockery, his death certificate gave his occupation as 'apprentice salesman'.[27]

Gustave Eiffel would surely have smiled at the irony that, of all the areas of life the Eiffel Tower has influenced, it is generally claimed to have had its greatest effect in the fields of art and literature. Quite apart from the commercial attractions already mentioned, the tower's abstract qualities, its very lack of obvious practical purpose, seemed to inspire a wide range of writers, painters and philosophers in particular; this in a city already crammed with grand architectural symbols. Worse than anything that could have been envisaged by Maupassant, the tower's ubiquitous presence was wholeheartedly adopted and celebrated by city, state and precisely the kind of intellectual elite that had formed the original, abortive protest. Its construction had given rise to dozens of popular songs (some actually mocking the Artists' Protest), with which some of the most popular artists, such as Maurice Chevalier and Mistinguett, became associated. The rigours of the First World War and the Nazi occupation of the Second World War (when all but Germans were barred from the tower, and there were fears that the potent symbol of French nationhood might be demolished by the occupying forces) served to ensure that songs declaring the tower's totemic status were employed at the forefront of Parisian defiance. Perhaps surprisingly, it was not until 1964, when André Malraux was Minister of Culture, that the tower was designated a national monument immune from casual commercial alteration or interference.

The anti-traditionalist surrealist poet Guillaume Apollinaire (originally Apollinaris Kostrowitzky, in his native Polish) referred to the tower as 'the shepherdess of the clouds'. In one of his 'calligrams' – in which the text of the poem is displayed graphically in the shape of the tower, making it particularly difficult to decipher for non-native French speakers – he took the opportunity deliberately to insult the occupying Germans. About the same time, Jean Cocteau wrote several works referring to the tower, but perhaps the most obsessed of the writers was the academic, diplomat and head of the French Ministry of Information, Jean Giraudoux, who wrote about the confidence of the engineer who defied gravity with a beautiful iron rope thrown by a fakir into the sky. Later sociologists and philosophers sought metaphor and explanation in the symbolism of the Eiffel Tower. Le Corbusier, Besset, Foliet and, most notably, the existentialist philosopher, writer and critic Roland Barthes analysed at length what the tower as national symbol actually represented. In his *Mythologies*, Barthes examined the semiology of such cultural phenomena as the tower, noting that just as Eiffel as a child had 'conquered' the city by discovering the magic of Paris, so does the visitor who climbs the tower to contemplate the view. He argued that, being fully useless, the tower was thus free of mundane, earthbound considerations and the requirement for rational description:

> In order to satisfy this great oneiric function, which makes it into a kind of total monument, the tower must escape reason. This first condition of this victorious flight is that the tower be an utterly useless monument. The tower's inutility has always been obscurely felt to be a scandal, i.e., a truth, one that is precious and inadmissible. Even before it was built, it was blamed for being useless, which, it was believed at the time, was sufficient to condemn it; it was not in the spirit of a period commonly dedicated to rationality and to the empiricism of great bourgeois enterprises to endure the notion of a useless object (unless it was declaratively an *objet d'art*, which was also unthinkable in relation to the tower); hence Gustave Eiffel, in his own defence of his project in reply to the Artists' Petition, scrupulously lists all the future uses of the tower; they are all, as we might expect of an engineer, scientific uses: aerodynamic measurements, studies of the resistance of substances, physiology of the climber, radio-electric research, problems of telecommunication, meteorological observations, etc. These are doubtless incontestable, but they seem quite ridiculous alongside the overwhelming myth of the tower, of the human meaning which it has assumed throughout the world. This is because here the utilitarian excuses, however ennobled they may be by the myth of Science, are nothing in comparison to the great imaginary function which enables men to be strictly human.[28]

Le Corbusier, who applauded the tower and its design proportions in particular, said:

I bear witness to the tower as an indefatigable pilgrim who has criss-crossed the world. In the cities, in the savanna, in the pampa, in the desert, on the gats and on the estuaries, everywhere and among the humble as among the others, the tower is in everyone's heart as the sign of a beloved Paris, beloved sign of Paris. Such homage is due to the qualities of a man, of a place and of an epoch.[29]

Garnier and Maupassant would have squirmed. The painters were even more prolific, and they were on the case quickly, with Seurat producing a first stunning pointillist canvas depicting the tower in 1889. The modernists saw in the new structure something of the same aesthetic sense that revered a painting or a sculpture or an object as an end in itself, stripped of the trappings of unnecessary explanation. The cream of European modernist painters – Pissarro, Bonnard, Chagall, Dufy, Rousseau, Picasso and Utrillo – all found fascination in the tower. The most obsessed was Robert Delaunay; his first painting of the tower in 1909 showed what had until then been the clear influence of Cézanne on his work, while the many spectacular later paintings demonstrate his more highly coloured and increasingly Impressionist and Cubist approaches. His friend the traveller, novelist and reluctant poet Blaise Cendrars described Delaunay's passion for his subject:

In 1911 Delaunay did, I believe, fifty-one canvases of the Eiffel Tower before getting the desired result. No art form could come close to the essence of the Eiffel Tower. Realism diminished the impression of height; the old laws of Italian perspective made it look skinny. When we viewed it from a distance, the Tower dominated Paris, as thin as a hat-pin; when we approached it, it seemed to bend and lean over us. Seen from the first platform it twisted like a corkscrew, and seen from the top it appeared to fold in upon itself, legs spread and neck pulled in. Delaunay wanted not only to show the Tower, but to situate it in Paris. Finally he took the Tower apart in order to place it in its natural framework. He truncated it and inclined it to give the impression of vertigo it inspires; he adopted ten different viewpoints, fifteen perspectives so that part of it is seen from below, part from above, while the buildings around it are shown from left and right, from above and below . . .[30]

In 1955, the relationship between the tower and the artists was uniquely celebrated with an exhibition, held on the first platform, of paintings of Paris by Utrillo; the press and critics waxed lyrical about the unique opportunity to put artistic impression side by side with reality.[31]

Cineastes will know that the international film industry has also made considerable use of the Eiffel Tower, both as a symbol of Paris, and as a unique location for action sequences. One thinks perhaps of such later movies as *Superman II* and *A View to a Kill*, but the entire gamut of the greatest French film directors have paid their homage at the Champ de Mars. Lumière, Méliès, René Clair (who insisted that '*La Tour Eiffel est le clocher de mon village*'), Abel Gance, Louis Malle, François Truffaut, Claude Chabrol, Claude Lelouch and many others have all made films at the tower, beginning with a documentary by Louis Lumière in 1897. René Clair had already made a science fiction film in 1924, but returned in 1928 to make *La Tour*, an inspired documentary which portrayed the structure in a highly abstract and physical manner.

Possibly the most memorable film, for a British audience, was the Ealing comedy *The Lavender Hill Mob*, directed in 1951 by Charles Crichton and starring Alec Guinness and Stanley Holloway, with Sidney James, Alfie Bass and momentary appearances by numerous unknowns, such as Audrey Hepburn, who played a cigarette seller. The film's title comes from the down-at-heel part of London where Guinness lives as a Bank of England employee, and it encompasses the classic features of the Ealing Comedy – ordinary people in extraordinary circumstances, circumventing disaster as they had done in wartime, while deriding those national institutions they were fighting to defend. Guinness hatches a plot to steal gold bullion and does a deal with

Holloway, who plays a manufacturer of solid lead, gold-painted paperweights in the form of the Eiffel Tower; in the scam, the paperweights will be made of melted-down gold and shipped to Paris. The pair head for the top of the Eiffel Tower, where Holloway's partner runs a stall selling the lead souvenirs. Typically, she has erroneously sold six of the gold towers to a party of English schoolgirls. Through numerous chases, twists and turns, the film reaches a conclusion in which it seems that Holloway is caught but Guinness escapes – until the final (and unnecessarily moral) twist sees him led off in handcuffs.

Today, the Eiffel Tower seems perhaps a little elderly, and that should be a comfortable realisation. This symbol of what, in its time, carried technological innovation to unthought-of extremes has maybe simply reached a kind of maturity, in an age when people have a dramatically reduced ability to understand the idea of men on huge ladders, high in the sky, beating red-hot rivets with hammers that, today, they themselves could not even think of lifting. We should remember that the man who imagined the tower in all its immensity, and who devised the endless intricacy of its making, knew no keyboard or CAD software. Yet the tower he built, with the other glories of Paris, has never ceased to exercise the minds of those seeking to redefine the significance of civic monuments:

. . . Whatever constitutes the nobility of our capital, it is neither its extent, its richness, nor its antiquity, it is the thought that it expresses. Paris is a city as in control of its direction as was Rome, because 'the ocean of houses' which shelters our material life, relatively low, uniform, is not allowed to be forgotten. The monuments which emerge set the tone and represent elements of the overall French ensemble. Notre-Dame is faith, the l'Institut, the University on Sainte-Geneviève hill are the spiritual life, the Pantheon is service rendered to the nation, l'Élysée is the State, the Louvre is Art and History, the Arc de Triomphe and the Dôme des Invalides are the glory. The Eiffel Tower, so often criticised, should be allowed also to make its statement; from the very start of the century it has affirmed the vitality of the technical culture which has maintained our position in modern competition . . .[32]

Somehow, without our noticing, the tower has passed from the realms of excitement and originality to those of nostalgia and a rather old-fashioned respect. No bad thing. Yet, plaything to even more touring masses than ever, the tower is still the same tower that was opened with such celebration in May 1889, and its future seems as secure as ever. Meanwhile, the name of the man who had appeared destined for provincial obscurity as a vinegar manufacturer, and whose name is uniquely synonymous with his creation, has become one of international renown.

TWELVE

Whither Tallest?

When Koechlin and Nouguier showed the first sketch for their proposed tower to Gustave Eiffel, it had already been determined that the exhibition would build the tallest man-made structure in the world. They had joined the ancient and mysterious urge to demonstrate power and authority by building high. They also intended to build a structure that would be iconic, and while it is no longer the tallest building, it retains its position as an icon of, and for, France, and a uniquely memorable feature in a world full of unique structures. One thinks perhaps of Roebling's Brooklyn Bridge in New York, the Taj Mahal, the Great Wall of China, the Forth Railway Bridge, the Statue of Liberty or, in a different way, the magnificent 125ft-high Statue of Christ of 1931 by Heitor da Silva and Paul Landowsky that envelops Rio de Janeiro in its outstretched arms from its position on Mount Corcovado almost two and a half thousand feet above the city.

The Eiffel Tower retained its position as the world's highest building until 1930, when, in the space of thirty minutes, a 180ft latticed-steel needle weighing 28 tons was lifted by crane to the top of the just-completed art deco Chrysler Building in New York, making it at 1,046ft the tallest building in the world (this was before the Eiffel Tower acquired its television antenna, which enabled it to reach 1,052ft 4in). The Chrysler was already under construction when it was broadcast that a new Bank of Manhattan building would reach two feet higher than the Chrysler's planned height – hence the added needle. Skyscraper mania had been apparent in New York long before the construction of the Chrysler building. At the turn of the nineteenth century, the famous Flatiron Building was erected (immortalised in an equally famous photograph by Alfred Stieglitz), to be followed in 1913 by the Woolworth Building, astutely described by its designer as 'the cathedral of commerce'. The desperation to outdo all others that was to become such a feature of skyscraper building was born. Cities, developers and architects have long argued about how to identify 'tallest'. Most now agree that only a structure primarily built for human occupancy may qualify; this would negate the claims of, for example, the 1975 CN Tower in Toronto (1,815ft) and, retrospectively according to some, the Eiffel Tower itself. Even with the main criterion decided in recent years, arguments persisted; if rooftop antennae were to be allowed, then the 1974 Sears Tower in Chicago, at 1,730ft would have been the highest. However, the acknowledged arbiter in these matters, the Council on Tall Buildings and Urban Habitat, based in Chicago, decided in favour of the 1997 twin Petronas Towers in Kuala Lumpur in Malaysia, which stand 1,483ft high.[1] Objectors nevertheless claim that the tops of these towers are wholly decorative, and that the Sears Tower deserved primacy, since it had the highest occupied floor (1,431ft) and the highest 'natural' roof (1,454ft).

The Chrysler Building did not maintain its 1930s blue-riband position for long. Within a year, New York's Empire State Building was topped out at 1,250ft – a height that included a 200ft 'mooring tower', allegedly intended to attract passing airships, but almost certainly added as a means of securing a height advantage that would preserve its pre-eminence for some time. By this time, New York's signature skyline was already well established, with nearly 200 skyscrapers, many of which were artificially heightened during construction by additional floors, pylons, antennae and decorative rooftop features, as news was received of the latest competitor. The scramble to join the sky bandwagon was intense, with new projects regularly announcing new attempts to break records. The only question in town, from developer to engineer, was 'how high can we go?' Scarcity of real estate on Manhattan was the excuse; the half-truth was macho self-promotion by builders and associated corporate desire for image. The real truth was that many such proposals never proceeded beyond the froth of the publicity launch. Those that did rise from the drawing-boards were often so precariously speculative that their futures were never anything other than highly doubtful. Even the celebrated Empire State Building, with thirty of its eighty-six floors still unoccupied eighteen months after opening, was widely lampooned as 'The Empty State Building'. Nevertheless, after its erection, the ideal of the Seven Wonders of the World was re-examined and the Empire State Building joined a list comprising the Great Pyramids, Hagia Sophia in Istanbul, the Leaning Tower of Pisa, the Washington Monument, the Eiffel Tower and the Taj Mahal.

Controversy continues over what height can be attained. Some believe that towers can be built a mile high using existing technology. Others claim that materials offering greater lightness and strength will be required, coupled with improved damping systems to reduce sway, and faster elevators built to more radical designs. However, the 'mile-high' concept is already fifty years old. In 1956, the visionary American architect Frank Lloyd Wright proposed the Illinois, a mile-high building sheathed in aluminium and stainless steel. The 528-storey tower would have accommodated 100,000 people, parking for 15,000 cars and sufficient office space to accommodate the entire state bureaucracy. This building never came near to reality, but Wright was adamant that it could be built using known technology of the period. Much high-flown rhetoric persists today in the realms of imaginative planning of future tall buildings, but there is an explanation if not a justification. Many proposed buildings have not materialised simply because they served essentially as conceptual models for technologies not yet attainable.

A feature of tall-building design that, more than any other, has dominated the issue of attainable height has been elevator design; the more obviously critical features, such as strength of construction materials and dynamic stability, have all been subordinated to that prickly question. 'Smart' elevators, which ascend at increasingly rapid speeds, or which allow transfer between express and local chains, do not solve the problem. As a building reaches higher, there are more people to transport and more floors to serve; as these two factors increase, elevator provision has to increase to match. The catch is that every elevator significantly reduces floor space, a factor that becomes increasingly critical as the building's height increases and achievable floor area decreases; this is the decisive financial equation that may be the final obstacle for developers. Standard theory set a limit at less than 150 floors; beyond that height it was reckoned that there would always be insufficient width to accommodate the number of elevators required. Another problem deriving from the need to have so many elevator shafts running vertically through buildings is that the structure demands more rigidity than would otherwise be required, simply to prevent elevators jamming in the shafts as the building flexes under normal wind conditions. As with Dr Hénocque and his physiological experiments at the Eiffel Tower, there are similar questions affecting the use of express lifts carrying people vertically at speed in enclosed spaces. A related area of continuing interest to skyscraper developers is the concept of what has become known as 'psychological waiting-time standards'.[2]

The 'Windy City' of Chicago looked set to gain the lead from the Petronas Towers with the expected construction of 7 South Dearborn, a slender, 1,567ft, mixed residential and office tower with television antennae bringing its total height to the suspiciously round figure of 2,000ft. However, the project was abandoned in early 2001 when financial arrangements disintegrated. Despite the aftermath of the atrocity of the destruction of the World Trade Center Twin Towers in New York in September 2001, the urge to build even taller has perhaps surprisingly not been halted, although new demands are increasingly likely to include additional pressurised stairwells for improved evacuation, and the provision of dedicated, protected, high-speed lifts reserved for rescue teams. Before 1930, all the world's tallest buildings were in the USA; today, the United States boasts only seven of the twenty tallest. More than ever, the impetus is coming from the Far East; in October 2003, Taipei 101 became the tallest building in the world when its 197ft spire was fixed in position, completing the structure of the 1,667ft steel, concrete and glass building. When completed, this two billion dollar, 90-storey building will house the Taiwan Stock Exchange, a shopping mall and offices for 12,000 people. Taipei 101 will have the world's fastest lifts, thirty-four double-decked cars travelling at 37mph, and while it has been constructed to withstand aeroplane attacks, severe storms and earthquakes above 7 on the Richter scale, it is a gloomy portent that in an earthquake during construction five people were killed when two cranes toppled from the building. Following its completetion, it is thought that the building may have initiated two recent earthquakes due to stresses exerted on the ground beneath; if this is so, there could be unforeseen and far-reaching implications for such man-made megastructures.

The pre-eminence of today's technology is largely unencumbered by the artistic backlashes of former decades; enormous financial implications constitute the main barrier to the continuing obsession with building high. Despite the apparent rush to continue seeking the grail of 'the world's tallest', there are concerns about falling public confidence. At a conference sponsored by the Council on Tall Buildings and Urban Habitat in Kuala Lumpur in the autumn of 2003, it was agreed that, in the aftermath of the destruction of the World Trade Center Twin Towers in New York, society was concerned about the safety and security of tall buildings, and that the international engineering community was expected to provide answers. Despite the huge technical and even-greater financial problems, the urge to continue building tall is usually claimed by architects and developers to be justified by demographic, cultural and even environmental concerns. In particular, population growth and rapidly increasing urbanisation are offered as the principal driving forces; perhaps it would be better for everyone if these two perfect examples of pressures on humanity were resisted and reduced rather than exacerbated.

Nevertheless, there continues to be what some regard as a surfeit of aspirational projects; Hong Kong has a conceptual Bionic Tower, mimicking structures found in trees, and planned to reach 4,029ft, four times the height of the Eiffel Tower. The designers of the World Trade Center are involved in what is expected to become the world's tallest building in 2008. The Centre of India Tower at Katangi in Madhya Pradesh, in the centre of the subcontinent, will be a 224-storey, 2,235ft, pyramid-shaped world headquarters for the Maharishi Mahesh Yogi. There are proposals for 1,970ft towers in both Tokyo and Dubai, and two 1,800ft towers in Seoul. One such scheme for a 'city within a city' includes shopping malls, entertainment and leisure, open spaces, pedestrian boulevards and even an 'old town'.

New ideas appear by the month and at any one time there are probably more than fifty proposals that would break the 'tallest' record. Some plans are for traditional skyscrapers that go relatively quickly into construction; others derive more from the ambitions of architectural, engineering and ecosystems theoreticians. The Japanese concept of the 'Ultima Tower' envisages a 2-mile-high 'sky city' accommodating a million people on 500 floors. This concept has a trumpet bell-shaped base of 7,000ft, capable of encompassing, for example, the entire financial district of San Francisco. It would contain four of the world's largest waterfalls surrounded by garden terraces in a series of interlinked ecosystems; 144 stacked elevators would stop at thirty floors simultaneously, and energy systems are suggested that are as imaginative as the overall concept. The skyscraping cost is in excess of 150 billion US dollars.[3] Tokyo has been the target of conceptual plans for projects by the name of Sky City, at 3,281ft, and Mother, at 4,333ft. An unfulfilled project by Sir Norman Foster for a massive, conical Millennium Tower in Tokyo Bay, with 170 storeys housing 52,000 people, would have been 2,625ft in height. Work on this self-contained city (deriving from the supposedly limitless Radiant City social engineering concept of Le Corbusier) never left the drawing-board, but there are hopes that potential financiers will still be identified; the same architect has plans for a similar 2,952ft tower in Shanghai. One equally inventive project that may be nearer to becoming reality is not a tower in the sense that it will house or accommodate people. This is an Australian plan for a convection tower 425ft wide and half a mile high, rising from a massive complex of greenhouses four and a half miles in diameter; the system will generate enough electricity for 200,000 houses by drawing warm air from its base through thirty-two turbines. The federal government in New South Wales placed the scheme in a fast-track planning process in August 2002, and the first electricity was expected to be generated in 2005.[4]

A hugely significant cultural and technological marker will be manifested by the rebuilding of the World Trade Center site in New York. The destruction of the Twin Towers in September 2001 was, apart from the associated horrors, a massive blow to the design and engineering community for the simple reason that the towers probably collapsed because of the advances in technology they exemplified: they were among the earliest skyscrapers to be built using no masonry whatsoever. The towers were essentially hollow steel tubes, comprising tightly packed steel columns with light steel floor trusses radiating from the core to the perimeter; this approach improved wind stability and, by eliminating interior columns, effectively increased floor space. Although the towers were built to withstand aircraft impact, what was not foreseen was deliberate attack by impacting aircraft fully loaded with up to 24,000 gallons of aviation fuel, which burns at temperatures up to 1,500°C. Fireproofing was completely inadequate against such hydrocarbon fire, and the lightweight steel floor trusses quickly succumbed, fatally damaging the entire structural integrity. Research has indicated three prime remedies – the need for stronger structures less vulnerable to the failure of individual elements leading to loss of integrity; better fire protection, coupled with gas-tight compartmentalisation to reduce the spread of fire; and greatly improved escape and evacuation facilities and procedures.

The decision to rebuild on the World Trade Center site was taken extremely rapidly. In a fevered atmosphere of public grief, blame and loss of confidence, development briefs were designed, an international competition held and the winning design by the Polish-born German architect Daniel Libeskind announced – all within eighteen months. Inspired by the Statue of Liberty, his proposal is for a 1,776ft Freedom Tower (commemorating the signing in 1776 of the Declaration of Independence) surrounded by a cluster of four smaller towers, due for completion in 2008 and costing almost two billion dollars. The destruction of the Twin Towers will be commemorated by creating a large open space, which will be illuminated by the sun each year on 11 September between 8.46 a.m., when the first hijacked plane crashed into the towers, and 10.28 a.m. when the second tower collapsed. Details of the construction seem destined not to be agreed for some considerable time, however, with the architect and the site's lease-holder and developers in continuing disagreement. At the time of writing, arguments over the proposal are still on-going, and there are complex financial problems involving the insurance payouts made after the collapse of the Twin Towers. Political power-broking has a long course to run; 8 million New Yorkers feel their voice should be more clearly heard, and the city seems headed for recession. It may be that the Freedom Tower will have a lengthy gestation.

Perhaps the day of the tower is drawing to a close, but one spectacular new theory of the tower as 'space elevator' for the end of the twenty-first century possibly owes its conception to the Eiffel Tower. In 1895, the Russian father of astronautics and rocket dynamics, Konstantin Tsiolkovsky, looked at Eiffel's masterpiece and envisaged a 'celestial castle' 22,400 miles in space, at the end of what he thought of as a 'space tower'. This idea, of a solid structure from the face of the earth into space, is now characterised as a 'space elevator' and would provide the ability to launch people, objects and materials into earth orbit without using rockets.[5] The concept was further developed in the 1960s by the Russian Yuri Artsutanov, and is currently being refined by Nasa's Marshall Space Flight Center at Huntsville, Alabama. In essence, such a system would build a 22,000-mile 'ladder' along which electromagnetic vehicles would transfer people and material from earth to a geo-stationary transfer station. As the vehicle rides along the 'ladder' it would attain orbit velocity, and so would maintain a geosynchronous orbit between the Earth and the destination space station. More-extremist theories suggest a space elevator from the Moon to the Earth, which would involve building the elevator cable 325,000 miles in length. Current research, involving carbon nanotechnology 100 times stronger than steel, is intended to prove the feasibility and advantages of such a space elevator system, and will also examine the potential for applying the concept to other engineering applications. Without doubt, while conventional skyscrapers and towers continue to be designed, argued over and built, passionate visionary engineers will continue to move technology forward in steps that will appear to be out of this world.

December 2004 saw the opening of the Milau Viaduct over the Tarn Gorge in the Massif Central near the old glove-making town of Milau on the A75 route from Paris to Barcelona. This spectacular, 2.4 km-long, cable-stayed bridge, is a brilliant example of collaboration between French and British designers and engineers. While challenging the design and engineering supremacy of Eiffel's Garabit Viaduct, it also constantly refers to his genius. It was designed by Norman Foster & Partners and Michael Virlogeux (designer of the Pont de Normandie) and engineered by Europe's sixth largest engineering consortium, Eiffage, which incorporates the Eiffel company. Like the Eiffel tower, the bridge displays an extraordinary, almost ethereal delicacy. The tallest of its seven trapezoidal piers is higher than the tower, and it is already the focus of the kind of international interest that the tower attracted. Although it was constructed and aligned with the aid of GPS instruments, most of the high-grade steel deck was prefabricated from thousands of accurately designed pieces in the Alsace workshops of Eiffage. Gustav Eiffel would undoubtedly have applauded that technique as much as the bold assertion that engineering in the landscape could indeed be a work of art.

Gustave Eiffel's zeal for his extraordinary tower has been vindicated in ways that he could never have imagined. This spectacular structure which, if many had had their way would have been swiftly demolished, has survived into its second century without the slightest hint of structural setback or popular objection. As a symbol of the City of Paris and the nationhood of France, it has endured war and enemy occupation and all manner of commercial exploitation. In addition, it has suffered the sadly predictable attention of exhibitionists and demonstrators who, recognising its supreme iconic status, have continued to attach their obsessions to the one structure that above all others would assure them of publicity. It has achieved unique worldwide recognition and popularity. During its first ninety-four years it welcomed 100 million visitors, but only another nineteen years passed before that number doubled, and in the winter of 2002 the anonymous 200-millionth visitor entered the massive iron maze as 1,200 VIPs attended a sumptuous celebratory dinner on the first platform.

Gustave Eiffel had confidence and pride in his work from the beginning, despite the passionate criticism directed against him during the Artists' Protest. Today, it is accepted that, with not a single extraneous feature, the tower is a perfect union of form and function. At the end of his life, Eiffel felt that he had at least reconciled engineers and scientists, if not the more volatile artistic community. Above all else, his own satisfaction was subsumed within a greater pride in the tradition of supreme French craftsmanship.

He was fiercely proud of his great tower, which he regarded as the most striking example of modern French national genius:

If judged by the interest they inspire, both in France and abroad, I believe that my efforts have not been fruitless and that we can tell the world that France remains at the forefront of progress, and that she has been the first to be able to realise such an often attempted and dreamed-of project. Man has always sought to erect buildings of a great height as a manifestation of power, but he soon recognised that the means were severely limited. It is only by the progress of science and art and of the metallurgical industry, which distinguishes our century, that we are able to overtake preceding generations by the construction of this tower, which will be one of the characteristics of modern industry, since the tower alone has made it possible.[6]

No other building or structure in history has borne the name of its designer and builder with such unique clarity of identity. It might amuse or exasperate Gustave Eiffel to witness the extent to which his masterpiece has become the plaything of millions; but this now elderly, somewhat ungainly edifice has earned for itself an exceptional place in history. It is right and proper to believe that the once mutually exclusive creeds of Art and Industry have both contributed to that historical appraisal. That would please *'le maître du fer'*.

Works by Eiffel's Company

(This list is based partly on that published by L'Association des Descendants de Gustave Eiffel on their website: www.gustaveeiffel.com)

Railway Bridges

1860–61	Bayonne Bridge, Bordeaux–Bayonne line, Pyrénées-Atlantiques, France
	Capdenac Bridge on the Lot, and Floriac Bridge on the Dordogne, Brive-Rodez line, Gers, France
1867	Bridges on the Orsay–Limours line, Essonne, France
	Bridges on the Poitiers–Limoges line, France
	Rouzat and Neuvial Viaducts, Allier, France
1869	Montpellier Bridge at Pauhlan, Hérault, France
	Mézy Bridge, Yvelines, France
	Bridges on the Cahors–Vibos line, Lot, France
1870	Bridges on the Latour-sur-Orb–Milhau line, Aveyron, France
	Bridges on the Brive–Tulle line, Corrèze, France
1872	Thouars Viaduct, Deux-Sèvres, France
	Bridges on the Jassy–Ungheni line, Romania
1873	Ornans Bridge, Doubs, France
	Champagne Bridge at Thémery, Marne, France
	Villandraut Bridge, Gironde, France
	Bridges on the Orléans–Gien line, Loiret, France
1874	Bridges on the Oroya, Peru
	Bridges on the Bressuire–Tours line, Deux-Sèvres, France

Magdalena Bridge, Colombia

Louviers Bridge, Eure, France

Amboise Bridge, Indre-et-Loire, France

Bridges at Chinon on the Vienne; at Tours on the Cher; and at Azay-le-Rideau on the Indre, France

1875 Bridges in the Bernese Jura, Switzerland

Bridge at Tombo de Viso, Portugal

Bridges on the Chinon–Joué line, Indre-et-Loire, France

Bridges on the Poitiers–Saumur line, Maine-et-Loire, France

Bridges on the Epinay–Luzarches line, Val-d'Oise, France

Clichy Bridge, Hauts-de-Seine, France

1876 Bridges on the Girona line, Spain

Maria Pia Bridge on the Douro, Portugal

1877 Bridges at Cavado, Ancora, Vianna, Ville Mea and Neiva in Portugal

Bridge on the Tâmega and the viaduct at Palla in Portugal

The Muga Bridge, Spain

Bridge on the Clain, France

1878 Bridges at Empalot, Valentine and Sarrieu, Haute-Garonne, France

Bridges on the Cáceres line, Spain

Bridges at Teticala and Cuenta, Mexico

Bergerac Bridge, Dordogne, France

Niherne Bridge, Indre, France

Buzançais Bridge, Indre, France

1879 Bridges on the Ploiesti–Predeal line, Romania

Bridge at Moutiers-sur-le-Lay, Vienne, France

1880 Bridges at Vaizeas, Trezaï, Côa, Deo, Beira Baixa, Frezse, Noemi, Meligroso, Criz, Cazillas, Perala, Tiétar, Gouveïa, Celerico and Breda on the Beira–Alta line, Portugal

Bridge on the Tagus, Spain

Bridges at Tamujoso, Grande, Val de Haza and

	Guadancil on the Cáceres line, Spain
	Bridges at Cazillas, Perala and Ollas, Spain
	Bridges at Binh-Dien, Tan-An and Ben-Luc in Vietnam
1881	Evaux Viaduct on the Tardes, Creuse, France
	Normanville Bridge, Calvados, France
1882	Conversion of the Bergerac Bridge on the Dordogne, France, to a road bridge
	Garabit Viaduct, Cantal, France
	Six bridges on the Asturias line, Galica y León, Spain
1883	Charenton Bridge, Val-de-Marne, France
	Transportable bridges, Senegal
1884	Three bridges at Alcántara, Spain
	Châteauroux Bridge, Indre, France
	Bridge on RN 121 at Chaudes-Aigues, Cantal, France
1885	Fifteen bridges on the Lisbon–Cintra line, Portugal
	Transportable bridges, Morbihan, France
	Bridge at La Fère, Aisne, France
1886	Collonge Viaduct on the Saône, Côte-d'Or, France
	Bridges at Evreux, Eure, France
1887	Thirty-seven bridges on the Fréjus–Saint-Raphaël line, Var, France
1888	Bridges on the Poco de Bispo–Carregado line, Portugal
1889	Bridges on the Nindas Novas–Santarém line, Portugal
1889–90	Conflans-Sainte-Honorine Viaduct, Yvelines, France
1890–92	Bridges at Almonda, Alviella, Asseca, Bleone, Ribeira, Modego and Cocuminho on the Lisbon–Badaroz line, Portugal
1891	Bridges on the Jaffa–Jerusalem line, Israel
	Bridges on the Saint-André–Nice line, Alpes-Maritimes, France
	Font Lauguières Viaduct on the Grasse–Mande line, Alpes-Maritimes, France
1892	Three viaducts on the Mezzana–Corte line, Corsica

	Decking for 108 bridges in China
1893	Bridge on the Vesle, Aisne, France
	Saint-Pierre-de-Vauvray Viaduct, Seine-Maritime, France
	Bridge at rue Chanteraine, Epinal, Vosges, France
1893–95	Bridges on the Saint-Pierre–les Andelys line, Eure, France
1894	La Taillée Viaduct on the Châteaubriant–Saint Nazaire line, Loire-Atlantique, France
1895	Two bridges on the Ryazan–Uralsk line, Russia
	Bridges on the Glos Montfort–Pont Audemer line, Eure, France
	Lou-Kou-Tiao Bridge, Petchili, China
1895–96	Bezons Bridge on the Seine, Val-d'Oise, France
	Bridges in Charente, France
	Bridge at Binh Dien, Vietnam
1895–97	Mahinady Bridge, Sudan
1896	Bridges on the Saint Jean and the Bras de la Plaine, La Réunion
1898–1900	Bridges on the Courcelles–Champ de Mars line, Paris, France

Road Bridges

1867	Bridge in the Buttes-Chaumont Park, Paris, France
	Bridge at La Rochelle, Charente-Maritime, France
1868–69	Bridge on the Marne at Château-Thierry, Aisne, France
1869	Footbridge, Aisne, France
	Footbridges on the dams on the Seine and the Yonne, France
	Footbridge on the Doloir, France
	Escurolles Bridge, Allier, France
1870	Swing Bridge at Dieppe, Seine-Maritime, France
1873	Salamleck Footbridge, Guiseh, Egypt
	Bridges on the Moselle, France
	La Paz Bridge, Bolivia

1876	Castelo Bridge, Portugal
1877	Footbridge at Port Said, Egypt
1878	Péault Bridge on the Lay, Vendée, France
	Footbridge on the Guell at Girona, Spain
1879	Savonnières Bridge on the Cher, Indre-et-Loire, France
	Bridge at Oued Djemma, Algeria
	Saint-Laurent-sur-Sèvre Bridge, Vendée, France
	Campina Bridge, Romania
1880	Cazères Bridge on the Adour, France
	Sidi Moussa Bridge, Algeria
	Cubzac Bridge on the Dordogne, France
1881	Szegedin Bridge, Hungary
1882	Messageries Bridge, Saigon, Vietnam
	Bridges at Ong Nui, Rach Lang and Dong Nhyen, Vietnam
1883	Sainte-Claire Bridge, Oléron, Charente Maritime, France
1884	Cholon Bridge, Vietnam
	Two canal bridges at Coimbra, Portugal
	Transportable bridges in Italy and Russia
	Bridge on the Michelotti, Turin, Italy
1885	Morannes Bridge on the Sarthe, Maine-et-Loire, France
1886	Montélimar Bridge, Drôme, France
	Bridge at Oued Seguin, Algeria
	Saint Pierre Bridge, Martinique
1887	Bridges at Lang Son and Binh Tay, Vietnam
	Castelsarrasin Footbridge, Tarn-et-Garonne, France
	Four bridges in Panama
	Footbridges on the Bonnard Canal at Cho Lon and at Logonn, Vietnam
1888	Monistrol-d'Allier Bridge, Haute-Loire, France
	Milagro Aqueduct, Spain
1889	Briare Canal Bridge, Loiret, France
	Quoi Duo Footbridge, Vietnam
1889–90	Lifting bridges at Tân An and My Tho, Vietnam

	Bridge at Venda Moras, Portugal
	Lifting bridge at Larrey, Dijon, France
1890	Footbridge of Notre Dame de la Garde, Marseilles, France
	Ayala Bridge on the Rio Passig, Manila, Philippines
	Santa Cruz Bridge, Laguna, Philippines
1891	Saint-Cloud Aqueduct, Hauts-de-Seine, France
	Bridges in Guinea and Mayotte
	Simala Bridge, Cebu, Philippines
	Bridge on the Bras Danon, La Réunion
	Bridge on the Ouenghi, New Caledonia
	Saint Pierre Bridge, Martinique
1891–93	Bridges at Oued Missa and Ighzer Sfaïa, Algeria
	Bridges at Rach Gia and Long Xuyen, Vietnam
1892	Bridges at Ainn Smara and Mencha, Algeria
	Bridge at Lai-Choueï-Hsien, China
	Bridge at Grenoble, France
1892–93	Bridges at Tanauan and Calamba, Batangas, Philippines
	San Miguel de Mayuno Bridge, Belacau, Philippines
	Bridges at Saint-Cyr and Gautreau on the Clain, Vienne, France
	Bridges at Saint-Martin-la-Rivière and Availles, Vienne, France
	Saint Aviol Bridge on the Charente, Vienne, France
1892–94	Four bridges on route No. 3, Cho Lon–Vaïco, Vietnam
	Two bridges on the Rach Cat and the Rach Can Tram, Vietnam
1893	Footbridge at Bry-sur-Marne, Val-de-Marne, France
	Ayala Bridge, Philippines
	Bridge on rue Michel Bizot, Paris
1893–95	Bridges on the Rach Cat, the Rach Tra and Rach Dong Trong, Vietnam
1894	Moussarah Bridge, Palestine
1894–97	Bridge on the Nile at Nag Abou Hamadi, Egypt
1895	Bridge on the Rio Janipan, Iloilo, Philippines

	Bridge at Puteaux, Hauts-de-Seine, France
1896	Folding bridge, Argentina
1897	Bridge in Sudan
	Bridge on the Khur Canal, Iraq
1897–98	Bridge on the Thanh Da Canal, Vietnam

Iron Buildings

1866	Railway Station at Toulouse, Haute-Garonne, France
	Railway Station at Agen, Lot-et-Garonne, France
1867	Beaux-Arts and Archaeology Galleries, 1867 Exposition, Paris
	Church of Notre Dame des Champs, Paris, France
	Synagogue in rue des Tournelles, Paris, France
1868–69	Church of Saint Joseph, Paris
1869	Railway Station at Verdun, Meuse, France
1870	Games hall at the Frères de Passy School, Paris, France
1871	Custom-house at Arica, Chile
1875	Pest Railway Station, Budapest, Hungary
	Chinon Railway Station, Indre-et-Loire, France
	Church of San Marcos, Arica, Chile
	Church at Tacna, Peru
	Church at Manila, Philippines
1876	Lycée Carnot, Paris, France
1877	Grand Vestibule and Domes for the Exposition of 1878, Paris, France
1878	Restoration at Portbou, Spain
1879	Extension of the Bon Marché, Paris, France
	Annexe to Grand Magasins of the Louvre, Paris, France
1881	Head office for Crédit Lyonnais, Paris, France
	Railway Stations at San Sebastián and Santander, Spain
1882	Capucins Market, Bordeaux, France
	Villaverde Studios, Madrid, Spain
1884	Galliéra Museum, Paris, France

Biscuit factory at île Saint Germain, Hauts-de-Seine, France

Steel workshops at Pagny sur Meuse, Meuse, France

1885   Railway stations on the Lisbon–Cintra line, Portugal

1889–90   Railway station workshops, Santa Polonia, Lisbon, Portugal

Locomotive restoration at Villa Nova and Gaia, Portugal

1892   Shops and docks at Beirut, Lebanon

Vinegar factory, Orléans, Loiret, France

1895   Factory workshops, Le Havre, Seine-Maritime, France

1896   Church of Santa Rosalina, Mexico

1897   Iron decking, Gare des Invalides, Paris

Gasworks

1868   Versailles and Poissy, Yvelines, France

Boulogne, Hauts-de-Seine, France

1869   Ternes and Courcelles, Paris, France

1873   La Paz, Bolivia, and Tacna, Peru

1876   La Villette, Paris, France

Yvry, Val-de-Marne, France

1878   Clichy, Hauts-de-Seine, France

1883   Rennes, Ile-et-Vilaine, France

1885   Vannes, Morbihan, France

Miscellaneous Construction

1868   Théâtre Les Folies, Paris, France

1869   Seine barrage Lock gates at Yonne, France

1870   Lighthouses, France

1872   Jetty at Arica, Chile

1874   Lock gates for dam at Moscow, Russia

1875   Casino at les-Sables-d'Olonne, Vendée, France

Windmill at Larrieu, France

Lighthouse at Dagenort

	Railway lighting gantries and reservoirs, France
1876	Jetty at Chala, Peru
1878	Department store, Mulhouse, Haut-Rhin, France
	Saint Nicholas lighthouse, Manila, Philippines
1881	Framework for the Statue of Liberty, New York, USA
1882	Mobile cupola for the Paris Observatory, France
1884	Dam on the Seine at Port Mort, Eure, France
1885	Cupola for the Nice Observatory, Alpes-Maritimes, France
	Locks at Port-Villez, Yvelines, France
1886	Market hall at Constantine, Algeria
	Cupola for Equatorial Telescope at Nice, France
	Market hall at Long Chau, Vietnam
	Department stores, rues de Lorraine and d'Alsace, Paris, France
1887	Market hall at Coalanh, Vietnam
1887–89	Eiffel Tower, Paris, France
	Locks for the Panama Canal
1888	Market halls at O Mon and Trahuse, Vietnam
1889	Market halls at Tân An and Tan Qui Dong, Vietnam
	Warehouse at Dunkirk, Nord, France
1890	Wharf at Pauillac, Gironde, France
	Meteorological laboratory at Sèvres, Hauts-de-Seine, France
1892	Club Equitos, Peru (originally a pavilion of the 1889 Exposition)
1894	Lock gates at Creil, Pontoise, France
1896–97	Wharves, Saigon, Vietnam
1899	Wharf at Tamatave, Madagascar
1901	Meteorological laboratory, Beaulieu, Alpes-Maritimes, France
1902	Meteorological laboratory, Vacquey, Gironde, France
1906	Meteorological laboratory, Ploumanach, Côte du Nord, France
1912	Aerodynamics laboratory, Paris, France
1917	Prototype single-seat aircraft

Eiffel's Honoured Scientists

The seventy-two names engraved on the four faces of the tower's frieze at the level of the first platform:

Opposite the Trocadéro:

1. Seguin (Mechanic)
2. Lalande (Astronomer)
3. Tresca (Engineer and Mechanic)
4. Poncelet (Geometrician)
5. Bresse (Mathematician)
6. Lagrange (Geometrician)
7. Belanger (Mathematician)
8. Cuvier (Naturalist)
9. Laplace (Astronomer)
10. Dulong (Physicist)
11. Chasles (Geometrician)
12. Lavoisier (Chemist)
13. Ampère (Mathematician and Physicist)
14. Chevreul (Chemist)
15. Flachat (Engineer)
16. Navier (Mathematician)
17. Legendre (Geometrician)
18. Chaptal (Agronomist and Chemist)

Opposite Grenelle

19. Jamin (Physicist)
20. Gay-Lussac (Chemist)

21. Fizeau (Physicist)
22. Schneider (Industrialist)
23. Le Chatelier (Engineer)
24. Berthier (Mineralogist)
25. Barral (Agronomist, Chemist, Physicist)
26. De Dion (Engineer)
27. Goüin (Engineer and Industrialist)
28. Jousselin (Engineer)
29. Broca (Surgeon)
30. Becquerel (Physicist)
31. Coriolis (Mathematician)
32. Cail (Industrialist)
33. Triger (Engineer)
34. Giffard (Engineer)
35. Perrier (Geographer and Mathematician)
36. Sturm (Mathematician)

Opposite the Military Academy

37. Cauchy (Mathematician)
38. Belgrand (Engineer)
39. Regnault (Chemist and Physicist)
40. Fresnel (Physicist)
41. De Prony (Engineer)
42. Vicat (Engineer)
43. Ebelmen (Chemist)
44. Coulomb (Physicist)
45. Poinsot (Mathematician)
46. Foucault (Physicist)
47. Delaunay (Astronomer)
48. Morin (Mathematician and Physicist)
49. Haüy (Mineralogist)
50. Combes (Engineer and Metallurgist)
51. Thénard (Chemist)
52. Arago (Astronomer and Physicist)
53. Poisson (Mathematician)
54. Monge (Geometrician)

Appendix 2

Opposite the view of Paris

55. Petiet (Engineer)
56. Daguerre (Painter and Physicist)
57. Wurtz (Chemist)
58. Le Verrier (Astronomer)
59. Perdonnet (Engineer)
60. Delambre (Astronomer)
61. Malus (Physicist)
62. Bréguet (Physicist and Constructor)
63. Polonceau (Engineer)
64. Dumas (Chemist)
65. Clapeyron (Engineer)
66. Borda (Mathematician)
67. Fourier (Mathematician)
68. Bichat (Anatomist and Physiologist)
69. Sauvage (Mechanic)
70. Pelouze (Chemist)
71. Carnot (Mathematician)
72. Lamé (Geometrician)

Films Featuring the Eiffel Tower

Year	Title	Director
1897	*Panorama Pendant l'Ascension de la Tour Eiffel* (Documentary)	Louis Lumière
1900	*Images de l'Exposition 1900* (Documentary)	Georges Méliès
1905	*La Course à la Perruque*	Georges Hatot
1912	*Fantomas*	Louis Feuillade
1923	*Paris qui Dort*	René Clair
1924	*La Cité Foudroyée*	Luitz Morat
1927	*Mystères de la Tour Eiffel*	Julien Duvivier
	La Tour (Documentary)	René Clair
1930	*La Fin du Monde*	Abel Gance
1939	*Ninotchka*	Ernst Lubitsch
1942	*Monsieur la Souris*	Georges Lacombe
1945	*A l'Assaut de la Tour Eiffel*	Alain Pol
1949	*The Man on the Eiffel Tower*	Burgess Meredith
1950	*The Lavender Hill Mob*	Charles Crichton
1952	*Bonjour Paris*	Jean Image
1955	*Marguerite de la Nuit*	Claude Autant-Lara
1956	*Le Chanteur de Mexico*	Richard Pottier
1959	*Tour Eiffel Idylle*	Louis Cuny
1960	*Zazie dans le Métro*	Louis Malle
1963	*Les Plus Belles Escroqueries du Monde: L'Homme qui Vendit la Tour Eiffel*	Claude Chabrol
1965	*The Great Race*	Blake Edwards
1966	*Les Cinq Dernières Minutes – La Rose de Fer* (Claude Loursais TV police series)	Jean-Pierre Marchand

	Un Idiot à Paris	Serge Korber
1968	*Paris Jamais Vu* (Documentary)	Albert Lamorisse
1980	*Superman II*	Richard Lester
1981	*Les Uns et les Autres*	Claude Lelouch
	La Tour Eiffel en Otage	Claude Guzman
1983	*Le Ruffian*	José Giovanni
	Vivement Dimanche	François Truffaut
1984	*Rive Droite – Rive Gauche*	Philippe Labro
1985	*A View to a Kill*	John Glen
1989	*Un Monde sans Pitié*	Eric Rochant
1994	*Un Indien dans la Ville*	Hervé Palud
1997	*Mars Attacks!*	Tim Burton
1998	*Le Loup-Garou de Paris*	Anthony Waller
	Armageddon	Michael Bay
2004	*Van Helsing*	Stephen Sommers
	Team America, World Police	Trey Parker
	Godzilla, The Final Wars	Ryuhel Kitamura
	The Eiffel Tower	Niklas Radstrom

Notes and References

Introduction

1. E. Heinle, *Towers: a Historical Survey* (London, Butterworth Architecture, 1989), p. 10

One: Beginnings

1. F. Poncetton, *Eiffel, Le Magicien du Fer* (Paris, Editions de la Tournelle, 1939), pp. 15–17
2. G. Eiffel, 'Généalogie de la famille Eiffel' (unpublished), p. 17 (quoted in H. Loyrette, *Gustave Eiffel* (New York, Rizzoli, 1985), p. 21)
3. Poncetton, *Magicien du Fer*, p. 46
4. Eiffel, 'Généalogie', pp. 49–50 (quoted in Loyrette, *Eiffel*, p. 23)
5. *Ibid.*, p. 52
6. Poncetton, *Magicien du Fer*, pp. 45–6
7. Eiffel, 'Généalogie', pp. 54–6 (quoted in Loyrette, *Eiffel*, pp. 24–5)
8. *Ibid.*, p. 64
9. J. Harriss, *The Eiffel Tower: Symbol of an Age* (London, Paul Elek, 1976), p. 33
10. Letter from Eiffel to his mother quoted in Loyrette, *Eiffel*, p. 29
11. Gustave Eiffel writing to his mother (quoted in Poncetton, *Magicien du Fer*, p. 53)
12. *Ibid.*, p. 57
13. *Ibid.*, p. 67
14. Eiffel, 'Généalogie', p. 94
15. Letter from Eiffel to his mother, 7 December 1855 (Eiffel collection, ARO 1981 1137(a)28) (quoted in Loyrette, *Eiffel*, p. 30)

Two: 'Iron, iron, nothing but iron'

1. Remark of Napoleon III to Victor Baltard from G.-E. Haussmann, *Mémoires 1890–93* (Paris, 1979), Vol. 2, p. 228 quoted in

Notes and References

B. Bergdoll, *European Architecture 1750–1890* OUP, 2000, p. 227

2. *Historical Dictionary of World's Fairs and Expositions 1851–1988*, ed. J.E. Findling (London, Greenwood Press, 1990), p. 16
3. L. Laborde, *Travaux de la Commission Française sur l'industrie des nations*, vol. viii, p. 234
4. The exhibition gates, made at Coalbrookdale, now separate Hyde Park and Kensington Gardens.
5. *Art Journal Illustrated Catalogue*, 1851 (facsimile edition 1995)
6. Napoleon III quoted in A. Chandler, 'The Paris Exposition Universelle of 1855', *World's Fair Magazine*, vi, no. 2 (1986)
7. *Historical Dictionary*, p. 16
8. Barrault, quoted in F.H. Steiner, *French Iron Architecture* UMI Research Epping Bowter, Ann Arbor, Michigan, 1984, p. 93
9. *Historical Dictionary*, p. 20
10. 'Rapport sur l'Exposition universelle de 1855 présenté à l'Empereur par S.A.I. Le Prince Napoléon, Président de la Commission' (Paris, 1857), p. 131, quoted in Chandler, 'The Paris Exposition Universelle of 1855'
11. G. Eiffel, 'Biographie industrielle et scientifique' (unpublished), vol. 1, p. 3 (quoted in Loyrette, *Eiffel*, p. 30)
12. Letter from Eiffel to his mother, 13 February 1856 (Eiffel collection ARO 1981 1139(a)6) (quoted in Loyrette, *Eiffel*, p. 32)
13. Poncetton, *Magicien du Fer*, p. 83
14. B. Lemoine, *Gustave Eiffel* (Paris, Editions Hazan, 1984), p. 20
15. Flachat's sheds at the Gare St-Lazare were the subject of several paintings by Monet
16. G. Eiffel, 'Les Grandes Constructions Métalliques' (lecture by Eiffel, 10 March 1888) l'Association Française pour L'Avancement des Sciences
17. Eiffel, 'Les Grandes Constructions Métalliques' (Paris, 1888)
18. Lemoine, *Gustave Eiffel*, p. 22
19. Within a few years, Nepveu's increasingly erratic behaviour confirmed an inability, predicted by many observers, to manage his business affairs, and he retired in 1860
20. British Patent No. 5071 of 1828
21. British Patent No. 1420 of 1784
22. British Patent No. 1667 of 1788
23. Burdon had patented a method of fastening cast-iron sections with wrought-iron straps, similar to a tongue-and-groove joint (patent

nos 2066 of 1795 and 2635 of 1802). It was not entirely successful: two bridges, including a 180ft span at Staines, collapsed. However, two Burdon bridges still survive at Spanish Town, Jamaica, and the Tickford Bridge at Newport Pagnell

24. Robert Stephenson quoted in Samuel Smiles, *Lives of the Engineers – Metcalfe and Telford* (London, John Murray, 1904), pp. 213–14

25. H. Straub, *A History of Civil Engineering* (Cambridge, Mass., MIT Press, 1964), pp. 174–5

26. *Ibid.*, p. 176

27. G. Eiffel, 'Les Grandes Constructions Métalliques' (Paris, 1888)

28. Hawkshaw wrote a highly favourable report in 1863 on the plans for the Suez Canal, leading Ferdinand de Lesseps to introduce him as 'the gentleman to whom I owe the canal'. He later condemned Lesseps' plans for the Panama Canal as unrealistic

29. Harriss, *Symbol of an Age*, p. 29

30. *New York Times*, 25 May 1970, p. 42

31. Poncetton, *Magicien du Fer*, pp. 86–9

32. Eiffel, 'Les Grandes Constructions Métalliques' (Paris, 1888)

Three: The Bridge-builder

1. Eiffel, 'Les Grandes Constructions Métalliques' (Paris, 1888). (The Crumlin Viaduct was demolished in 1965.)

2. Lemoine, *Gustave Eiffel*, p. 26

3. Loyrette, *Eiffel*, p. 36

4. Letter from Eiffel to his mother (quoted in Lemoine, *Gustave Eiffel*, p. 27)

5. Eiffel, 'Les Grandes Constructions Métalliques' (Paris, 1888)

6. *Ibid.*

7. Loyrette, *Eiffel*, p. 41 and Lemoine, *Gustave Eiffel*, p. 36

8. Eiffel, 'Les Grandes Constructions Métalliques' (Paris, 1888). (Exchange Station was closed in 1977 and later demolished; its fine masonry façade still stands.)

9. Loyrette, *Eiffel*, p. 53

10. Lemoine, *Gustave Eiffel*, p. 37

11. *Exposition Universelle de 1878, Notice*, p. 28 (quoted in Loyrette, *Eiffel*, p. 53)

12. Loyrette, *Eiffel*, p. 60

13. Lemoine, *Gustave Eiffel*, p. 50

14. G.G. Scott, *Remarks on Secular and Domestic Architecture*, 1858)

(quoted in A. Briggs, *Iron Bridge to Crystal Palace: Impact and Images of the Industrial Revolution* (London, Thames & Hudson, 1979), p. 169)

15. T. Seyrig, *Le Pont du Douro à Porto* (Paris, 1878) (quoted in Lemoine, *Gustave Eiffel*, p. 50)

16. Henri de Dion had been made Chevalier of the Légion d'Honneur in 1854 for his use of iron in saving Bayeux Cathedral from collapse

17. Loyrette, *Eiffel*, p. 62

18. *Exposition Universelle de 1878, Notice*, p. 39 (quoted in Loyrette, *Eiffel*, p. 71)

Four: 'The Shapes Arise!'

1. From 'Song of the Broad-Axe' in Walt Whitman, *Leaves of Grass*, 1856 Dent edn, 1947

2. K. Frampton and Y. Futagawa, *Modern Architecture 1851–1945* (New York, Rizzoli International, 1983), p. 36

3. Lemoine, *Gustave Eiffel*, p. 54

4. Eiffel, 'Les Grandes Constructions Métalliques' (Paris, 1888)

5. 'Préfecture de la Lozère, décision ministérielle, 14 juin 1879' (quoted in Loyrette, *Eiffel*, p. 76)

6. Lemoine, *Gustave Eiffel*, p. 54

7. Poncetton, *Magicien du Fer*, p. 136

8. Commissioner Rothery quoted in R. Hammond, *The Forth Bridge and its Builders* (London, Eyre & Spottiswoode, 1964), p. 29

9. Sir George Airey quoted in L.T.C. Rolt, *Victorian Engineering* (London, Pelican,) p. 191. (When initial work was undertaken on the Forth Bridge, wind-gauge readings done on-site indicated 34lb per sq. ft; so much for the notions of the Astronomer Royal.)

10. Airey in Hammond, *The Forth Bridge*, p. 32

11. 'Tay Bridge Disaster', report by Rothery quoted in J. Thomas, *The Tay Bridge Disaster: New Light on the 1879 Tragedy* (Newton Abbot, David & Charles, 1972), p. 177

12. Harriss, *Symbol of an Age*, p. 46

13. Lemoine, *Gustave Eiffel*, p. 70

14. Eiffel, 'Les Grandes Constructions Métalliques' (Paris, 1888)

15. Bouguereau, quoted in R. Rudorff, *Belle Epoque: Paris in the Nineties* (Hamish Hamilton, 1972), p. 99

16. 'Introduction, rapports du jury international, Exposition universelle internationale de 1878 à Paris' (Jules Simon, 1880) (quoted in M.R. Levin, *When the Eiffel Tower was New: French*

Visions of Progress at the Centennial of the Revolution (Mount Holyoke College Art Museum/University of Massachusetts Press, 1989), pp. 21–2

Five: 'Liberty'

1. B. Levine and I.F. Story, *Statue of Liberty*, US National Park Service Historical Handbook Series, No. 11 (Washington DC, 1954); see also the website of the New York Trust Co., www.endex.com/gf/buildings/liberty/nytc/solnytc1943.htm
2. *The Manufacturer and Builder*, vol. 8, no. 11, November 1876, 259 (courtesy of Cornell University Library, Making of America Digital Collection)
3. Bartholdi, quoted at www.endex.com/gf/buildings/liberty/nytc/solnytc1943.htm
4. Congressional resolution, quoted at www.endex.com/gf/buildings/liberty/nytc/solnytc1943.htm
5. *Scientific American*, 13 June 1885, p. 375
6. Levine and Story, *Statue of Liberty*
7. *Ibid.* www.endex.com/gf/buildings/liberty/nytc/solnytc1943.htm
8. Pulitzer was discharged from the US Army and after becoming penniless in St Louis, became a reporter, and was elected to the Missouri state legislature. After buying up several newspapers, he endowed the Columbia University School of Journalism, and in his will established the Pulitzer Prize for literature, drama, music and journalism. The often sensationalist style of his newspapers led to the introduction of the term 'yellow press'
9. *Harper's New Monthly Magazine*, 71, no. 423, August 1885, 476 (courtesy of Cornell University Library, Making of America Digital Collection)
10. 'The Great Statue of Liberty and the Pedestal Fund', *The Manufacturer and Builder*, 17, no. 6, June 1885, p. 140 (courtesy of Cornell University Library, Making of America Digital Collection)
11. Cleveland, quoted at www.endex.com/gf/buildings/liberty/nytc/solnytc1943.htm
12. Emma Lazarus who had been invited to submit a poem in a fundraising effort for the pedestal, was from a prominent New York Jewish family; she had initially declined, but later relented, taking as her inspiration the horror of the anti-Jewish pogroms in Russia
13. *New York Times*, 6 April 2004

14. *The Statue of Liberty Revisited* ed. W.S. Dillon (Smithsonian Institute Press, 1994, p. 155)

Six: 'A tower of very great height'

1. *Historical Dictionary*, p. 109
2. *Journal Officiel* (2 May 1886) quoted in Harriss, *Symbol of an Age*, p. 11
3. Koechlin quoted in Lemoine, *Gustave Eiffel*, p. 86
4. H. Loyrette, 'La Tour de 300 Metres' in *1889 – La Tour Eiffel et L'Exposition Universelle, Paris*, pp. 220–2
5. G. Eiffel, *La Tour de Trois Cents Mètres* (2 vols, Paris, Société des Imprimeries Lemercier, 1900), vol. 1, p. 4
6. *Engineering*, 3 May 1889, p. 430
7. Eiffel, *La Tour de Trois Cents Mètres*, vol. 1, p. 1
8. *Morning Herald*, 11 July 1833
9. *The Builder*, 1 May 1852, p. 280
10. Heinle, *Towers: a Historical Survey*, p. 214
11. Eiffel, 'Les Grandes Constructions Métalliques' (Paris, 1888)
12. Eiffel, *La Tour de Trois Cents Mètres*, vol. 1, p. 3
13. Eiffel, quoted in Lemoine, *Gustave Eiffel*, p. 90
14. G. Eiffel, *La Tour Eiffel vers 1900* (Paris, Masson et Cie, 1902), p. 9
15. Harriss, *Symbol of an Age*, p. 13
16. L. Jardine, *On a Grander Scale: the Outstanding Career of Sir Christopher Wren*, pp. xi, 316–21
17. 'Monuments and Microscopes: Scientific Thinking on a Grand Scale in the Early Royal Society' in *Notes & Records of the Royal Society of London*, vol. 55, no. 2, 2001
18. Eiffel, *La Tour vers 1900*, pp. 17–19 (quoted in Harriss, *Symbol of an Age*, p. 102)
19. Janssen, quoted in G. Tissandier, *The Eiffel Tower, a Description of the Monument, its Construction, its Machinery, its Object and its Utility, with an Autographic Letter of M. Gustave Eiffel* (London, 1889, p. 86)
20. Loyrette, *Eiffel*, p. 121
21. Charles Gounod, interviewed in *Le Matin*, 8 May 1889
22. Eiffel, quoted in J. Allwood, *The Great Exhibitions* (London, Studio Vista, 1977), p. 77
23. 'Artists against the Eiffel Tower', *Le Temps*, 14 February 1887, quoted in *Engineering*, 3 May 1889, p. 428
24. Eiffel, 'Les Grandes Constructions Métalliques' (Paris, 1888)
25. Eiffel, *La Tour de Trois Cents Mètres*, vol. 1, p. 7

26. Eiffel, 'Les Grandes Constructions Métalliques' (Paris, 1888)
27. G. Monod, 'Contemporary Life and Thought in France', *The Living Age* (23 April 1887), 232 (courtesy of Cornell University Library, Making of America Digital Collection)
28. Lockroy's reply to Alphand, reported in Alfred Picard, *Exposition Universelle Internationale de 1889 à Paris; Rapport Générale,* *1891*, pp. 270–1 (quoted in Harriss, *Symbol of an Age,* pp. 23–4)
29. Eiffel's reply to the protest, *Le Temps*, Paris, 14 February 1887
30. Vogüé, *Remarques sur l'Exposition*, pp. 24–5, quoted in Loyrette, *Eiffel*, p. 174

Seven: The Tower Rises

1. www.printsgeorge.com/ArtEccles_Aeronauts1.htm
2. *Les Révolutions de Paris*, no. 106 (16–23 July 1791); (source: http://chnm.gmu.edu/revolution/d/389/)
3. Gazette Nationale, no. 262 (10 June 1794); (source: http://chnm.gmu.edu/revolution/d/436/)
4. M. Nansouty, *La Tour Eiffel de 300 Mètres à l'Exposition Universelle de 1889* (Paris, Bernard Tignol, 1889), p. 28
5. Eiffel, *La Tour de Trois Centre Mètres*, vol. 1, p. 100
6. *Engineering*, 3 May 1889, p. 430
7. *From the Rapport Général of M. Alfred Picard*, reproduced in Eiffel, *La Tour de Trois Cent Mètres*, vol. 1, p. 101
8. M. de Nansouty of the Génie Civil, quoted in Tissandier, *The Eiffel Tower*, pp. 63–5
9. J. Morlaine, *La Tour Eiffel* (Paris, Pierre Belfond, 1978), p. 56
10. Eiffel, quoted in Tissandier, *The Eiffel Tower,* pp. 38–9
11. T. F. Peters, *Building the Nineteenth Century* (Cambridge, Mass., MIT Press, 1996), p. 266. Meccano was actually patented in the UK as 'Mechanics Made Easy' by Frank Hornby in 1901, and renamed in 1907
12. Benjamin Baker, address to British Association, Montreal, 1884
13. Nansouty, *La Tour Eiffel de 300 Mètres*, p. 104
14. Eiffel, *La Tour de Trois Cents Mètres*, vol. 1, p. 108
15. *Ibid.*, p. 118
16. Newspaper account quoted in R. Poirier, *The Fifteen Wonders of the World*, trans. M. Crosland (London, 1960, p. 252)
17. Nansouty, *La Tour Eiffel de 300 Mètres*, p. 105

18. W.H. Bishop, 'A Paris Exposition in Dishabille', *Atlantic Monthly*, 63, no. 379 (May 1889), 624 (Courtesy of Cornell University Library, Making of America Digital Collection)

19. Journalist Emile Goudeau, 'Ascension à la Tour', p. 282, quoted in the official Eiffel Tower website: www.toureiffel.fr/teiffel/uk/documentation/dossiers/page/ construction.html

20. H. Le Roux, *L'Exposition de Paris, 1889*, 1 (1 April 1889), 58

21. *Ibid.*, 58–9

22. *New York Times*, 25 February 1889

23. *Le Temps*, March 1889 (quoted in C. Braibant, *Histoire de la Tour Eiffel* (Paris, 1964), p. 76)

24. *Engineering*, 12 July 1889, p. 42

25. *Le Figaro*, 1 April 1889

26. *Ibid.*

27. *Le Monde Illustré*, 13 April 1889

28. *Illustrated London News*, 13 April 1899, p. 459

29. Eiffel, *La Tour de Trois Cents Mètres*, vol. 1, p. 311

30. *Ibid.*, p. 312

31. *Ibid.*, p. 319

Eight: 'Unique, strange and truly grandiose'

1. *Scientific American*, 2 February 1889, p. 65

2. *Engineering*, 3 May 1889, pp. 433–4

3. *Scientific American*, 29 June 1889, p. 402

4. Charles Otis telegram to Eiffel, quoted in 'Elevator systems of the Eiffel Tower, 1889', *United States National Museum Bulletin*, (228, 1961), 28

5. *Engineering*, 3 May 1889, p. 436

6. See Appendix 2

7. Tissandier, *The Eiffel Tower*, p. 92

8. Poncetton, *Magicien du Fer*, p. 207

9. W. Denker and F. Sagan, *The Eiffel Tower* (London, Deutsch, 1989), p. 10

10. Unattributed quotation in Denker and Sagan, *Eiffel Tower*, p. 5

11. *Ibid.*

12. *Illustrated London News*, 4 May 1889, p. 558

13. *Scientific American*, 15 June 1889, p. 376

14. *Ibid.*, p. 375

15. Ironically, Carnot was later to be a victim of assassination: in 1892 he was fatally stabbed by an Italian anarchist in Lyons
16. *The Times*, 6 May 1889, p. 11
17. *Ibid.*, p. 7
18. *Le Matin*, 9 May 1889
19. *Historical Dictionary*, p. 111
20. *The Times*, 7 May 1889, p. 5
21. *Le Figaro*, 6 May 1889 (Special Edition), p. 1
22. *The Times*, 7 May, 1889, p. 5
23. *L'Exposition de Paris, 1889*, p. 82
24. *Glasgow Herald*, 14 June 1889
25. Eiffel, *La Tour de 300 Mètres*, vol. 1, p. 285
26. *The Times*, 9 May 1889, p. 5
27. *The Spectator*, 11 May 1889, p. 632
28. Harriss, *Symbol of an Age*, p. 116
29. *Scientific American*, 14 September 1889, p. 166. (Film shot by Edison of an ascent of the tower by elevator, and other sequences filmed by him at the Exhibition, can be seen at the Internet site http://memory.loc.gov/; see also www.britishpathe.com)
30. *Le Figaro*, 7 May 1889
31. *Ibid.*, 11 July 1889
32. *Scientific American*, 7 September 1889, p. 149
33. *The Spectator*, 15 June 1889, p. 815
34. G. de Maupassant, *La Vie Errante*, p. 5 in *Oeuvres Complètes*, 1909
35. *The Spectator*, 6 April 1889, pp. 475–6
36. W.A. Eddy, 'The Highest Structure in the World', *Atlantic Monthly*, 63, no. 380 (June 1889), 725 (courtesy of Cornell University Library, Making of America Digital Collection)
37. William Clark, 'In Paris at the Centennial of the Revolution', *New England Magazine*, 7 (September 1889), 98 (courtesy of Cornell University Library, Making of America Digital Collection)
38. *Ibid.*, p. 99
39. German correspondent in *Le Figaro*, 28 October 1889
40. W.C. Brownell, 'The Paris Exposition – notes and impressions', *Scribner's Magazine*, 7, no. 1 (January 1890), 25 (courtesy of Cornell University Library, Making of America Digital Collection)
41. 'Loitering through the Paris Exposition', *Atlantic Monthly*, 65, no. 389 (March 1890), 373–4 (courtesy of Cornell University Library, Making of America Digital Collection)

Notes and References

Nine: The Panama Plunder

1. Allwood, *The Great Exhibitions*, p. 181
2. Nansouty, *La Tour Eiffel de 300 Mètres*, pp. 113–14
3. *Nature*, 7 August 1890, p. 353
4. 'Loitering through the Paris Exposition', *Atlantic Monthly*, 65, no. 389 (March 1890), 360 (courtesy of Cornell University Library, Making of America Digital Collection)
5. M.J. Simon, *The Panama Affair* (New York, Scribner's, 1971), p. 35
6. Ferdinand de Lesseps, 'The Interoceanic Canal', *The North American Review* (January 1880), 2
7. The Panama Canal website: www.pancanal.com/eng/history/history/french.html
8. Lesseps, 'The Panama Canal', *North American Review* (August 1880), 77
9. *Ibid.*, p. 76
10. Braibant, *Histoire de la Tour Eiffel*, p. 100
11. Resolution of the International Congress; source: the Panama Canal website: www.pancanal.com/eng/history/history/french.html
12. 'M. de Lesseps and his Canal' *North American Review* (February 1880)
13. Lesseps, 'Interoceanic Canal', p. 9
14. *The Times*, 12 March 1884
15. *Scientific American*, 22 August 1885, p. 118
16. *Ibid.*, 1 August 1881, p. 65
17. Philippe Bunau-Varilla, *Panama The Creation, Destruction and Resurrection* (London, Constable & Robinson, 1913), p. 66
18. Braibant, *Histoire de la Tour Eiffel*, p. 101
19. *Engineering*, 1 November 1889, p. 513
20. Braibant, *Histoire de la Tour Eiffel*, p. 102
21. Poncetton, *Magicien du Fer*, p. 237
22. Bunau-Varilla, *Creation, Destruction and Resurrection*, p. 87
23. *Engineering*, 1 February 1889, p. 115
24. *Ibid.*, p. 115
25. Simon, *The Panama Affair*, p. 79
26. *Engineering*, 1 February 1889, p. 115
27. *Ibid.*, 11 January 1889, p. 30
28. Braibant, *Histoire de la Tour Eiffel*, p. 104
29. 'The Great Forth Brige – its Formal Opening for Traffic', *The*

Manufacturer and Builder, 22, no. 4 (April 1890), 89 (courtesy of Cornell University Library, Making of America Digital Collection)

30. J. Gies, *Bridges and Men* (London, Cassell, 1963), p. 218
31. Baker, quoted in Rolt, *Victorian Engineering*, pp. 194–5
32. S. Mackay, *The Forth Bridge: a Picture History*, pp. 111–12
33. *Transactions of the National Association for the Advancement of Art and its Application to Industry*, Edinburgh meeting, 1889 (London, 1890)
34. *Engineering*, 28 February 1890, p. 218
35. *The Scotsman*, 4 March 1890
36. Rolt, *Victorian Engineering*, p. 194
37. *The Scotsman*, 5 March 1890
38. Simon, *The Panama Affair*, p. 102
39. Bunau-Varilla had been the French canal project engineer in 1884. He had organised attempts to form a new French company, and, when these failed, he arranged the eventual sale to the USA. A highly political operator – he was fiercely anti-German – in 1903 he sided with insurrectionists in their successful Colombian revolution and became the first Colombian minister to the United States
40. Philippe Bunau-Varilla, *Creation, Destruction and Resurrection*, p. 104
41. *The Times*, 23 November 1892, p. 5
42. *The Spectator*, 26 November 1892, p. 756
43. *Le Temps*, 22 November 1892
44. *Ibid.*
45. Bunau-Varilla, *Creation, Destruction and Resurrection*, p. 114
46. *The Spectator*, 24 December 1892
47. *Ibid.*, 14 January 1893, p. 33
48. *The Times*, 10 January 1893, p. 5
49. *Ibid.*, 12 January 1893, p. 5
50. *Ibid.*, 10 February 1893, p. 5
51. *Ibid.*, 13 February 1893, p. 5
52. *The Spectator*, 11 February 1893, p. 178
53. Bunau-Varilla, *Creation, Destruction and Resurrection*, p. 541
54. *The Times*, 13 March 1895, p. 5
55. *Ibid.*, 1 March 1893, p. 5
56. *Ibid.*, p. 5
57. Simon, *The Panama Affair*, p. 233
58. G. Eiffel, *Transactions de M. G. Eiffel avec la Liquidation de Panama*, pp. iii–vi
59. *Ibid.*

60. *Ibid.*, p. 23
61. *Ibid.*, p. 24
62. Statement by Gustave Eiffel to general meeting of the Eiffel Company, 1 March 1893 (quoted in Lemoine, *Gustave Eiffel*, p. 112)

Ten: New Directions

1. A. Shaw, 'Paris, the typical modern city', *The Century*, 42, no. 3 (July 1891), 463 (courtesy of Cornell University Library, Making of America Digital Collection)
2. *Ibid.*
3. Paris Observatory website: www.obspm.fr/histoire/montblanc/
4. Eiffel, 'Biographie' (unpublished), vol. 3, p. 1 (quoted in Loyrette, *Eiffel*, p. 206)
5. Eiffel, *La Tour de Trois Cents Mètres*, vol. 1, p. 240
6. *Ibid.*
7. Eiffel, *La Tour de Trois Cents Mètres*, vol. 1, p. 310
8. *Harper's New Monthly Magazine*, October 1892, p. 730
9. G. Eiffel, *Dix Années d'observations météorologiques à Sèvres, 1892–1901*, pp. 1–5
10. *Ibid.*
11. Loyrette, *Eiffel*, p. 164
12. *The Times*, 21 October 1901, p. 4
13. *Ibid.*
14. *Ibid.*
15. P. Hoffman, *Wings of Madness: Alberto Santos-Dumont and the Invention of Flight* (London, Fourth Estate, 2003), p. 142
16. For Santos, see www.rudnei.cunha.nom.br/FAB/eng/index.html
17. G. Eiffel, *Recherches expérimentales sur la résistance de l'air à la Tour Eiffel* (Paris, L. Maretheux, 1907), pp. 1–2
18. 'Air Resistance Experiment Described', *The Times*, 8 January 1908 (Engineering Supplement), p. 8
19. Eiffel, *La résistance de l'air*, pp. 89–90
20. Lapresle's words in *l'Aéronautique* (quoted in Poncetton, *Magicien du Fer*, p. 274)
21. Eiffel, *La Tour de Trois Cents Mètres*, vol. 1, p. 297
22. *The Times*, 28 May 1913 (Engineering Supplement) p. 25
23. *Electrical Review and Western Electrician*, 11 April 1914, p. 745
24. G. Eiffel, *Inauguration du Nouveau Laboratoire Aérodynamique*, L. Maretheux, Paris, 1912, p. 5

25. Robins was an able communicator and writer, and was probably the man who edited one of the greatest publishing successes of the eighteenth century, *A Voyage Round the World by George Anson*. This was written from Anson's notes of the four-year circumnavigation, and attributed to his chaplain, Richard Walter, who sailed on the voyage

26. For wind tunnel history, see websites: www.centennialofflight.gov and www.hq.nasa.gov

27. G. Eiffel, 'Later Experimental Research at the New Laboratory at Auteuil', a paper for the Société des Ingénieurs Civils de France, July 1912, published in his *Resistance of the Air and Aviation; Experiments Conducted at the Champ de Mars Laboratory*, trans. J.C. Hunsaker (London, Constable, 1913), pp. 229–32

28. G. Eiffel, *Later Experimental Research* (1913), pp. 234–6

29. Smithsonian Institution: Record Unit 45, Correspondence Series I, Box 35 ? 3–6: see also website www.memory.loc.gov/learn/features/flight/flying. html, pp. 9–10

30. *The Times*, 26 July 1911 (Engineering Supplement), p. 23

31. Letter to Eiffel from P.E. Flandin (quoted in Poncetton, *Magicien du Fer*, p. 287)

32. *Science and Technology in France*, no. 16, August 2002

33. Harriss, *Symbol of an Age*, p. 176

34. Loyrette, *Eiffel*, p. 211

Eleven: The International Icon

1. Perhaps ironically for a composer who had a reputation for harmonic clarity, Satie followed Matisse's idea tht there was a need for forms of art as undistracting as an easy chair. Satie's biographer said that his first piece, 'Musique d'ameublement', consisted of fragments of popular refrains from 'Mignon' and 'Danse Macabre' and isolated phrases repeated over and over again, like the pattern of wallpaper; [it] was meant strictly to be nothing more than a background and was not intended to attract attention in any way.' (R.H. Mayers, *Erik Satie* (New York: Dover, 1948, 1968), p. 60)

2. Adolphe David's Opus 63 described in Loyrette, *Eiffel*, p. 188

3. Maupassant, *La Vie Errante* (Paris, Louis Conard, 'Lassitude', 1902), pp. 1–2

4. See website www.latinreporters.com/expeeiffel12072002.html

5. J.A. Keim, *La Tour Eiffel* (Paris, Editions Tel, 1950), p. 7

Notes and References

6. Le Corbusier, who admired Eiffel's instinct for proportion, devised a system which he called 'le Modulor', which employed standardised units calculated on the proportions of the human figure

7. Harriss, *Symbol of an Age*, p. 226; source: C. Cordat, *La Tour Eiffel* (Paris, Editions de Minuit, 1955)

8. Braibant, *Histoire de la Tour Eiffel*, p. 96

9. *Ibid.*, p. 97

10. B. Maddox, *Rosalind Franklin, The Dark Lady of DNA*, p. 94

11. Harriss, *Symbol of an Age*, pp. 212–13

12. G. Headley and W. Meulenkamp, *Follies: A Guide to Rogue Architecture in England, Scotland and Wales* (London, Jonathan Cape, 1990), p. 387

13. 'Blackpool's Tour de Force' in *History Today*, 44 (June 1994)

14. Watkin was an extraordinarily innovative and open-minded railway promoter, a 'Europhile' in today's terminology. As well as promoting a Channel Tunnel capable of running 250 trains each way every day as early as 1869, he also proposed a railway tunnel between Scotland and Ireland and a ship canal from Dublin to Galway

15. Eiffel, *La Tour de Trois Cents Mètres*, p. 322

16. *Nature*, 8 May 1890, p. 36

17. See www.brent.gov.uk/wembley.nsf and http://www2.umist.ac.uk/sport/3_art3.htm

18. *Las Vegas Sun*, 2 September 1999

19. 'Eiffel Tower II', *Modern Steel Construction* (June 2001)

20. Braibant, *Histoire de la Tour Eiffel*, p. 181

21. Morlaine, *La Tour Eiffel*, p. 111–13

22. *Ibid.*, p. 133

23. *Le Figaro*, 20 June 1957

24. *Ibid.*, 6 July 1965

25. *L'Aurore*, 12 September 1969

26. Harriss, *Symbol of an Age*, p. 211

27. J.F. Johnson (with F. Miller), *The Man who Sold the Eiffel Tower* (New York, Doubleday, 1961)

28. R. Barthes, *The Eiffel Tower and Other Mythologies*, trans. R. Howard (New York, Hill and Wang, 1979), pp. 5–6

29. Le Corbusier, quoted in Harriss, *Symbol of an Age*, p. 226; source: Cordat, *La Tour Eiffel*

30. Morlaine, *La Tour Eiffel*, p. 137

31. *Le Figaro*, 6 May 1955
32. *Ibid.*, 30 December 1971

Twelve: Wither Tallest?

1. The Council on Tall Buildings and Urban Habitat has a website at www.ctbuh.org
2. A useful website is www.elevator-world.com, and a helpful overview of the issue of elevator provision in tall buildings is at www.gmu.edu/departments/safe/mega.html
3. For the Ultima Tower, see website www.tdrinc.com/ultima.html
4. *Guardian*, 19 August 2002
5. Space elevators, see www.liftoff.msfc.nasa.gov and www.flightprojects.msfc.nasa.gov/fd02_towers.html
6. *Ibid.*, p. 186

Bibliography

Books

Allwood, J. *The Great Exhibitions*, London, Studio Vista, 1977

Auerbach, J.A. *The Great Exhibition of 1851: a Nation on Display*, New Haven/London, Yale University Press, 1999

Barthes, R. *The Eiffel Tower and Other Mythologies*, trans. R. Howard, New York, Hill and Wang, 1979

Bennett, D. *The Creation of Bridges*, London, Aurum Press, 1999

Berlioz, H. *The Memoirs of Hector Berlioz: Member of the French Institute, Including his Travels in Italy, Germany, Russia and England, 1803–1865*, trans. D. Cairns, London, Gollancz, 1969

Braibant, C. *Histoire de la Tour Eiffel*, Paris, 1964

Briggs, A. *Iron Bridge to Crystal Palace: Impact and Images of the Industrial Revolution*, London, Thames & Hudson, 1979

Brontë, C. *The Brontës: Life and Letters*, ed. C. King, London, Shorter, 1908

Bunau-Varilla, P. *Panama: the Creation, Destruction and Resurrection*, London, Constable & Robinson, 1913

Burton, R.D.E. *Blood in the City: Violence and Revolution in Paris, 1798–1945*, Ithaca and London, Cornell University Press, 2001

Carlyle, T. *Early Letters of Thomas Carlyle*, ed. C.E. Norton, London, Macmillan, 1886

Davis, J.R. *The Great Exhibition*, Stroud, Sutton, 1999

Denker, W. and Sagan, F. *The Eiffel Tower*, London, Deutsch, 1989

Dickens, C. *The Uncollected Writings of Charles Dickens: 'Household Words', 1850–1859* ed. with an introduction and notes by H. Stone, London, Allen Lane, 1969

Eiffel, G. *L'Architecture Métallique*, Paris, Maisonneuve et Larose, 1996

——. *Dix années d'observations météorologiques à Sèvres (Seine-et-Oise)*, Paris, 1904

——. *Les grandes constructions métalliques* (lecture to French Association for the Advancement of Science), Paris, 1888

——. *Inauguration du nouveau laboratoire aérodynamique*, L. Marethoux, Paris, 1912

——. *Recherches expérimentales sur la résistance de l'air à la Tour Eiffel*, Paris, L. Marethoux, 1907

——. *The Resistance of the Air, and Aviation: Experiments Conducted at the Champ de Mars Laboratory*, trans. J.C. Hunsaker, London, Constable, 1913

——. *La Tour de trois cents mètres*, 2 vols, Paris, Société des Imprimeries Lemercier, 1900

——. *Transactions de M. G. Eiffel avec la liquidation de Panama*, Paris, 1900

Findling, J.E. *Historical Dictionary of World's Fairs and Expositions, 1851–1988*, London, Greenwood Press, 1990

Frampton, K. (and Futagawa, Y.) *Modern Architecture*, New York, Rizzoli International, 1983

French, Y. *The Great Exhibition, 1851*, London, Harvill Press, 1950

Friebe, W. *Buildings of the World Exhibitions*, trans. J. Vowles and P. Roper, Leipzig, 1985

Gibbs-Smith, C.H. *The Great Exhibition of 1851: a Commemorative Album*, London, HMSO, 1950

Gies, J. *Bridges and Men*, London, Cassell, 1963

Gordon, J.E. *Structures, or Why Things Don't Fall Down*, London, Pelican, 1978

Hammond, R. *The Forth Bridge and its Builders*, London, Eyre & Spottiswoode, 1964

Harriss, J. *The Eiffel Tower, Symbol of an Age*, London, Paul Elek, 1976 (first published 1975 in the USA by Houghton Mifflin as *The Tallest Tower*)

Headley, G. and Meulenkamp, W. *Follies: A Guide to Rogue Architecture in England, Scotland and Wales*, London, Jonathan Cape, 1990

Heinle, E. *Towers: a Historical Survey*, London, Butterworth Architecture, 1989

Hobhouse, H. *The Crystal Palace and the Great Exhibition: Art, Science and Productive Industry, a History of the Royal Commission for the Exhibition of 1851*, Athlone, 2002

Hoffman, P. *Wings of Madness: Alberto Santos-Dumont and the Invention of Flight*, London, Fourth Estate, 2003

Jardine, L. *On a Grander Scale: the Outstanding Career of Sir Christopher Wren*, London, HarperCollins, 2002

Jennings, H. *Pandaemonium: the Coming of the Machine as seen by contemporary observers*, ed. M.-L. Jennings and C. Madge, London, Andre Deutsch, 1985

Johnson, J.F. (with F. Miller) *The Man who Sold the Eiffel Tower*, New York, Doubleday, 1961

Bibliography

Keim, J.A. *La Tour Eiffel*, Paris, Tel, 1950

Laborde, L. *Travaux de la Commission Française sur l'industrie des nations*, Paris, 1858

Lanza, J. *Elevator Music*, London, Quartet Books, 1995 (first published 1994 in the USA)

Leapman, M. *The World for a Shilling: How the Great Exhibition of 1851 Shaped a Nation*, London, Headline, 2002

Lemoine, B. *Gustave Eiffel*, Paris, Hazan, 1984

Levin, M.R. *When the Eiffel Tower was New: French Visions of Progress at the Centennial of the Revolution*, Mount Holyoke College Art Museum/University of Massachusetts Press, 1989

Levine, B. and Story, I.F. *Statue of Liberty*, Washington DC, US National Park Service, Historical Handbook Series, No. 11, 1954

Loyrette, H. *Gustave Eiffel*, trans. R. and S. Gomme, New York, Rizzoli, 1985 originally published 1985 as *Eiffel – Un Ingénieur et son oeuvre*, Office du Livre SA, Fribourg, Switzerland

Mackay, S. *The Forth Bridge: A Picture History*, HMSO, Edinburgh, 1993

Maddox, B. *Rosalind Franklin, the Dark Lady of DNA*, Harper Collins, London, 2002

Marrey, B. *Gustave Eiffel, Une Entreprise Exemplaire*, Institute, Paris, 1989

Maupassant, G. de. *Oeuvres Complètes de Guy de Maupassant*, Paris, Louis Conard, 1909

Meeks, C.L.V. *The Railroad Station: an Architectural History*, Yale University Press, 1956

Morlaine, J. *La Tour Eiffel*, Paris, Pierre Belfond, 1978

Myers, R.H. *Erik Satie*, New York, Dover, 1968

Nansouty, M. *La Tour Eiffel de 300 Mètres à l'Exposition Universelle de 1889*, Paris, Bernard Tignol, 1889

Nasmyth, J. *Autobiography*, ed. S. Smiles, London, John Murray, 1883

Pacelle, M. *Empire: A tale of Obsession, Betrayal and the Battle for an American Icon*, New York, Wiley, 2001

Pannell, J.P.M. *An Illustrated History of Civil Engineering*, London, Thames & Hudson, 1964

Peters, T.F. *Building the Nineteenth Century*, Cambridge, Mass., MIT Press, 1996

Poirier, R. *The Fifteen Wonders of the World*, trans. M. Crosland, London, 1960

Poncetton, F. *Eiffel, Le Magicien du Fer*, Paris, Editions de la Tournelle, 1939

Richards, J. and MacKenzie, J.M. *The Railway Station: a Social History*, Oxford University Press, 1986

Rolt, L.T.C. *Victorian Engineering*, London, Pelican, 1974

Rudorff, R. *Belle Epoque: Paris in the Nineties*, London, Hamish Hamilton, 1972

Sabbagh, K. *Skyscraper: the Making of a Building*, London, Macmillan, 1989

Shirley-Smith, H. *The World's Great Bridges*, London, Phoenix House, 1964

Simon, M.J. *The Panama Affair*, New York, Scribner's, 1971

Smiles, S. *Lives of the Engineers* (Metcalfe and Telford), London, John Murray, 1904

Sparling, T.A. *The Great Exhibition: a Question of Taste*, New Haven, Conn., Yale Center for British Art, 1982

Straub, H. *A History of Civil Engineering*, trans. E. Rockwell, Cambridge, Mass., MIT Press, 1964

Thackeray, W.M. *Miscellaneous Prose and Verse*, vol. 1, London, Bradbury & Evans, 1855

Thomas, J. *The Tay Bridge Disaster: New Light on the 1879 Tragedy*, Newton Abbot, David & Charles, 1972

Tissandier, G. *The Eiffel Tower, a Description of the Monument, its Construction, its Machinery, its Object, and its Utility; with an Autographic Letter of M. Gustave Eiffel*, London, Searle & Rivington, London, 1889

Tuchman, B. *The Proud Tower, A Portrait of the World before the War, 1890–1914*, Macmillan, 1980

Whyte, I.B. (with A.J. MacDonald and C. Baxter) *John Fowler, Benjamin Baker, Forth Bridge*, Stuttgart and London, Axel Menges, 1997

Wilson, K. *Channel Tunnel Visions, 1850–1945: Dreams and Nightmares*, London, Hambledon, 1994

Woods, M. and Warren A.S. *Glass Houses: a History of Greenhouses, Orangeries and Conservatories*, London, Aurum Press, 1988

Dictionnaire de Biographie Française, Paris, Librairie Letouzey et Ané, 1970

L'Exposition de Paris 1889; publiée avec la collaboration d'écrivains spéciaux; édition enrichie de vues, de scènes de réproductions d'objets d'art, de machines, de dessins et gravures par les meilleurs artistes. Paris, La Librairie Illustrée, 1889

The Faber Book of Reportage, ed. J. Carey, London, Faber, 1987

The Great Exhibition (Facsimile of the illustrated Catalogue of 1851, published by the *Art Journal*), New York, Gramercy Books, 1995

The Great Exhibition of 1851; New Interdisciplinary Essays, ed. L. Purbrick, Manchester University Press, 2001

Bibliography

1889 – La Tour Eiffel et L'Exposition Universelle, Paris, Editions de la Réunion des Musées nationaux; Ministère de la culture, de la communication, des grands travaux et du bicentenaire, 1989

Newspapers, Journals and Pamphlets

Atlantic Monthly (Boston)
The Builder
Catalogue Sommaire Illustré du Fonds Eiffel, Musée d'Orsay, Paris, 1989
The Century (New York)
Engineering
L'Exposition Universelle, 1889, publiée avec la collaboration d'écrivains spéciaux, etc. Paris, sold at the Librairie Illustrée, 1889
Le Figaro
The Forth Bridge (paper read by Benjamin Baker at meeting of the British Association in Montreal, 1884)
Les Grandes Constructions Métalliques, conference instigated by Gustave Eiffel, Association Française pour l'Avancement des Sciences, Paris, 1888
Glasgow Herald
Illustrated London News
John Bull
Le Matin
Le Monde Illustré
New England Magazine (Boston)
New York Times
News Chronicle
North American Review (New York)
Notes & Records of the Royal Society of London
Presidential Address by Benjamin Baker, British Association meeting, Aberdeen, 1885
Proceedings, Institution of Civil Engineers
Scientific American
Scotsman
Scribner's Magazine (New York)
The Spectator
Le Temps
The Times
World's Fair Magazine

Websites

www.brantacan.co.uk: an excellent website packed with information on, and outlining the principles of, bridge-building and related architecture; also has a useful catalogue of bridges and other structures.

www.kuleuven.ac.be/bwk/materials/Education/master/wg01b/10410.htm and 10430.htm: two web pages from the Department of Civil Engineering at the Katholieke Universiteit Leuven, at Heverlee in Belgium, which contain excellent illustrated lectures on the Historical Development of Iron and Steel in Structures, and in Buildings.

www.tour-eiffel.fr the excellent official Eiffel Tower website, available in an English language version.

www.cr.nps.gov/history/online_books/hh/11 the excellent US National Parks Service website for the Statue of Liberty.

Secret history of Wembley, see www.brent.gov.uk/wembley.nsf

Creating Wembley: The Construction of a National Monument, by Jeff Hill, Nottingham Trent University and Francesco Varrasi, De Montfort University, see

http://www2.umist.ac.uk/sport/3art3.htm

Index

advertising, on Eiffel Tower; 226–7
aerodynamics:
    'free-fall' experiments, 197–200
    wind tunnels, 203–9
Airey, Prof. George; 13, 56, 168
Alphand, Charles Adolphe (Paris
        Dir. Of Works), 87
    addressee of Artists' Protest, 95
    ascent of Tower, 123
American Committee for Statue of
        Liberty; 68, 70
Anderson, Robert Rowand,
        architect; 166
Anderton Boat Lift, 159
Apollinaire, Guillaume, 229
Arrol, William, engineering
        contractor, 167
'Art v. Industry'; 13, 15, 47, 58–9,
        63–4
    and the Eiffel Tower, 79
    and the Artists' Protest', 94–101
    and the Forth Bridge, 165–6
Artsutanov, Yuri; engineer; 242
Auteuil Laboratory;
    Eiffel's second wind tunnel,
        205–9
    Eiffel gift to France, 208
aviation; 193–7, 206–8

Babel, Tower of; x
Baker, Benjamin; civil engineer;
    on aesthetics of Forth Bridge, 112
    contract for Forth Bridge, 164
    response to William Morris, 165
    describes cantilever principle,
        166–7
    English Channel Bridge, 187
    and Sir Edward Watkin, 220

Baltard, Victor; architect; 19, 28–9
Barrault, Alexandre; engineer; 15
Barthes, Roland; writer & critic;
        212, 230
Bartholdi, Frederic Auguste;
        sculptor;
    Statue of Liberty ideas, 65–6
    design objectives, 69–70
    uncertainty, 69
    unveils Statue's face, 73
    sees early drawing of Tower, 79
    visits Eiffel Tower, 142
Becquerel, Edmond; engineer; 140–1
Bedloe's Island, New York Harbor;
        66, 73
Bell, Alexander Graham; honours
        Eiffel's aeronautical work, 207
Berlin; radio tower, 222
Berlioz, Hector, composer; 16
Bessemer, Henry; 23
Bischoffsheim, Raphael;
        philanthropist; 62–3
Blackpool Tower; 219–20
Blackpool Winter Gardens Co.;
        219–20
Bloy, Léon; writer & critic; 97, 213
Boenickhausen, Jean-René (great-
        great grandfather); 1
Bogardus, James; inventor &
        engineer; 83
Boileau, Louis-Charles; architect;
        52
Bonaparte, Charles Louis Napoléon;
        6–7, 12–16, 28–9
Bordeaux Bridge, over the Garonne;
        20, 29–31, 33–5
Bouch, (Sir) Thomas; engineer;
        55–7, 168

Bouguereau, William Adolphe; painter; 64, 95

Bourdais, Jules; architect; 84–8

Boyer, Léon; architect;
at Garabit, 53
dies in Panama, 159

Bréguet, Louis; aircraft designer; 207–8

Britannia Bridge, Menai Strait; 27

Brooklyn Bridge, New York City; 45

Broseley, Shropshire; 24

Brown, Captain (Sir) Samuel; engineer; 26

Brunel, Isambard Kingdom; engineer; 33

Brunet, Joseph-Mathieu; receiver; 163–4

Budapest, Nyugati Station; 43–4

'Buffalo Bill' Cody; 142

Buildwas, Shropshire; 26

Bunau-Varilla, Philippe; engineer & politician;
appalled by Panama prosecutions, 170–1
scathing of Eiffel's treatment, 173–4
castigates Appeal Court, 178

bungee jumping; 223

Burton, Charles; architect; 82–3

Cailletet, Louis Paul; Academician; 152

caissons; in foundation working;
for Bordeaux Bridge, 32–3
for Eiffel Tower, 106

calligrams (graphic poems by Appolinaire); 229

Carlisle Citadel Station; railway crash; 169

Carnot, President Marie François;
assassination attempt, 136
opens Expo 1889, 138
ascends Eiffel Tower, 144

cast iron; 21–23

Cendrars, Blaise; poet & novelist; 231–2

Champ de Mars; 12, 92–3, 102–5

Chevalier, Maurice; actor & singer; 229

Chrichton, Charles; film director; 232

Citroën, André Gustave; motor engineer; 226

Clair, René; film director; 232

Clemenceau, (Prime Minister) Georges; 153, 174

Cleveland, US President Grover; 73

Coalbrookdale, Shropshire; 12, 23–4

Collège Sainte Barbe, Paris; 5–6

Collin, Joseph (brother-in-law); 8, 10, 46

Collot, Léon; aviator; 224

Compagnie Universelle du Canal Interocéanique;
shares issue opened, 153–4
dissolution, 163

Compagnon, Jean; construction supervisor; 46, 54
directs assembly of Eiffel Tower, 108
makes celebratory ascent, 122

Company of Scotland Trading to Africa and The Indies, 154–5

Congrès International d'Etudes du Canal Interocéanique; 155–7

Conwy Castle Bridge; 26

Coppée, François; poet; 95, 97

Cort, Henry; ironmaster; 22–3

Cortez, Hernando; conquistador; 154

Council on Tall Buildings and Urban Habitat; 236, 239

Couvreux & Hersent; engineering contractors; 158

Craigellachie Bridge, over the River Spey, Scotland; 26

Crumlin Viaduct, Wales; 32

Crystal Palace, London; 12–13, 82–3

Cubitt, William; civil engineer; 33

Culmann, Karl; engineer; 54–5

Index

Darby, Abraham, III; ironmaster; 24

Darien, Isthmus of Panama; 155

David, Adolphe; composer; 211–12

De Dion, Henri; structural engineer; 47–9, 133

Delahaye, Jules; French National Assembly member; 171

Delaunay, Robert; painter; 231–2

Delmaet, Hyacinthe-César; photographer; 216

Deneuve, Catherine; actress; 222

Déroulède, Paul; French National Assembly member; 174

Desmaret, Nicolas; engineer; 27

Dijon, ancient capital of Burgundy; 2–5

Dornon, Silvain; 223

Drumont, Edouard; anti-semite; 169

Ducretet, Eugène; radio pioneer; 200

Dundonald, Thomas Cochrane, Earl of; 33

Durandelle, Louis-Emile; photographer, 216–17

Ecole Centrale, Paris; 7–9

Edison, Thomas A; inventor; 92
in Eiffel's apartment on the Tower, 134
on Eiffel's achievement, 142–3

Edoux elevators; 128, 130–1

Eiffage Construction; 243

Eiffel, Alexandre (father); 1–2, 9, death of 54

EIFFEL, ALEXANDRE GUSTAVE
family history, 1–10
childhood, 3–7
youth, 7–10
early debt problems, 11, 29
seeks employment, 16–18
leaves Nepveu's employment, 20
praises English iron bridges, 27, 30
on workers' safety, 33–4, 114
employment worries, 35–9
marriage and children, 35

becomes self-employed, 36
defines elasticity principles for iron, 37
establishes workshops, 38
early work undertaken, 38–40
develops new techniques, 39–40
company name changes, 40
politics affects business, 41–2
work in South America, 42–3
work on Maria Pia Bridge; 44–7
uncertainty in collaboration, 47–8, 78–80,
importance of calculation, 46, 107–9, 191–2, 206–8
'art' in engineering, 44, 47, 58–9,100–1
work for Paris Expo 1878, 48–50
Légion d'Honneur awards; Cross, 49; Officer, 124; exonerated, 181–2
Garabit Viaduct; 52–5, 57–9
effect of family deaths, 53–4
and 'graphic statics', 55
impact of Tay Bridge collapse, 57–8
significance of design & method, 57–9
work in Indo-China, 59–60
growing confidence & wealth, 60
work in other countries, 61
his favourite work, 62–3
contacted by Bartholdi, 69
first reaction to Tower idea, 78–80
indebtedness to others, 79–80
on construction materials, 84–5
accepts financial burden of Tower, 88
'usefulness' of Tower, 88–91, 188–90
contractual commitment to Tower, 91–2
response to Artists' Protest, 97–8, 100–1
use of pistons on Tower, 107
accepts insurance liability, 110–1

concern for safety on Tower, 110–1

provides worker's canteen, 113–4

extols French abilities, 115–6

his organisational genius, 121–2

celebratory ascent of Tower, 122–3

addresses guests, 123

honours workmen and French national heroes, 133, 255–7

his sense of triumph with Tower, 150

opposes de Lesseps' Panama canal plan, 156–7

contracts to rescue canal works, 160

agreement with receiver, 164

attends opening of Forth Bridge, 164–9

home raided in Panama scandal, 170

indicted on Panama charges, 171

his evidence in court, 175–6

court verdict, 177

legal appeal, 178

survives Légion d'Honneur inquiry, 181–2

his reaction to Panama case, 182–3

abandons engineering, 183–4

plan for Paris Metro, 185–6

proposes Channel Tunnel, 187

Mont Blanc Observatory, 187–8

buys Paris mansion, 188

work in meteorology, 188–192

his properties, 192, 209

air resistance experiments, 197–9

wind tunnel at Tower, 203–5

wind tunnel at Auteuil, 205–8

proves air-flow principles, 205

designs fighter plane, 207–8

retirement, 208–9

death, 210

dispute over Tower imagery, 214–6

and 'Watkin's Folly', 220

Eiffel, Catherine (mother); 2–3, 5–6, 8, 10, 29, death of 54

Eiffel, Claire (daughter); 35, 50,144, 188

Eiffel, Laure (sister); 2, 8, 11, death of 36

Eiffel, Marie (sister); 2, 8–10, 34–35, 55

Eiffel, Marie (wife, née Gaudelet; known as Marguerite); 35, 46, death of 50

Eiffel Tower

genesis of, 77–81

construction materials, 84–5

decision to proceed, 87–8

contracts, 91–2

site, and public reaction, 92–4

the Artists' Protest, 94–100

foundations, 105–7

work on tower begins, 107

wind resistance and methodology, 108–9, 111

public anxiety, 110–12

completion of first stage, 112–13

safety issues, 114–15

higher levels, 115–21

industrial action, 115

early visitors, 116–20

topmost features, 121

celebration ascent, 122–5

fitting out & elevators, 126–36

opinions of visitors before opening, 133–6

opening of Expo, 136–50

tower opens late, 142–3

symbolism for French, 148–9

Eiffel's personal triumph, 150

success at end of Expo, 151–2

meteorological experiments, 189

physiological experiments, 190

during 1900 Expo, 192–3

early aviation, 193–6

Santos-Dumont's flight, 194–6

'free-fall' experiments, 197–9

radio, 200–203

wind tunnel, 203–5

Index

ownership passes to Paris, 204
as icon, 211–34
commercial imagery, 214–18
photography, 216–17
commercial products, 217–18
scale models, 218
engineering replicas, 218–23
suicides & publicity seekers,
  223–6
advertising, 226–7
con men, 227–8
art, literature & cinema, 229–33
Nazi occupation, 229
national monument, 229
painters, 231–2
films, 232–3, 258–9
passage of time, 233–4
Eiffel Tower Symphony, 211–2
Einstein, Albert; 222
elevators on Eiffel Tower; 128–32
elevators, principles of, 127–8,
  237–8
English Channel, tunnel plans;
  27–8, 187
Expo Universelle, Paris
  1855; 10–12
  1867; 36–7
  1878; 44, 48–50
  1889; 76–7, 93–4, 135–50,
    151–3, 213
  1900; 192–3
Exposition International des Arts et
  Techniques dans la Vie
  Moderne, 1937; 226

Fairbairn, Sir William; engineer;
  27
Ferrié, Captain Gustave; military
  officer; 201, 210
Ferry, (Prime Minister) Jules; 76
'Le Figaro'; newspaper at Eiffel
  Tower; 126, 138–9, 142–4
films; 232–3, 258–9
Flachat, Eugène; engineer; 19, 29,
  33
Forth Railway Bridge, Scotland;

wind resistance techniques, 57–8
comparative construction
  methods, 59, 109–110
aesthetic views, 112
Eiffel attends opening, 164–9
opening ceremony, 167–8
as icon, 211
Fowler, John; civil engineer; 165–8,
  187
Franco-American Union, to
  undertake Statue of Liberty,
  66
Franklin, Rosalind; crystallographer;
  217
French National Assembly; refuses
  Panama rescue, 163
funding for 'Liberty' in USA; 70–2
'furniture music'; 211

Gaget, Gauthier & Cie; 67
Gamond, Thome de; engineer; 27–8
Garabit Viaduct; 52–5, 57–9
Garnier, Charles; architect; 15
  Nice Observatory, 63
  Artists' Protest, 95–101
Gauguin, Paul; artist; 134
Giraudoux, Jean; academic, writer;
  229
Gounod, Charles; composer; 211
  and Liberty project, 66
  on siting of Tower, 92–3
  Artists' Protest, 95
  retracts protest, 134
Great Exhibition, London 1851;
  12–14
'graphic statics'; 55
Grasset, André; architect; 226
Guiard, Emile; playwright; 66
Guinness, Alec; actor; 233

Hackett, A.J.; 223
'Halles, Les'; 19, 28–9
Hari, Mata; spy; 201–2
Haussmann, Baron Georges Eugène;
  administrator; 14, 28–9
Hawkshaw, Sir John; engineer; 28

Hénocque, Dr. Albert; (brother-in-law); 42, 50, 54, 190, 238
Hertz, Cornelius; financier; 169, 171
Hodgkinson, Eaton; engineer; 27
Hooke, Robert; chemist, physicist & architect; 89
Horeau, Hector; engineer; 27
Hugo, Victor; poet & writer; 28
Hunt, Richard M; architect; 66
Hussonmorel, Armand; (brother-in-law); 8–9, 34, 42
Huysmans, Joris-Karl; novelist; 97

Indo-China; 59–60
Iquitos, Peru; 213
iron; 21–9

Jacopozzi, Fernand; lighting engineer; 226
Jaluzot, Jules; businessman; 215–6
Janssen, Pierre Jules; astronomer & Academician; 90–1, 187–8

Koechlin, Maurice; engineer; 54, 69, 78–80, 108, 110, 235
Krantz, Jean–Baptiste; engineer; 37, 49

Laasan, Silesia; bridge on Strieguer Wasser; 26
Laboulaye, Edouard; republican historian; 65–6, 70
Labric, Pierre; 223
Labrouste, Henri; architect; 15, 28
Lafayette, Marie Joseph; reformer & politician; 104
Langley, Samuel Pierpoint; astronomer & aeronautical pioneer; 199, 204
Las Vegas, New Mexico; 222–3
'The Lavender Hill Mob'; 233
Lazarus, Emma; poet; 74
Le Corbusier; architect; 214, 229–31, 240
Légion d'Honneur: 49, 124, 181–2
Lelièvre, M; 42–3

Lépinay, Adolphe Dodin de; state engineer; 156–7
Lesseps, Ferdinand, Vicomte de; diplomat; 36, 148
  and 'Liberty'; 65, 70–1, 73–4
  and Panama; 155–63, 168–73, 175–8, 180
  death of, 181
Lesseps, Charles de; 157, 163, 171, 174–9
Libeskind, Daniel; architect; 241
Lincoln, US President Abraham; 65–6
Liverpool Exchange Station; 41
Lockroy, Edouard; administrator & politician;
  demands tower for Expo, 77–9
  chairs committee, 87
  reply to Artists' Protest; 99–100
  support of Eiffel acknowledged, 116
  at opening of Expo; 136–7
London, Great Exhibition of 1851; 10–12
Loubet, Prime Minister Emile; 170
Lustig, Victor; con–man; 227–8

Magasin au Bon Marché, Paris department store; 52
Mallarmé, Stéphane; symbolist poet; 134
Malraux, André; writer, republican; 229
Maputo, Mozambique; 213
Marconi, Guglielmo; radio pioneer; 200
Maria Pia Bridge, Porto; 44–8
Massenet, Jules; composer; 95
Mathieu, Albert; engineer; 27
Maupassant, Guy de; novellist & critic; 95, 97, 146, 212, 212–4, 217, 229, 231
Maxwell, James Clerk; physicist; 200
Maxwell & Tuke; engineers; 219
Menai Suspension Bridge; 27

Index

Merrimac River Bridge, Massachusetts; 26

Meurthe, Henri Deutsch de la; entrepreneur; 193

Milau Viaduct; 243

Mistinguette; dancer & singer; 229

models for 'Liberty'; 67

Mollerat, Jean-Baptiste (uncle); 4–5, 8–9

Mont Blanc; observatory project; 187–8

Montgolfier brothers; aeronautical inventors; 102–3

Monument, to Great Fire of London; 89

Morris, William; artist & critic; 165

Morton, Levi P.; US diplomat; 70–1

Nansouty, Max; engineer; 109–10, 113, 151–2

Neilson, James Beaumont; ironmaster; 21

Nepveu, Charles; engineer; 17–20, 29–30

New Brighton Tower; 221–2

New York City; Brooklyn Bridge; 45

'New York World'; newspaper; 71–2

Nice Observatory; 62–3

Nordling, Wilhelm; engineer; 39, 44

Nouguier, Emile; engineer; 46, 54, 78–80, 108, 122, 235

Nyugati Station, Budapest; 43–4

Otis elevators; 127–32

Paine, Tom; writer, reformer & revolutionary; 24–6

painters, and the Tower; 231–2

Palais de l'Industrie (1855); 14–15

Panama Canal; 154–64, 169–81
   disease & conditions; 154–6, 158
   early financial troubles; 157–8
   Eiffel contracted; 160
   extent of losses; 161–3
   works halted; 164

scandal becomes political; 169–71
   legal proceedings; 172–5
   Eiffel in court; 175–6
   verdicts; 177–80
   attempts to revive project; 180–1
   project abandoned to USA; 181

Panama, Isthmus of; 154–7

Paris, city of;
   Eiffel's first visit, 5
   Second Empire of Napoléon III, 6
   Eiffel's student years, 6–9
   Champ de Mars; 12, 92–3, 102–5
   regeneration of city; 14–16, 185–6
   Les Halles, 19, 28–9
   Pont des Arts, 26, 28
   Pont d'Austerlitz, 26
   Bibliotheque Sainte-Genevieve, 28
   Bibliotheque Nationale, 28
   Levallois-Perret district, 38
   political strife in 1871, 42
   Expo Universelle 1878, 44, 48–50
   Expo Universelle 1889, 76–7, 93–4, 135–53, 213
   reactions to Tower, 140–4
   development of the Metro, 185–6
   Expo Universelle 1900, 192–3

Paris, Texas; 222–3

Paxton, Joseph; gardener, architect; 12–13, 82–3

Philadelphia, Pennsylvania; 68, 83

Phoenix Bridge Company; 83–4

photography; 216–7

Prague; 219

Printemps, department store; 215

Proust, Antonin; public servant; 77, 79

Poisson, André; contractor; 228

'portable bridges'; 59–60

Porto, Portugal; Maria Pia Bridge; 44–7

publicity seekers & suicides; 223–6

Pulitzer, Joseph; newspaper proprietor; 71

radio; 200–203

railways in France; 17–20

Regneau, Edouard; 3, 35, 43

Reeves, David; engineer; 83

Reichelt, ——; tailor; 225

Reinach, Baron Jacques de; financier;
160, 169, 171–2, 174

Rennie, George; engineer; 23

Ridley, Sir Matthew, MP; 219

Rivière, Henri; photographer; 216

Robespierre, Maximilien de;
revolutionary; 105

Roche-Tolay, Stanislas de la;
engineer; 30, 34

Roebling, Washington; engineer; 45

Rohe, Ludwig Mies van der;
architect; 29

Le Roux, Hugues; journalist; 117–19

Roux-Combaluzier elevators; 128–9

Robins, Benjamin; mathematician;
204

Royal Albert Bridge, Saltash; 33

Saint-Simon, Comte de; socialist
philosopher; 5, 19

Salles, Adolphe; (son-in-law); 50,
188, 210

San Gimignano, Italy; ix

Santos-Dumont, Alberto;
aeronautical pioneer;
historic flight round Eiffel Tower,
194–6
dispute over timing, 196
lunch with Eiffel, 196
arrested as spy, 197
suicide, 197

Satie, Erik; composer; 211

Sauvestre, Stephen; architect; 49,
78–80

Schuykill River Bridge,
Pennsylvania; 25

Scott, Sir George Gilbert; architect;
47

Sebillot, ——; electrical engineer; 84

Séguin, Marc; engineer; 26–7

Sèvres, Seine-et-Oise; 191–2

Seyrig, Théophile; engineer; 40,
43–5, 47–8, 51, 53, 58, 60

Simon, Jules; statesman &
philosopher; 64

skyscrapers; xiii, 235–42

Société d'Exploitation de la Tour
Eiffel; 218

Society of Arts of London;11

'space elevators'; 242–3

'The Spectator'; 141–2, 145–6

St. Petersburg (Leningrad), Russia;
219

Stair Climbing Championship; 223

Stephenson, Robert; engineer; 19,
25, 27, 41

Stewart MacLaren & Dunn;
engineering consultants; 221

Statue of Liberty;
proposals, 66
US confusion, 67–8
and Philadelphia, 67
design models, 67
US funding problems, 68, 71
US committee, 68
Congressional resolution, 68
Bartholdi contacts Eiffel, 69
construction, 69–70
gifted to USA, 70–71
role of 'New York World', 71–2
Joseph Pulitzer, 71
statue crosses Atlantic, 72
formal dedication, 73
Emma Lazarus poem, 74
iconic status, 74–5

Suez Canal, Egypt; 155, 158, 168

Suicides on Tower, 223–6

Sully-Prudhomme, René François;
poet; 95, 124, 133-4, 211

Sunderland High-Level Bridge; 25

swindles on Eiffel Tower; 227–8

Tay Bridge, Scotland; 40, 55–7

Tall Buildings, 235–42
by name;
Chrysler Building, 235–6
Bank of Manhattan, 235

Index

Flatiron Building, 236
Woolworth Building, 236
CN Tower, 236
Sears Tower, 236
Petronas Towers, 236
Empire State Building, 236–7
'The Illinois', 237
7 South Dearborn, 238
World Trade Center, 238, 241–2
'Taipei 101', 238–9
Taiwan Stock Exchange, 239
Bionic Tower, 239
Centre of India Tower, 240
'Ultima Tower', 240
'Sky City', 240
'Mother', 240
Millennium Tower, 240
'Radiant City', 240
convection tower, 240–1
'space elevators', 242–3
Talleyrand, Charles Maurice de; statesman; 103
Telford, Thomas; engineer; 26
Thiébaud, Georges; businessman; 180
Tirard, Prime Minister Pierre; 123–4, 138
Tissandier, Gaston; aviation pioneer & photographer; 133–4
towers (general); ix–xiii, 235–42
Trevithick, Richard; engineer; 81–2, 95
Tricolour; 122–3, 137, 139, 225–6
Tsiolovsky, Konstantin; aerodynamics & rocket pioneer; 242

Union Bridge, Berwick-on-Tweed; 26
US Congress; 68

Viollet-le-Duc, Eugène; architect; 69
De Vogüé, Eugène, Marquis de; archaeologist & diplomat; 101

Waldeck-Rousseau, Pierre; jurist & politican; 175
Waterhouse, Alfred; architect; 165
Watkin, Sir Edward; railway promoter; 220–2
'Watkin's Folly'; 220–2
weather & lightning (on Eiffel Tower); 140–1
Wenham, Frank Herbert; engineer & inventor; 204
Whitman, Walt; poet; 51
wind tunnels; 204–8
world iconic structures, 235–41
World Trade Center Towers; 238–9, 241–2
Wren, Sir Christopher; architect; 89
Wright, Frank Lloyd; architect; 237
Wright, Wilbur; aeronautics pioneer; 197
wrought iron; 22–3
Wyse, Louis Napoléon Bonaparte; canal promoter; 157

Zelle, Margarete Gertrude (Mata Hari); spy; 201–2
Zola, Emile; novellist; 29